What Shall We Tell the Children?

International Perspectives on School History Textbooks

What Shall We Tell the Children?

International Perspectives on School History Textbooks

Edited by

Stuart J. Foster

and

Keith A. Crawford

**INFORMATION AGE
PUBLISHING**

Greenwich, Connecticut 06830 • www.infoagepub.com

Library of Congress Cataloging-in-Publication Data

What shall we tell the children? : international perspectives on school history textbooks / edited by Stuart J. Foster and Keith A. Crawford.
    p. cm.
  Includes bibliographical references.
  ISBN 1-59311-509-1 (pbk.) – ISBN 1-59311-510-5
  1. History–Study and teaching. 2. History–Textbooks. I. Foster, Stuart J., 1960- II. Crawford, Keith, 1950-
  D16.25.W53 2006
  907.1–dc22

                                                  2006006667

Printed in the United States of America

For

Joe Henry Foster
Jennifer

CONTENTS

FOREWORD

I welcome this timely and important book. The unfortunate succession of violent events in the first few years of the 21st century has reminded us powerfully that learning to live together is as important an outcome of schooling as the more traditional aims of learning to be, to know and to do. Children learn to live together in many ways, not only from what they are taught in the classroom but also from the atmosphere of their school and from the life of their community. Their school textbooks are, however, a very important vehicle for shaping their understanding of the world, not least because they perceive that textbooks represent the "official" point of view of grown-ups.

For this very reason textbooks can also be a source of tension between countries. A country may feel that it is misrepresented in the textbooks of its neighbor or that the books present a tendentious account of the neighbor's own history. Sometimes countries seek the help of the UN system, particularly UNESCO, to mediate in conflicts over the presentation of history or the portrayal of neighbors in textbooks. Although such mediation can be helpful, as it was many years ago in the case of Germany and Poland, it is difficult because it requires that the countries concerned really want to address the issues and agree to the involvement of an international body. These conditions are usually not met.

The surest way to develop textbooks that are not contentious with neighboring states and that help children learn to live together harmoniously is to give textbook writers the tools to write internationally acceptable material in the first place. The most important tool for these writers is to have, as a point of reference, an international academic community that subjects textbooks to dispassionate analysis and publishes its findings. In addition to alerting writers to the issues that they should monitor and providing a code of good practice, such academic analysis is also the best way of deflating the claims made by those for whom selective criticism of textbooks is a propaganda tactic for sustaining tensions.

This kind of book, and the academic community behind it, can do far more than the international community to improve the textbooks through which children learn about the world. I congratulate the authors on their work.

—Sir John Daniel,
President and CEO, "Commonwealth of Learning," Vancouver
formerly Assistant General Director, UNESCO

PREFACE

Textbooks and other books of texts have been both important and ubiquitous in schools across many hundreds of years. They continue to be central to schools' curricula and instruction at almost all grade levels in almost all countries.

I fully recognize the importance of textbooks as well as books of texts to my instruction, in both schools and universities, throughout my career. I have used them in some form during every term that I have taught. Not unlike other teachers, I hope that I used them well, but I recognize that I probably misused some of them. I have been involved with textbooks and the nature of textual narratives in other ways, too.

Some years ago, I led an author team that prepared a series of elementary level social studies textbooks; I also wrote one of the books and parts of others. In addition, I have conducted and supervised research about textbooks. Throughout my university teaching career, I have encouraged—with too little success—increased research about textbooks. I have advocated that some of this research should focus on the nature of the textual narratives, e.g., their accuracy, as well as dimensions of their formats, e.g., the value to students' learning of illustrations. I also have walked that talk. That is, I have conducted research about several aspects of texts and textbooks. I firmly believe that increased knowledge about textbooks can and will facilitate understanding of the actual school curriculum in practice.

Increased understanding through research can and should be productive. On the other hand, particularly in education, such understanding, by itself, is almost never enough to justify the investment of scarce resources in research endeavors. Additionally, research findings seem altogether insufficient, never robust enough, and seldom meaningful enough to serve as evi-

What Shall We Tell the Children?, pages xi–xiv
Copyright © 2006 by Information Age Publishing

dence on which educators and publishers can make reliable decisions about curriculum policy and practice. Quests for increased understanding of curriculum and instruction resources, therefore, must be coupled with serious intentions to act on that understanding, e.g., to prepare and to publish better textbooks, to use textbooks more productively in classrooms.

Beyond all the theory and attempts at theorizing about curriculum lies the reality of classrooms and interactions of students and teachers and texts. That reality, across schools and societies, is easily recognized.

Classrooms are quite unlike other architectural spaces used in education. They exist for the instruction of students in class groupings that are comprised by concerns, among others, about talent, previous experience, grade-levels, gender, or age. In different places and contexts, classrooms differ in characteristic ways. Some are large, almost cavernous, and others are distinguished by cubicles intended for individuals' private study. They display decorations differently, too. Some are conspicuously bare, devoid of students' work or prominently feature a photograph of the current national leader and, perhaps, a national symbol, a flag, perhaps. On the other hand, some classrooms are brightened by students' work, for example, essays posted on a nearby wall space, drawings hung unevenly between the windows, science projects carefully arranged on tables, and a student-made time-line in the process of completion throughout the year. Many classrooms are known by their neat lines of desks or benches or tables and chairs whereas others feature movable furniture arranged in clusters suitable for student discussion and small group projects. School places and space, however embellished and organized, are not constitutive of classrooms. The addition of teachers, students, and textbooks to school space, in so many ways, makes them so.

Likely the most common elements in the classroom lives of teachers and students are textbooks and their texts. Almost everyone easily recognizes textbooks. Thin or weighty, colorful or black printing on white paper, textbooks contain a variety of narratives or exercises of different kinds bound in volumes. Simply, they are books of texts. However, textbooks are not just collections of texts. These books, probably like no others with the exception of dictionaries and encyclopedias, are ordered in tight sequences of topics. Normally textbooks contain only the basic texts or narrative sequences required by the authorized syllabus. Hosts of teachers find textbooks to be their most useful guides with which to plan and to offer their instruction. With textbooks, and in some schools only with textbooks, students study, memorize, recite and only, sometimes, truly discuss texts in these books. Also and long before the recent institution of accountability testing, students routinely have expected to be tested on all or most of the knowledge that their textbooks contain. Textbooks are powerful, crucially important elements of what David Tyack and Larry Cuban have called the "grammar of schooling."

Textbooks derive their power not from their ubiquitous presence in classrooms.

If they did although they do not, chalkboards and pencils and paper would share textbooks' potency. Textbooks are powerful not because of the nature of the texts that they include. Simply, textbooks are powerful because they contain the information that society expects students to know. These expectations, commonly, are ones enunciated by governing officials, sometimes elected, but frequently by bureaucrats. As Michael Apple has so aptly noted, the knowledge in almost all textbooks, however written, compiled, and published, properly may be classified as "official knowledge." Such knowledge carries impressive weight and most teachers neither dismiss it nor publicly substitute other knowledge for it.

The powerful official-ness of textbook knowledge surely is not completely known by decisions made by elected officials, by bureaucrats, or by publishers. Public opinion also exercises a particularly impressive agency. Certainly in the United States, notice must be accorded to the impressive influence of special interest groups. Spokespersons for all manner of causes and "watch-dog groups" track textbook adoption and use and routinely sound alarmist cries because, to identify only three reasons, they perceive textbooks not to advocate desired forms of patriotic or religious sentiments and displays, do not promote the exclusivity of particular economic, political, or religious interpretations, or fail to display the equivalence in textual narrative and accompanying illustrations of individuals of different ethnic groups. The fruits of the insistence on official knowledge in textbooks are not the sole creation of government.

Permission is accorded in only a few countries for teachers to select the instructional materials, including textbooks that they and their students use. However, many, maybe even most, classroom teachers exercise their personal power, especially when the classroom door is closed, to emphasize some rather than other knowledge embedded in the adopted textbook. They also stress or dismiss interpretations and/or even entire selections according to the warrants of their own sentiments. Teachers, consequently, also create official knowledge.

Although students may not recognize that textbook knowledge is "official" in the sense known by many educators, children learn early in their schooling that textbook knowledge is both important as well as true even though both conclusions may be seriously contested. When confronted in school, for example, with information from textbooks that is inconsistent with that obtained from television or even parents, most students commonly choose their textbook as the authoritative source and reject as invalid knowledge from an alternate source. Moreover, if information and interpretation is not in the textbook, most students quickly come to understand that no necessity exists for them to learn this knowledge.

Research attention to official knowledge, to inadequate or incorrect knowledge, however, does not exhaust concerns and wonders about school textbooks. In fact, the general paucity of research about textbooks constitutes an extremely serious, not just an unfortunate, dimension of studies about school curricula. This situation surely will not abate even if instructional programs are packaged into laptop computers and this technology substitutes for printed text on pages bound into books. Still, research about school textbooks or their technological equivalents will continue to be needed—particularly as this research is joined with actions based on decisions about educational practice.

Stuart J. Foster, Keith A. Crawford, and their associates offer a provocative beginning to one aspect of needed research on textbooks. These scholars intentionally focus on the nature and adequacy of the knowledge incorporated in school history textbooks used in ten nations in different regions of the world. Moreover, their portrayals provide researchers and teachers as well as general readers a set of penetrating international perspectives. I invite mindful attention to this book's insightful, research-based essays. Such attention certainly informs. Additionally, it can be productive in the improvement of instructional practices as well as for interpretations, even theory development, within the curriculum field.

—O. L. Davis, Jr.
Catherine Mae Parker Centennial
Professor of Curriculum and Instruction
The University of Texas at Austin

THE CRITICAL IMPORTANCE OF HISTORY TEXTBOOK RESEARCH

Stuart Foster and Keith Crawford

History is one of the few curriculum subjects commonly mandated in education systems throughout the world. Furthermore, the use of history textbooks to support student learning is almost universally accepted practice. However, the widespread international presence of the humble history textbook should not disguise its ideological and cultural potency. Indeed, essential to understanding the power and importance of history textbooks is to appreciate that in any given culture they typically exist as the keepers of ideas, values, and knowledge. No matter how neutral history textbooks may appear, they prove ideologically important because often they seek to imbue in the young a shared set of values, a national ethos, and an incontrovertible sense of political orthodoxy.

Textbooks stand as cultural artefacts that in their production and use embody a range of issues associated with ideology, politics and values which in themselves function at a variety of different levels of power, status and influence. Embedded in history textbooks are narratives and stories that

What Shall We Tell the Children?, pages 1–23
Copyright © 2006 by Information Age Publishing

nation states choose to tell about themselves and their relationships with other nations. Typically they represent a core of cultural knowledge which future generations are expected both to assimilate and support. As a consequence to think about the content of textbooks and how they are authored, published, and used is to think about the purposes of schooling. So dominant are textbooks in most education systems that Boyer has suggested that choosing and using textbooks "Is the closest thing that we have to systematic debate over what schools should be teaching."[1]

Not surprisingly in many nations' debates over the content and format of school textbooks are sites of considerable educational and political conflict. Evidence from national education systems across the globe strongly suggests that the manufacture of textbook content is the result of competition between powerful groups who see it as central to the creation of a collective national memory designed to meet specific cultural, economic and social imperatives.[2] Abundantly clear, however, is that the process of textbook production and distribution is not a simplistic top-down process in which the knowledge valued by prevailing political leaders is distributed instrumentally into classrooms in uniform ways. Undoubtedly, the ways in which textbooks are selected and deployed in classrooms across nations is extremely complex and, although textbook research in this area is expanding, not enough is known about the influence of dominant cultural, political, and economic forces on textbook content, production, and deployment.

As a consequence one of the purposes of this book is to begin to address this fundamental gap in our knowledge. Through the informed perspective of leading international scholars, this book explores the way in which historical, cultural, political and socioeconomic factors influence the selection of knowledge that appears in a range of history school textbooks. It also investigates how societal forces (e.g., governments, politicians and pressure groups) influence the way school knowledge is selected and how that knowledge is presented in the form of history textbooks. Finally, this book pays critical attention to what knowledge is included and rejected in history textbooks and how the transmission of this selected knowledge often attempts to shape a particular form of national memory, national identity and national consciousness.

SCHOOL TEXTBOOKS AND THE "PREACTIVE" CURRICULUM

The relationship between history textbooks and the school curriculum is an important one. Following Goodson's claim that in order to understand curriculum we need to develop a sense of history, a focus on the "preactive" definition of a written curriculum enables us to analyze the relationship between historical antecedence and the exercise of power and agency at the micro-level of curriculum implementation.[3] The notion of curriculum as that which is taught in schools and its relationship with the manner in which curriculum is constructed outside school is poorly documented. Young developed two views of curriculum: "curriculum as fact" and "curriculum as practice." For Young, "curriculum as fact" views curriculum as an uncontested and uncontroversial given, a historically located response to particular socioeconomic conditions. Young saw "curriculum as practice" as reductionist in the sense that because it focuses upon interpretation within schools, it ignores the wider socioeconomic, ideological and political concerns that help construct curriculum.[4]

Goodson's contribution to curriculum theory demonstrates how taking curriculum as an abstract and unquestioned given ignores the "Antecedent struggles over the preactive definition of curriculum."[5] Goodson defines the preactive curriculum as, "The visible, public and changing testimony of selected rationales and legitimating rhetorics of schooling."[6] From this perspective Goodson has produced an extensive body of work focusing on the social construction of curriculum subjects. Goodson claims that: "The conflicts over the definition of the written curriculum offer visible, public and documentary evidence of the continuing struggle over the aspirations and purposes of schooling."[7]

This book applies this perspective to the idea that school history textbooks are examples of preactive curriculum documents that are socially constructed. The view of social constructionism adopted in this book is based upon the notion that social action is the product of the manner in which individuals and groups create and sustain their social world. From this viewpoint the setting, the participants, their motives and intentions and the socioeconomic, cultural and historical context are important variables in shaping meaning and behavior. This approach has similarities to Foucault's analysis of social constructionism. Foucault takes the view that knowledge is historically and culturally specific and emphasizes the constructive power of language. Foucault does not talk of truth but of "discourses of truth" in the construction of a "regime of truth." Foucault was also interested in the status of truth and the economic and political role it plays. For Foucault truth operates within hegemonic, social, cultural and economic contexts. True and truth can mean different things in different contexts. He writes, "Every educational system is a political means of maintaining or of modifying the appropriation of discourses with the knowledge and power it carries with it."[8] Studying the construction of history textbooks and their use in school from a social constructionist viewpoint allows for the exploration of the views, values and interests involved in the making of curriculum, of the political maintenance of power and knowledge and, crucially, of the sociohistorical context within which curriculum is constructed.

TEXTBOOKS AS IDEOLOGICAL DISCOURSES

School textbooks are a vital element in the implementation of curriculum in schools and are a representation of political, cultural, economic and political battles and compromises. As Apple rightly acknowledges, "Textbooks are...conceived, designed and authored by real people with real interests" and are "...published within the political and economic constraints of markets, resources and power."[9] As such school textbooks are based upon the cultural, ideological and political power of dominant groups that tend to enforce, and reinforce, cultural homogeneity through the promotion of shared attitudes and the construction of shared historical memories. The construction of textbook knowledge is an intensely political activity and debates, controversies and tensions over the construction of school textbooks involve a struggle over the manufacture and control of popular memory. School textbooks are one vehicle through which attempts can be made to disseminate and reinforce dominant cultural forms. Griffin and Marciano have claimed, "Textbooks offer an obvious means of realizing hegemony in education...within history texts...the omission of crucial facts and viewpoints limits profoundly the ways in which students come to view history events."[10]

School textbooks, inherently, are social constructions and during the production process authors and publishers inevitably find themselves responding to the expectations of competing interests concerning what constitutes legitimate curriculum knowledge. Although individuals or teams of authors write them, textbooks routinely present broader cultural "messages" and in terms of their social function are often afforded the same authority as government policy documents.[11] Scholars also have claimed that the function of textbooks is to "...tell children what their elders want them to know"[12] and to "...represent to each generation of students a sanctioned version of human knowledge and culture."[13]

One of the most important problems for those exploring the social construction of curriculum knowledge is to find methods and techniques for understanding and interpreting it from an ideological perspective. The difficulty stems from the fact that curriculum can be misleading. On the surface level it is there to be seen, read, used and discussed; it is visible in the form of textbooks, teacher guides and pupil exercises. However, these manifestations of curriculum are, in a sense, hollow shells to which little in the way of meaning can be attributed. Understanding curriculum through the forms in which it is publicly presented also requires identifying, analysing and critiquing earlier stages of curriculum construction. This involves investigating the work of authors, editors, publishers, teachers and students as they struggle to create meanings. The content of the curriculum is always a source of social conflict. The pedagogy that accompanies the curriculum and the allied assessment procedures are subject to analysis and commentary by competing groups who invariably hold distinctly different educational and ideological visions. As Walker and Soltis put it, "In deciding what and how to teach our children, we are expressing and thus exposing and risking our identity—personal, social, and cultural."[14]

Central in the process of constructing textbook knowledge is what Williams called a "selective tradition," where from the vast store of available knowledge the school curriculum is manufactured to reflect the values considered important by powerful groups.[15] Thirty years ago Bernstein identified the hegemonic power of curriculum in claiming that "How a society selects, classifies, distributes transmits and evaluates the educational knowledge it considers to be public reflects both the distribution of power and the principles of social control."[16] As authors in this book illustrate, in a variety of national contexts history textbooks are shaped by competing ideological and cultural forces that heavily influence what knowledge gets "selected."

THE DISCOURSE OF HISTORY TEXTS

The particular concern of this book is the extent to which textbook construction influences the teaching and learning of history. While one may reasonably argue that textbooks in other subjects (e.g., geography, English, science, mathematics) are worthy of detailed empirical study, history textbooks serve as the focus because they provide a crucial context for analysing the interplay of power and culture. Giroux has identified this area as one which involves "...challenging, remapping and renegotiating those boundaries of knowledge that claim the status of master narratives, fixed identities and an objective representation of reality."[17] The history curriculum is traditionally regarded as the vehicle through which nations seek to store, transmit and disseminate narratives that define conceptions of nationhood and national culture; as such they are crucial sites for investigation.

The fact that nation states seek to define their sense of identity by drawing upon the experiences and lessons of the past is not surprising. In seeking to establish and to maintain a physical, political and cultural sense of belonging, nations place great store in articulating what has traditionally bound them together and what makes them different from their neighbors. This is particularly so when conceptions of national identity and place are seemingly threatened by ideological, political and cultural change. What is more interesting, because it is more problematic and because of what it reveals about a nation, is the process through which states socially construct images of themselves for national and international consumption by re-negotiating and re-inventing their pasts.

The intellectual and emotional relationship between a nation's present, future and past is shaped through the selection, manufacture and transmission of powerful narratives promoting a sense of history and identity based upon a mixture of myth, remembrance and official knowledge. When an individual tells a story about their past they tend not to tell it the way it happened but the way they choose to remember it—nations do exactly the same.

Nations rarely tell "the truth" about themselves, what national stories provide are claims to truth, the publicly available record of a nation's past does not provide accounts of what actually happened; rather they represent what it chooses to remember and what it chooses to tell as its national story. What follows from this is that selecting a national past is an intensely political and ideological process. Politicians of all persuasions have long recognized that controlling the present and shaping the future relies to some extent upon controlling the manner in which the past is presented. During periods of socioeconomic, political and cultural crisis governments invariably evoke some aspect of the national past to convince the populace to support, or not to support, an issue, to vote, or not to vote for something. The past is even reified to induce individuals to die, or make somebody else die, in the service of national salvation.

Selecting a national past also involves a de-selection process. Choosing to highlight some aspect of the national past at the expense of other aspects inevitably produces conflict as history is re-made by competing interest groups each seeking a dominant voice in constructing what counts as popular memory. This process is ongoing for the only non-negotiable fact about the past is that it is always open to interpretation as it is continually re-written and re-designed to comply with contemporary issues. National pasts are never manufactured within a vacuum. While many national stories exist, powerful individuals and groups, in their pursuit of particular hegemonic goals, always construct what is presented as the national story. National governments and their agencies, to varying degrees, frequently lie, misinform and either manipulate, or ignore, the past in pursuit of their goals. One outcome is that the history taught to children is often a watered-down, partial, sometimes distorted, and sometimes fictional, view of a national past based upon cultural, ideological and political selection.

In some nation states history teaching is used openly and unashamedly to promote specific ideologies and sets of political ideas. In other countries, under the guise of patriotism, the history of a nation served up for student consumption is what its leaders decide it is to be. In states which consider their existence to be under threat, or in states which are struggling to create an identity, or in those which are re-inventing themselves following a period of colonial rule, teaching a nationalistic and mono-cultural form of history can prove to be the cement which binds people together. In its worst form the manufacture and teaching of such an official past can create, sponsor, maintain and justify xenophobic hatred, racism and the obscenity of ethnic cleansing. More subtly, nations which give the appearance of stability, cohesion and well established liberal traditions also re-visit and re-invent aspects of their past to promote particular forms of domestic behavior and to support the creation of a particular form of national and/or international identity. Xenophobia, racism and the manipulation of national histories are not confined to fledgling nations or to one-party totalitarian states.

This selective tradition ensures that some knowledge receives privileged and authoritative status. As a result through a process of textual inclusion and exclusion, one group's cultural knowledge is given an official stamp of approval. Unfortunately this narrow construction of social representation, historical memory and identity inevitable ensures the absence of alternative knowledge. Thus, often missing or marginalized in school textbooks is a plurality of discourses and narratives that might emerge from oppositional histories. In practical terms these cultural and historical silences reveal themselves through what Apple calls "mentioning" where "...limited and isolated elements of the history and culture of less powerful groups are included in the texts."[18]

The process through which historical factual knowledge is transformed into legitimate curriculum knowledge for pupil consumption typically involves two stages. First, factual historical knowledge, those issues, themes, and problems which form the core of official knowledge to be transmitted through the curriculum, is selected, reproduced, and structured around specific sets of cultural, socioeconomic and ideological aims.[19] In analysing the maturation of Environmental Studies into a curriculum area, for example, Goodson reflected on its salience at a time when environmentalism became a social movement. Goodson quotes Gomm who claimed that the "Climate of opinion which made environmental studies a credible label for curriculum innovation . . . is best understood in terms of the historical circumstances of post-war capitalism."[20]

Whitty makes a similar case in charting the growth of the Social Studies curriculum claiming that one of its aims was to "Fit the changing demands of British capitalism and democracy."[21] More recently, Washburn's study of U.S. textbook portrayal of slavery between 1900 and 1992 identified a pronounced shift of emphasis from the multicultural texts of the 1960s and 1970s generated within a climate of liberal reform based around the civil rights movement to the more conservative representations of the 1980s and 1990s produced within the political context of the neo-conservative Reagan and Bush administrations.[22]

The second stage of textbook development is concerned with how the selected historical text is modified through constraints often placed upon textbook authors and editors. Routinely history textbooks are scrutinized and simplified in order to satisfy the demands of textbook publishers. Textbooks are economic commodities often published for economic rather than intellectual reasons.[23]

School textbook sales in the United States are a multi-billion dollar business with many books, chiefly adopted for a five to seven year period, benefiting from lucrative repeat print runs. Significantly, in Russia, Alexander Krutik, a leading figure in the Dorfa publishing company that publishes 30% of the textbooks used in Russian schools was, in August 1997, shot dead by a sniper outside his apartment. The leading suspects were the "Russian Mafia" said to be anxious to gain control of a profitable textbook market, as books were re-written in a post-communist world.[24]

The economics of textbook publishing has a considerable influence upon the work of authors in terms of content, emphasis and pedagogy and subsequently, upon the representation of the past presented to pupils. Authors write textbooks within a clearly designed set of economic constraints. In most cases they begin their work having been told that their book will have a prescribed number of pages and will include a certain number of illustrations, maps and questions. The aim of textbook publishing is to produce a product accessible to a particular audience and, in a competitive and volatile market, a product that conforms closely to requirements such as national curriculum programs of study. Managing this process successfully does not involve the production of knowledge but its reproduction in a form that reinforces a selective tradition. Central in this process is the construction of what counts as knowledge and, crucially, what counts as being "true."

THE CONSTRUCTION OF TRUTH AND KNOWLEDGE IN INTERNATIONAL SETTINGS

What appears in school textbooks is legitimately sanctioned knowledge that has been allocated an official stamp of "truth"; but what textbooks offer are not truths but claims to truth. Foucault provides a definition of "truth" which is helpful in this context:

> Truth is a thing of this world... Each society has its regime of truth, its "general politics" of truth: that is, the types of discourse which it accepts and

makes function as true; the mechanisms and instances which enable one to distinguish true and false statements, the means by which each is sanctified; the techniques and procedures accorded value in the acquisition of truth; the status of those who are charged with saying what counts as true.[25]

For Foucault "'Truth'... is the issue of a whole political debate and social confrontation (ideological struggles)."[26] It is generally assumed that what appears in textbooks is accurate (factually) and true. Yet, the evidence from a number of national studies is such that it is not possible to conclude that textbooks offer "truthful" or accurate accounts. Indeed, the notion of "claims to truth" often is problematised in analyses of school textbooks. Most textbook critics fully appreciate that knowledge must never be viewed as accurate and definitive, but rather as temporary and transitory.

In some societies the manufacture of textbook knowledge is achieved through direct political control, in other nations the control is less explicit resulting in more pragmatic responses. Paradoxically, perhaps, in the most powerful of democracies, the United States, the selection of textbook knowledge ostensibly is centrally controlled.[27] Unquestionably textbooks are often viewed as important weapons in fiercely fought cultural wars. Accordingly, Apple has written: "There is considerable pressure to... standardise their content, make certain that the texts place more stress on "American" themes of patriotism, free enterprise and the "Western tradition...""[28]

In a similar vein, in his critique of United States history textbooks, Loewen claims that the teaching of history is dominated by textbooks whose contents are predictable, uncontroversial and exclude material that "...might reflect badly on our [United States] national character."[29] For Loewen, the American past is presented as a morality tale with textbooks encouraging students to believe that "...history is facts to be learned."[30] Most textbook publishers in the United States ensure that the content of their textbooks will be approved by state textbook adoption committees (not all states have such committees but many do, particularly in the southern states) especially those in the highly populated states of Texas and in California and Florida, which exert tremendous power over what counts as official knowledge nationally. For example, as Delfattore revealed, Texas legislation asserts that textbook content will:

promote citizenship and understanding of the essentials and benefits of the free enterprise system, emphasizing patriotism and respect for recognized authority, and promote respect for individual rights...Finally, textbooks approved for use in Texas shall not encourage lifestyles deviating from generally accepted standards of society.[31]

In many states textbook adoption is a public process during which different pressure groups mobilize populist support in an attempt to exert influence on the content and format of individual texts. Huyette noted that at one California history/social science adoption meeting over 200 individuals spoke for two minutes each, the most vocal groups were those representing ethnic, religious, woman's and homosexual organizations.[32] This is a process that often results in revisions being made to books including the removal of text or illustration considered by a group to be inappropriate or offensive.[33]

Political, social, and cultural influences on textbooks are not exclusive to the United States. For example, Bates has described how in Indian social studies textbooks Muslims and Christians are described as "alien villains" and how textbooks in the state of Gujerat extol the Aryan race, ignore Jewish persecution and call for an increase of "national spirit."[34] Behera similarly has analysed how ruling regimes in Pakistan have tried to re-write the national past to suit present political ideologies.[35]

Following Hong Kong's return to Chinese control in 1997, China's vice-premier, Qian Qichen, confirmed that existing "colonial" history textbooks not conforming to Chinese principles would be revised. In China history textbooks present an unflattering image of colonial rule in Hong Kong and credit the Chinese for the former colonies' economic success. Within China itself textbook writing is closely monitored by the state to ensure that books provide pupils with a foundation for the development of ideological and moral character in accordance with the interests of the socialist state.[36]

Citing similar ideological biases, Lisovskaya and Karpov document how history textbooks employed under communist rule were distorted in order to match the ideological dogma of Leninism. Under Gorbachev's perestroika, textbooks, the authors noted, continued to support communism but included topics that hitherto had been forbidden such as sharp critiques of Stalinism. Since the collapse of the Soviet Union concepts such as capitalism, economic entrepreneurship, political freedom and the rights of individuals increasingly have found their way into textbooks.[37]

From Israel evidence emerges that textbooks paint a simplistic picture of the Arab–Israeli conflict and are profoundly ethnocentric. Research at Tel Aviv University analysed one hundred and twenty four history, geography and civics textbooks approved by the Ministry of Education and found evidence of a widespread belief in Israeli victimisation and the negative stereotyping of Arabs. For example, one textbook states that "They [the Arabs] are extremists and we are more moderate. They murder indiscriminately and we defend ourselves."[38] On the other side of this tragic divide, Reading, Writing and Hate, a study of three hundred and thirty Egyptian, Jordanian, Syrian and Palestinian textbooks by Susan Sachs, found that reference to Arab-Israeli co-existence was ignored; Egyptian textbooks did not name Israel on maps and Jordanian textbooks contained evidence of anti-Semitism.[39]

Kallis reached a similar conclusion in his study of German, Italian and Greek textbooks.[40] In Spain problems over the selection of content and bias are even more pronounced in a nation where textbook publishers have to provide seven versions of history texts in response to regional demands. For example, Castille and Catalan have very different views on the role of Ferdinand and Isabella's contribution to financing the voyages of Columbus and history texts in the Basque region describe France *and* Spain as neighbors.[41]

Limited empirical research has focused on the construction of textbook knowledge in the United Kingdom (UK). What evidence there is suggests that UK history textbooks often suffer from a strong ethno-centric bias that perpetuates stereotypical images of events, issues and alternative cultures. For example, Coman claimed that a sample of history textbooks which focused on World War Two portrayed Germans as "crude and thoughtless" and declared that, "None of the texts used German primary sources... [and] only three asked pupils to consider the Germans' position..."[42] Coman concluded that as a result primary aged children "...understood the war to have involved unprovoked, irrational and unchallenged German aerial bombardment of British civilians."[43]

Evidence also exists that Second World War images of a victorious Britain shape definitions of what it means to be British.[44] Furthermore, some have argued that British children lack a moral understanding of the Second World War as a result of the neglect of sensitive issues like the Holocaust and uncritical attention to such events as the Blitz.[45] Such narrow foci might explain why the British continue to mythologize the war and why Michael Naumann, the then German culture minister, could reasonably claim that, "There is only one nation in the world (Britain) that has decided to make the second world war a sort of spiritual core of its national self, understanding and pride."[46]

METHODOLOGICAL ISSUES

The methodological principles that underpin textbook research are not well developed and the area remains under-theorised. Narrow conceptions of the field have sometimes resulted in too much emphasis on quantitative forms of analysis in which scholars present statistical evidence on, for example, the number of pages devoted to particular themes, the number of photographs presented in texts and their positioning, or the percentage of text devoted to multi-cultural and gender issues. Too often absent from textbook studies are reports which contextualise the social construction of textbooks within broader and deeper socioeconomic and cultural parameters. Simply put, in order to develop further our knowledge and understanding of school textbooks as cultural artefacts, emphasis must be placed not only on analysing what is presented in history textbooks, but crucially on why certain knowledge is, or is not, presented.

Rather than provide a freestanding chapter that explores methodological approaches to textbook analysis, the chapters in this book conceptualise the field through reference to case studies of particular themes, issues and methodological principles typically set within national contexts. However, the book does broadly employ an empirical and theoretical model that is designed to provide it with shape, purpose and a sense of direction. The model is drawn from the work of Ball et al. and their analysis of educational policy sociology where their work has made a significant contribution to understanding the relationship between the formation of educational policy and its implementation in schools.

In their analysis of the 1988 Education Reform Act in England and Wales, Bowe and Ball with Gold identify three sites within which they claim the construction and reconstruction of educational policy takes place:

1. *The Context of Influence:* where the ideological and political basis of policy is debated and decided by government and powerful interest groups;
2. *The Context of Text Production:* where texts deemed to represent policy are constructed by powerful interest groups;
3. *The Context of Practice:* the professional sites within which policy, in the form of policy texts, are interpreted by teachers and pupils.[47]

This framework provides a useful model from within which to mount studies of textbook construction both within individual contexts, and crucially, in terms of structural, ideological and political inter-relationships, between different contexts. Two of the three policy contexts (i.e., the context of influence and text production) are centrally featured in this book.

The context of influence provides the arena within which educational policy is initiated and policy discourses are constructed, the context where "Interested parties struggle to influence the definition and social purposes of education."[48] It is at this level, the level of the political, ideological and educational state, that cultural wars are conducted and where a selective tradition is formed. Within the framework of textbook analysis, this context could be seen as one within which national socioeconomic, ideological and cultural goals are established which then provide quite specific parameters for the social construction of textbook knowledge. As a result textbooks frequently respond to national, and sometimes nationalistic, agendas. Based upon this model, within the context of influence textbook studies might usefully focus upon:

(a) The influence of state control over school knowledge and the nature of the structural (historical, economic, cultural, ideological and political) constraints that impinge upon textbook construction;

(b) The relationship between the exercise of power, the selection of curriculum knowledge and its classroom implementation.

In the context of text production individual policy texts are seen as, "The outcome of struggle and compromise."[49] Focus here might be on how and why textbook authors, publishers and pressure groups influence and legitimise curriculum knowledge through the vehicle of school history textbooks. Within the context of text production, key questions include: what is the process through which textbook knowledge is constructed? What claims to truth and knowledge are presented? Who are the characters, heroes and villains? How does the process of textual inclusion and textual exclusion work? Is what is presented nationalistic or national history? Are accounts "safe" and uncontroversial excluding material that reflects badly on national sensitivities? Does a dominant elite suppress the development of a critical historical consciousness? Here the focus also might broaden to include:

(a) Who is it that selects school textbook knowledge and what are the ideological, economic and intellectual relationships between these different interest groups?

(b) Through what process is textbook knowledge declared to be official knowledge and how is it filtered through sets of political screens and decisions before it is declared legitimate?

(c) What voices are heard in textbooks? Whose knowledge is included? Which group(s) receives the most sustained attention? Whose story is being told?

(d) To what extent do school textbooks act as a filter that ignore other views and perspectives? Do texts exclude or marginalize particular groups who are part of a nation's history (e.g. those representing social, cultural, religious, economic, ethnic or geographical groups)?

Of course it would be wrong to assume that what is written in textbooks gets either taught or learnt. A number of critical ethnographies of school and classroom have shown that written texts are subject to a multiplicity of readings and that the manner in which a text is received varies considerably.[50] For example, Apple talks of "dominant," "negotiated," and "oppositional" readings. Dominant readings result in the reader accepting the text uncritically; in a negotiated reading the reader accepts the basic premise and accuracy of the text even if doubts exist over certain elements; in an oppositional reading the text is rejected outright.[51] Within the context of practice useful areas of investigation might focus upon:

(a) The extent to which teachers re-select, re-define and re-interpret textbook knowledge in their teaching. For example, are elements of texts rejected, ignored or deliberately misunderstood?

(b) The pedagogic approaches teachers adopt and their impact on the presentation of textbook knowledge as "writerly" or "readerly." Key questions include what evidence is there of dominant, negotiated or oppositional readings? To what extent do teachers engage in interpretation and meaning making and creative and novel readings?

(c) The impact of teacher belief and values systems on curriculum delivery;

(d) The structural limitations on teachers' work (e.g., regulations, accountability mechanisms, bureaucratic pressures) that influence how and why textbooks are used.

Although examination of the context of practice is not a primary focus of this book this does not, however, undervalue its importance. Indeed, because of the paucity of research in this area more studies are needed on how textbooks are used in the history classroom and on the complex ways that students process and understand the "stories" history textbooks tell to young people.

HISTORY TEXTBOOKS IN DIFFERENT CONTEXTS

Authors in this book principally attend to textbook issues and developments in different countries across different continents. As such they offer a fascinating insight into debates over the role and importance of history textbooks in contemporary societies. To suggest, however, that history textbooks have similar value and authority in different countries would be misleading for two important reasons. First, coverage issues and the place and status of history in different countries ensure that like-for-like comparisons are not easily made. The situation is further complicated by awareness of the complex relationship between the production, selection, and deployment of history textbooks and the relative influence of government agencies, national curricula, standardised testing, and the practices of individual schools and teachers in different countries.

For example, in England, although a national curriculum and national testing regime is in place, individual schools (and sometimes individual teachers) can select history textbooks from an assortment of private publishers. By contrast in the United States no federally mandated national curriculum exists and individual states are able to determine how textbooks are selected. In the two dozen "textbook adoption states," agencies provide a list of "approved" state textbooks from which local school districts can choose. However, the situation is further clouded by the fact that most states do not have uniform state adoption policies. Illustrating yet another approach to textbook adoption, in Japan non-governmental publishers submit textbooks to the Ministry of Education for approval. Textbooks have to conform to national curriculum standards and are examined by specialists at the Ministry of Education and the Textbook Authorization Council. Textbooks that meet the standards established by the Ministry are authorized for use and are subsequently selected by individual schools in accordance with their respective educational needs. As many authors in this book illustrate, the vagaries of local and national education systems and their relationships to central and regional governments determine that textbooks are developed and employed in different ways in different national settings.

The second reason why history textbooks are not an internationally standardised entity stems from the fact that they are typically fashioned and employed for different reasons and for different purposes in individual nations. Often they perform multiple functions simultaneously. For example, they are used to cover mandated historical topics, to conform to curriculum needs, and to address the demands of standardized tests. Sometimes, they are used as a support mechanism and as the primary source of information for teachers, students, and parents. Occasionally they are used critically as an example of one representation, among many, of a particular historical perspective. Nevertheless, no matter for what reason they are employed, textbooks inescapably represent a powerful means to render a particular version of a nation's past in the history classroom. Accordingly this book, which provides a detailed analysis of how history is represented in different national contexts, offers intriguing and illuminating perspectives on how nationalistic bias, particularistic cultural and geopolitical perspectives, and powerful socio-political agendas dramatically influence and shape what historical stories are told to children in different nations across the world.

In Chapter 1, Ed Vickers examines recent trends in history textbook development in mainland China. He focuses principal attention on the way in which Chinese nationhood is defined, explicitly or implicitly, through the selection of particular historical narratives involving "minority" groups or "Special Administrative Regions" (SAR). Vickers offers a fascinating critique of the ways in which the histories of Tibet, Mongolia, Taiwan and Hong Kong are distorted in textbook accounts in order to reinforce a nationalist vision of a united China. Vickers illustrates that, despite the existence of complex and disputed "minority nationalities," central authorities in the state-controlled Chinese education system use history education as a vehicle to reinforce the "One China" message—an intensely state-centerd and homogenising vision of Chinese national identity. In its pursuit of its unifying goal, Vickers charts an interesting shift in China's educational policy which involves a move away from an emphasis upon Marxist interpretations of class struggle towards a distinctively celebratory nationalist narrative that subsumes minority groups into a highly selective and xenephobic version of China's "national" story. The chapter concludes with a very relevant discussion of the implications of this "national" vision for relations between the Han majority on the mainland and the minority communities that exist, both politically and geographically, on China's periphery.

Keith Crawford's incisive analysis of the construction of official memory in Japanese history textbooks is the subject of Chapter 2. At the core of the chapter is an exploration of how and why the Japanese Ministry of Education has consistently proved reluctant to fully acknowledge and address unsavoury and horrific episodes in Japan's wartime past. In particular the author draws attention to official textbook accounts of the activities of Unit 731, responsible for bacteriological warfare in China, the experiences of Chinese and Korean "comfort woman," sexual slaves used by Japanese soldiers, and the Nanking Massacre in 1937, that some historians have argued saw the brutal killing of over 250,000 Chinese civilians and soldiers. The chapter illustrates that, despite repeated challenges from liberal critics and textbook academics, Japanese textbooks tend to offer sanitized and nationalist interpretations of Japan's wartime actions. Crawford persuasively argues that this selective attention to the past can only be explained by understanding powerful socio-political, cultural, and ideological agendas in the present. In particular he argues that the renaissance of conservative nationalism in recent years has led to increased demands for patriotic unity, celebratory history, and pride in Japanese achievement and identity. Accordingly, state control over textbook content offers the political right a convenient and useful means to maintain a particular form of hegemonic and ideological control over contemporary Japanese society.

In Chapter 3, Misook Kim's analysis of North and South Korean elementary school textbooks focuses on the construction of gendered national identities on either side of the 38th parallel. The chapter illuminates three important features of Korean textbooks. First, textbooks on both sides of the divide often serve as vehicles to draw together members of a national community. Typically this is achieved through appeals to national symbols, traditions and experiences through the metaphors of land and family. It is also achieved by differentiating between what unites a people and what divides them and by emphasizing the "otherness" of traditional and emerging enemies. Second, the chapter explores the ways in which national images and portrayals commonly are created to celebrate masculinity and patriarchy and thereby affect the social structure of the two Koreas. Accordingly, emphasis is placed on the achievements of males in textbook portrayals of military heroes, influential leaders, and national role models. Third, the study demonstrates that, despite obvious differences between textbook accounts in the North and South, clear evidence exists to suggest that a softening of the vehement hostility between the two sides has occurred in recent decades. Indeed, Kim concludes the chapter by looking positively to a period of greater Inter-Korea political and social reconciliation and the emergence of textbooks that encourage greater mutual understanding and tolerance.

Whereas most authors concentrate textbook analysis on one nation, in Chapter 4, Jason Nicholls offers thoughtful insights into the differing portrayals of World War II across five countries: Japan, United States, England, Italy, and Sweden. Significantly, Nicholls illustrates how history textbooks in each nation select, emphasize, and present wartime events in strikingly different ways. His analysis further illustrates the irony that, although textbooks in many nations portray historical events as fixed, objective and certain, historical events are by their very nature open to a variety of interpretations. The chapter is particularly illuminating because it offers a critical analysis of the role of national and transnational perspectives in history textbook construction and masterfully exposes how current history textbooks often "appear anchored in the international politics of the present." Furthermore, Nicholl's addresses head on vital issues of epistemological and critical orientation in textbook analysis. Nicholls invites the reader to think carefully not only about how and why textbook portrayals are variously constructed in different nations, but also to consider the complexities that textbook scholars face in meaningfully analysing the potency, value, and appropriateness of any given text in national and international settings. Ultimately his appeal for history textbooks that encourage students to critically engage with multiple perspectives is both thought provoking and persuasive.

In Chapter 5, Yasemin Soysal offers a fascinating exploration of the concept of Europeanness and European identity as articulated through the educational curriculum and history textbooks in Germany, France, Britain and Turkey. In her discussion, Soysal examines contemporary and historical attempts by various social and political institutions and agencies to advance a common European past and a shared cultural tradition based on universalistic principles (e.g., democracy, progress, human rights, gender equality). Soysal's analysis of school history and civics textbooks in many European countries clearly demonstrates a shift away from unapologetic nationalism, emphasis on military conflict, and the mythology of national heroes to a softer, more conciliatory, more interconnected, and more

European representation of the past. Soysal's work, however, underlines the complexity of identity formation, the slippery relationship between national and transnational history, and the problematic construction of a shared European identity.

In Chapter 6, Falk Pingel examines the teaching of National Socialism and the Holocaust in German schools from both contemporary and historical perspectives. Drawing on his extensive knowledge of educational developments in post-War Germany, Pingel skilfully demonstrates how National Socialism and the Holocaust have received contrasting treatments in history textbooks, curricula, and pedagogic practice in various historical periods from the end of the war to the present. In particular, he delineates how treatment of these two issues is largely determined by the prevailing sociopolitical context. In the 1950s, for example, the Holocaust and National Socialism receive cursory attention. According to Pingel, horrors committed during the 1930s and the Second World War were typically attributed to a small group of Nazi leaders who had led astray "the people." By contrast contemporary schools offer a more sophisticated, open, and honest interpretation of the Holocaust and Nazi rule. Today, increased attention is given to issues such as the persecution of the Jews, responsibility for the ascendancy of National Socialism, and the uncomfortable moral choices faced by many German citizens. In his examination of this sensitive and vital issue Pingel underscores the moral complexity of the Holocaust and National Socialism and offers intelligent insight into the challenges of pedagogy, the development of appropriate teaching resources, and the construction of meaningful history textbooks.

In an adaptation of a study first published in *History of Education* (Volume 28, 3), in Chapter 7, Stuart Foster takes a broad historical look at more than two hundred years of American school history textbooks. Particular attention is given to the status and contribution accorded to immigrant groups in the unfolding story of the U.S. nation. Critical examination of the balance between, on the one hand, celebrating America's multiethnic and diverse past and, on the other, representing a shared and united experience, is an essential feature of the chapter. Foster argues that despite changes in textbook presentation, focus, and style, the central story line remains strikingly consistent across generations. Indeed, in order to conform to the pressures of a highly competitive market, to prevent vehement criticism from the increasingly influential political right, and to appease powerful conservative interest groups, textbook publishers continue to produce books that trumpet national achievements, venerate the Western tradition, and emphasize a shared and heroic American experience.

Chapter 8 shifts the geographical focus to south Asia. Here Yvette Rosser, offers a sharp and poignant critique of the Islamization of Pakistani social studies textbooks in recent decades. In particular Rosser attends to the continuing impact on education of the eleven years of General Zia-ul-Haq's military rule between 1977 and 1988. She laments the replacement of the traditional subjects of history and geography with Pakistan Studies (during this period and beyond) and criticizes the introduction of a systematic policy of "chauvinistic Islamic nationalism" that continues to dramatically shape educational practice in contemporary Pakistan. Zia's legacy, Rosser argues, is the widespread existence of a policy of indoctrination in which textbooks play a significant role. Above all she illustrates how Pakistani textbooks now promote the superiority of Islamic values, a deeply religious conservatism and fundamentalism, a hatred of Western ideologies, vehement anti-Hinduism, and a fervent belief in the heroic destiny of the Pakistani nation. In an age when Islamic and Western nations appear increasingly divided over cultural, political and religious differences, Rosser's contribution is a timely reminder of how textbooks often are viewed as powerful weapons in ideological and religious battles for the hearts and minds of young people.

Dan Porat's analysis of the changing representations of the Second Temple era in Israeli history textbooks from the early 1950s to the 1990s is the focus of Chapter 9. Here, Porat skilfully demonstrates how Israeli textbooks written since the 1950s have undergone subtle but important changes in recent decades. Despite these changes, however, Porat illustrates how textbooks typically are constructed to serve dominant social, political, and cultural imperatives in the present (e.g., to promote national unity by recounting a noble, heroic, and worthy experience shared by all Jews). Chief among Porat's concerns is that Israeli textbooks have too often promoted a monolithic, "best story," and authoritative account of the past. Accordingly he concludes by arguing for textbooks that aim not to assist in the formation of a national collective memory, but rather that invite students to view the past through a disciplinary perspective which accepts and encourages alternative and contrasting interpretations of historical events.

In Chapter 10, Jonathan Kriener pursues the issues discussed by Porat from a comparative perspective in his analysis of Israeli and Palestinian social studies textbooks. Here Kriener examines the manner in which the politicisation of textbooks within Israeli and Palestinian culture have been marked by contradiction and argument and illustrates how the construction of textbooks is solidly grounded in intense and long standing ideological and political disagreement. Kriener also points to an aspect of textbook construction that is not always acknowledged by comparative studies, the widely differing interpretations that exist *within*, as well as *between* states. What is clear from Kriener's contribution is that powerful and historically located cultural interests are at work in Israel and Palestine that make the creation of meaningful dialogue extremely problematic as both nations seek to establish, maintain and develop a sense of national identity in a region wracked with violence, political and religious tensions.

The post-Apartheid era in South Africa is the setting for Chapter 11. Here Rob Siebörger critically explores issues of curriculum development and the construction of history textbooks in the new South Africa. Siebörger carefully describes the collective vision of two significant textbook colloquia that aimed to examine and to explore what textbooks in the new South Africa might become in an era of rapid change and considerable promise. Key among the aspirations of colloquia participants was the desire for textbooks that were more responsive to historical scholarship, more sensitive to the disciplinary process of history, and more inclusive of the histories of ordinary people. Appeals also were made for a more transparent and participatory process of textbook selection. Siebörger points out that much remains to be done to accomplish the vision of improved history textbooks. In particular he argues for the establishment of clear guidelines and criteria to govern the textbook approval process, the need for a widespread replacement policy which systematically purges old textbooks, increased opportunities for black writers to contribute to textbook construction, and an end to the dominance of Afrikaans-owned textbook publishing companies. Undoubtedly school history textbooks continue to have a vital presence in contemporary South Africa, Siebörger's hope is that textbooks of the future will embrace the recommendations of the textbook colloquia and effectively and sensitively respond to the considerable challenges of the present.

Finally, the pages of this book illustrate that as instruments of socialization and sites of ideological discourse textbooks are powerful artefacts in introducing young people to a specific historical, cultural and socioeconomic order. Crucially, exploring the social construction of school textbooks and the messages they impart provides an important context from within which to critically investigate the dynamics underlying the cultural politics of education and the social movements that form it and which are formed by it.

The school curriculum is essentially the knowledge system of a society incorporating its values and its dominant ideology. The curriculum is not "our knowledge" born of a broad hegemonic consensus, rather it is a battleground in which cultural authority and the right to define what is labelled legitimate knowledge is fought over. As each chapter in this book illustrates curriculum as theory and practice has never been, and can never be, divorced from the ethical, economic, political, and cultural conflicts of society which impact so deeply upon it. We cannot escape the clear implication that questions about what knowledge is of most worth and about how it should be organized and taught are problematic, contentious and very serious.

NOTES

1. Quoted in M. J. Chambliss and R. C. Calfee, *Textbooks for Learning: Nurturing Children's Minds* (Oxford: Blackwell, 1998), p. 2.

2. See, P. G. Altbach, et al., *Textbooks in American Society* (New York: State University Press, 1991); W. E. Marsden, *The School Textbook: geography, history and social studies* (London: Woburn Press, 2001).

3. I. Goodson, "Subjects for Study: Towards a Social History of Curriculum," in *Defining the Curriculum*, I. Goodson and S. Ball eds. (Lewes: Falmer Press, 1984).

4. See, M. F. D. Young, *Society, State and Schooling: readings on the possibilities for radical education* (Ringmer: Falmer Press, 1977).

5. I. Goodson, *The Making of Curriculum: collected essays,* (Lewes: Falmer Press, 1988) p. 15.

6. Ibid., p. 16.

7. op.cit., p. 12.

8. M. Foucault, *The Archaeology of Knowledge* (London: Tavistock Press, 1972).

9. M. Apple, *Official Knowledge: Democratic Education in a Conservative Age* (London: Routledge, 1993), p. 46.

10. W. L. Griffin and J. Marciano, *Teaching the Vietnam War* (Monclair, N.J: Allenhead Osmun, 1979), p. 35.

11. See J. Anyon, "Ideology and United States History Textbooks," *Harvard Educational Review* 49 (1979): 361–86; S. De Castell, "Literacy as Disempowerment: The Role of Documentary Texts," in *Philosophy of Education 1990*, ed. D. P. Ericson, (Normal, Illinois: Philosophy of Education Society, 1991).

12. F. Fitzgerald, *America Revised: History Schoolbooks in the Twentieth Century* (New York: Vintage Press, 1979), p. 47.

13. S. De Castell, 1991, Ibid., p. 78

14. D. F. Walker and J. F. Soltis, *Curriculum and Aims* (New York: Teachers College Press, 1986), p. 14.

15. R. Williams, *The Long Revolution,* (London: Chatto and Windus, 1961).

16. B. Bernstein, "On the Classification and Framing of Educational Knowledge," in *Knowledge and Control*, ed. M. Young (London: Collier-Macmillan, 1971), p. 47.

17. H. Giroux, *Border Crossings: cultural workers and the politics of education* (London: Routledge, 1992), p. 26.

18. M. Apple, 1993, Ibid., p. 56.

19. See for example, R. Arnove, "Education as contested terrain in Nicaragua," *Comparative Education Review,* 39 (1995): 28–53; J. D. Jansen, "The state and curriculum in the transition to socialism: The Zimbabwean experience," *Comparative Education Review,* 35 (1991), pp. 76–91; S. Oispuu, "Teaching History in Estonia," *Teaching History: A Journal of Methods,* 17 (1992), pp. 4–10, and I. Silova, "De-Sovietization of Latvian textbooks made visible," *European Journal of International Studies,* 7 (1996), pp. 35–45.

20. I. Goodson, I. and S. Ball. (eds.), 1984, Ibid., p. 41

21. G. Whitty, *Sociology and School Knowledge: Curriculum theory, research and politics* (London: Methuen, 1985), p. 36.

22. L. Washburn, "Accounts of Slavery: An analysis of the United States history textbooks from 1900–1992," *Theory and Research in Social Education* 25 (1997).

23. See M. Apple, "Culture and commerce of the textbook" in *The Politics of the Textbook* eds. M. Apple and L. Christian-Smith (New York: Routledge, 1991).

24. *The Times*, 28th August 1997; *Times Educational Supplement,* 22nd May 1999.

25. M. Foucault, *Power/Knowledge* (Sussex: Harvester Press, 1980), p. 131.

26. Ibid. p. 132.

27. Although we recognise that in the United States approved textbooks are not mandated or produced by the federal government, textbook control ostensibly is centralised for two reasons. First, a remarkable similarity exists across the United States in the content, provision, and deployment of history textbooks. Second, the enormous power and influence of the large textbook production companies ensures that textbooks typically follow a consistent pattern. Significantly, even schools within the non-textbook adoption states commonly employ history textbooks that are either identical to those use used in other states or have striking similarities.

28. M. Apple, 1993, op. cit., p. 52.

29. J. Loewen, *Lies My Teacher Told Me: everything your American history textbooks got wrong* (New York: Simon and Schuster, 1995), p. 13.

30. Ibid., p. 16.

31. J. Delfattore, *What Johnny Shouldn't Read* (New Haven: Yale University Press, 1992), p. 139.

32. See, F. Huyette, "The Politics of Textbook Selection in California," *Internationale Schulbuchforschung,* 17, (1995) pp. 130–133.

33. See M. Apple and L. Christian-Smith, *The Politics of the Textbook* (London: Routledge, 1991); M. Apple, *Teachers and Texts: A Political Economy of Class and Gender Relations in Education* (New York: Routledge and Kegan Paul, 1986); J. G. Herlihy, ed. *The Textbook Controversies: Issues, Aspects and Perspectives* (Norwood, NJ: Ablex Publishing, 1992).

34. S. Bates, "Anger at growing textbook bias in India," *The Guardian,* 25th January 2000.

35. N. C. Behera, "Perpetuating the Divide: political abuse of History in South Asia," South *Asia News* 5, (Issue 2, 1996), pp. 191–205.

36. Liu Bin Speech at the conference for the Inspection and examination of the curriculum and the textbooks for mandatory education, *Chinese Education and Society* 27, (Issue 2, 1994), pp. 6–27.

37. E. Lisovskaya and V. Karpov, "New Ideologies in Postcommunist Russian Textbooks," *Comparative Education Review* 43 (November, 1999), pp. 522–541.

38. Quoted in S. Surkes, "Hostile Stereotypes Persist despite the peace process," *Times Educational Supplement,* 11th April 1997, p. 4.

39. S. Surkes, "Textbooks Keep the Old Hostilities Alive," *Times Educational Supplement,* 26th January 1996.

40. A. Kallis, "Coping with the uncomfortable past: a comparative analysis of the teaching of World War Two and the role of historical education in the construction of a "European" Identity," unpublished paper given at *Children's and Young People's Social, Political and Economic Learning and Understand-*

ing within the European Context conference (University of North London, May 1999)

41. S. Mackay, "Nationalist History Relaxed," *Times Educational Supplement,* 14th November, 1997

42. P. Coman, "Reading About the Enemy: school textbook representations of Germany's role in the war with Britain during the period from April 1940 to May 1941," *British Journal of Sociology of Education* 17, (1996). p. 335.

43. Ibid. p. 335.

44. A. Calder, *The Myth of the Blitz* (London: Pimlico, 1995).

45. See *Times Educational Supplement,* 5th May 1995. See also, C. Cullingford. and H. Husemann , eds. *Anglo-German Attitudes* (Aldershot: Palgrave,1995).

46. *The Sunday Times,* 19th February, 1999, p. 11.

47. R. Bowe and S. J. Ball with A. Gold, *Reforming Education and Changing Schools* (London: Routledge, 1992).

48. Ibid., p. 19.

49. op.cit., p. 21.

50. R. Barthes, *The Pleasure of Text* (London: Cape, 1976).

51. See, M. Apple, 1991, Ibid.

CHAPTER 1

DEFINING THE BOUNDARIES OF "CHINESENESS"

Tibet, Mongolia, Taiwan, and Hong Kong in Mainland History Textbooks

Edward Vickers

INTRODUCTION—DEFINING "CHINESENESS" IN CHINA TODAY

The language of nationalism is everywhere in contemporary China: in the state-controlled (or state-supervised) media, in commercials for products ranging from cigarettes to long-life milk, in the propaganda associated with the national space program or the 2008 Olympic Games, and in the museums and monuments that welcome growing numbers of domestic and foreign tourists. Now that the label *socialist* carries even less meaning in China than the designer logos sported by urban youths, the state is increasingly appealing to symbols and narratives associated with ancient national traditions. Thus Confucius, subjected to a bizarre campaign of posthumous vilification during the Cultural Revolution in the 1970s,[1] has been rehabilitated, and honored by the construction of a lavish new "Confucius Research Center" in his home town of Qufu. Meanwhile, traditional

What Shall We Tell the Children?, pages 25–48
Copyright © 2006 by Information Age Publishing
All rights of reproduction in any form reserved.

heroes from the ruling elite, previously condemned in history textbooks on class grounds, have been readmitted to the nationalist pantheon.[2] History education in the People's Republic constitutes one front in a broader nationalist campaign whereby the Communist regime is seeking to harness and tame the latent patriotism of its citizens in order to bolster its own legitimacy.

Most nationalist writing, official or unofficial, on the nature of "the Chinese nation" or "Chineseness" tends to assume that the definition of "China" is singular and clear-cut. As with national identities everywhere, however, the picture is actually rather more complex. For example, Beijing's official spokesmen frequently lecture foreign journalists and politicians on the sanctity of the "One China Principle"—the doctrine that there is one legitimate Chinese state, single and indivisible, and that Taiwan (or Tibet, or Xinjiang) has always been and forever will remain part of it. However, many Taiwanese (not to mention Tibetans or Uighurs) these days take a rather different view, and some historians point to the fact that their island was only settled by Chinese immigrants from the early seventeenth century onwards, initially under the auspices of Taiwan's Dutch colonial government. Advocates of full independence from China have also placed increasing emphasis on Taiwan's aboriginal heritage—pointing out that the island's population prior to Chinese colonization was actually Malayo-Polynesian. The remaining aboriginal tribes, formerly rendered near invisible by the Kuomintang regime's Han chauvinism, have seen their culture increasingly celebrated (indeed some would say appropriated) by the ethnic Chinese as the latter seek to construct a mythology of "multicultural" Taiwanese nationalism.[3]

Meanwhile, on the mainland, the predominant mode of thinking about national identity amongst politicians and intellectuals (and most ordinary Chinese) remains "primordialist"; in other words, national identity is seen as bound up with a concept of homogenous and immemorial "Chineseness," defined in cultural and often pseudo-racialist terms. The extremes to which primordialism can be taken in China are reflected in the plans for the Olympic torch procession in 2008. The torch is to begin its journey into the city of Beijing from the "Peking Man Site" to the Southwest of the capital. This is where archaeologists in the 1930s discovered the remains of a hominid that was duly christened "Peking Man," and who, in defiance of the "Out of Africa" theory, was subsequently adopted as a prehistoric national ancestor. The precise nature of the relationship between "Peking Man" and modern-day Chinese is seldom probed, but the fact that history textbooks in the People's Republic generally start their narratives with descriptions of "Peking Man" and prehistoric China reflects a desire to reinforce notions of the unique antiquity and genetic homogeneity of the Chinese "race-nation."[4]

The concept of an ethnoculturally homogenous "race-nation" (*minzu*) continues to enjoy a powerful appeal among ethnic Chinese both within and beyond the borders of the People's Republic.[5] However, it clashes with other manifestations of national or sub-national identity, both long established and of more recent origin. On the one hand, there are the numerous "minority nationalities" (*xiaoshu minzu*), including Tibetans, Uighurs and Mongols, of whom no less than 53 are officially recognized by the Chinese authorities. These are all, by definition, ethnocultural constructs, though the work of Soviet-trained Chinese anthropologists during the 1950s and 1960s identified some minority nationalities whose parameters, or even whose very existence, came as something of a surprise to members of the communities in question.[6] Nevertheless, most of these groupings do manifest clear and more or less ancient cultural traits distinguishing them from the Han majority.

Meanwhile, the homogeneity of the "Chinese nation" has also been subject to challenges from self-consciously "Han" communities in Hong Kong and Taiwan. In the latter case, a full-blown nationalism has emerged over the past twenty years, with debates continuing between those who attempt to construct a Taiwanese identity along ethnocultural lines, and others who argue for a more civic-based notion of Taiwaneseness, as a sense of belonging and loyalty to the island community and its institutions—discussions further complicated by calculations as to the prudence of expressing a sense of Taiwanese distinctiveness (given Beijing's strident opposition). For Hong Kong, independence—*de facto* or *de jure*—has never been an option, but Hongkongers have nonetheless manifested a very strong sense of what distinguishes them from "mainlanders," and have come to possess a consciousness of "Hongkongese" identity centered around the local lifestyle, popular culture, and certain values or practices associated with the territory's institutions, such as the rule of law.[7] To declare that one is a "Hongkonger" or a "Taiwanese" first and foremost (as most inhabitants of Hong Kong and Taiwan now do) does not necessarily imply any denial of one's Chineseness, but it does involve perceiving this Chineseness primarily as a cultural rather than a political attribute. This sits uneasily, to say the least, with the absolute and totalizing definition of Chinese nationhood to which Beijing continues to subscribe.

In this chapter, I look at recent developments with respect to history textbooks in mainland China, focusing in particular on the way in which Chinese nationhood is defined, explicitly or implicitly, through the narration of particular events or topics involving minority groups or Special Administrative Regions (SAR). I examine some of the ways in which the histories of Tibet, Mongolia, Taiwan and Hong Kong are distorted in textbook accounts in order to reinforce the One China message—an intensely state-centered and homogenizing vision of Chinese national identity. The chapter concludes with a consideration of the possible implications of this vision for relations between the Han majority on the mainland and these communities on China's periphery.

NATIONALISM AND POLITICS IN CONTEMPORARY CHINA

On the mainland, phenomena such as the rehabilitation of Confucius and, more broadly, the return to a more positive evaluation of China's traditional culture, have been accompanied by (and in part have been responses to) calls for the Chinese Communist Party (CCP) to transform itself from a revolutionary into a ruling party. Communism took root in China during the May 4th Movement of the 1920s, an intellectual current characterized by a radical critique of Chinese tradition, and calls for the more or less wholesale repudiation of the indigenous heritage in favor of post-Enlightenment Western values and models. This repudiation took its most extreme form in the Cultural Revolution of 1966–1976, which rejected not only Chinese tradition, but all tradition, looking instead to build a brave new world on the basis of "Mao Zedong Thought." The aftermath of the Cultural Revolution initially witnessed a renewed flirtation on the part of China's intellectuals with Western, and especially American, political ideas, but this culminated in the bloody crushing of the Students" Movement in 1989. Since then, many Chinese intellectuals, and elements within the CCP itself, have increasingly taken issue with the radical May 4th critique of Chinese tradition, and have argued for the elaboration of a new political philosophy drawing heavily on elements from indigenous traditions, not least Confucianism.[8] Ironically, in so doing they are engaging in a project very similar to that pursued by Chiang Kai-shek in the 1930s with his pseudo-Confucianist "New Life Movement," a program much derided by Communists at the time and since. There are also similarities with attempts made by Hong Kong's British colonial government in the 1930s, and again from the 1950s onwards, to promote ultra-conservative "Confucian values" as a means of encouraging political quiescence and damping down anti-colonial resentment.[9] The Kuomintang, the British, and more recently the CCP, have all seen in Confucianism a useful resource for bolstering their fragile legitimacy by inculcating the virtues of respect for authority and a family-oriented social ethic.

Nevertheless, the rise of popular nationalism and the renewed interest in traditional culture in post-Tiananmen China have by no means been simply a state-orchestrated phenomenon. Among the main factors behind this has been the reaction in China to the collapse of Communism in Eastern Europe, and especially to the chaos and instability that this caused in post-Soviet Russia and the former Yugoslavia during the 1990s. Not only the CCP, but also many intellectuals and opinion formers, drew the lesson that China should at all costs avoid the sort of headlong rush towards democratization and reform witnessed in Russia. China's brand of authoritarianism started to appear less like a throwback to feudal times, and more as a bulwark against political and social collapse.[10] At the same time, events such as the First Gulf War and the NATO intervention in Kosovo appeared to raise the spectre of untrammeled Western hegemony, especially when blended in Chinese minds with memories of 19th century Western imperialism and 20th century Japanese aggression. Episodes such as the bombing of China's Belgrade embassy in 1999 and protests over the Japanese "occupation" of the Diaoyutai/Senkakuji islands (uninhabited islets to the north of Taiwan) showed that the strength of popular nationalist sentiment could sometimes go far beyond what the CCP was prepared to tolerate or condone. Peter Gries has argued that underlying the sometimes hysterical anti-Westernism of such outbursts is a psychological need for recognition—a sense among many Chinese that their country is still not accorded the respect it deserves in the international arena, particularly by its most significant "others," the United States and Japan.[11]

The popular appeal of strident and xenophobic nationalism in the post-Tiananmen era casts the Communist regime in the role of Sorcerer's Apprentice: decades of propaganda (not least that purveyed through history textbooks) have established as unchallenged orthodoxy a vision of China as a violated innocent, the victim of repeated assaults by evil imperialists. The very success of its own propaganda has contributed to the pressure to which the regime now finds itself subjected from a newly vocal public opinion: pressure manifested in the popularity of such books as *China Can Say No!*, that call for the nation to "stand up to" foreign (especially Japanese and American) aggression, and to assert itself more forcefully on the international stage.[12] Internet chatrooms, an arena for freer speech that the government has struggled to control since the mid-1990s, are swamped with expressions of hate for Japan (including calls for a war with the despised enemy) at every perceived slight inflicted by China's Asian neighbor. However, while such Chinese nationalism is a double-edged sword for the Communist authorities in terms of their relations with neighboring states, the simultaneous rise (since the 1980s) of separatist sentiment in areas such as Tibet and Xinjiang, as well as the pro-independence movement in Taiwan, constitute challenges to the integrity of the state that appear to demand a nationalist response. The problem is that the vision of Chinese nationhood that the state attempts to promote in the "minority" areas—a multicultural, inclusive concept of a "Great Chinese National Family" based on "solidarity" among the various ethnic communities—sits uneasily, to say the least, alongside the Great Han Chauvinism that is the salient feature of nationalism in its more popular (and populist) manifestations.

Though nationalism has in recent years tended to dominate much of the discourse over China's past and present place in the world, the parameters of political and intellectual debate are far wider now than they once were. For example, self-styled "postmodernists," influenced by the writings of Edward Said and others, seek to deconstruct Western "dominant discourses," though significantly they do not accord similar treatment to dominant discourses *within* China, since then postmodernist (or postcolonialist) theory might be used by intellectuals from "minority nationalities" to cause trouble.[13] Nevertheless, some criticism of the regime's policies (though not of the regime itself) is tolerated in the media, if only sporadically and uncertainly—so long as it stops short of personal criticism of the key Party leaders, and so long as it does not question the "One China Principle." Thus a prominent liberal, Li Shenzhi, was able to circulate scathing criticisms of the lavish 1999 National Day celebrations, and of the unwillingness of the government to open official archives on the June 4, 1989 suppression of the student movement. "The cost [of suppressing the truth about such events]," he wrote, "is the national loss of memory and the loss of the ability to think logically about the past."[14]

Such open criticism remains relatively rare, and its influence on the portrayal of history in school textbooks on the Chinese mainland is minimal or non-existent. However, it is worth bearing in mind, when discussing the school curriculum that the national discourse on history in the world outside the classroom is no longer quite as monolithic and controlled as it once was. Inside the classroom, it is still a different story. Since 1950, curriculum development for China's secondary schools has been a highly centralized affair, the responsibility—except during the interlude of the Cultural Revolution (1966–1976)—of the editors at the People's Education Press (PEP) in Beijing. Until very recently, this meant that students across China used the same textbooks for each subject—one subject, one textbook. Since the mid-1990s, this one-size-fits-all model has been modified or abandoned for subjects such as English language, with the more "advanced" coastal regions and large cities adopting more challenging courses, while rural areas and inland provinces make do with the old PEP books.[15] For history, however, the move towards textbook diversity has been far more cautious.

Nor is this caution entirely or simply a product of political sensitivities (though of course that has a great deal to do with it); it is also a reflection of a strong cultural orientation in China towards the idea that history, particularly as taught in schools, should embody "correct" verdicts about the past, as well as providing "correct" moral exemplars (a key function of Confucian historiography). Disputes over historical interpretation among intellectuals are one thing, but the function of history as a school subject in China has always been to moralize, as much as (or more than) to afford access to the truth about the past. Moreover, the interpretation of history has traditionally been a matter in which the Chinese state has taken an intimate interest; indeed, the keeping of historical records, and the issuing of "correct verdicts" on past events and historical figures, has traditionally been the province of an organ of the central government. This does not mean that official historiography has always held the field unchallenged—far from it. However, it has led to a deeply ingrained expectation that the state has a role in supplying a "correct" version of the past, and an assumption that this will be enshrined in the history curriculum for schools.[16]

TEXTBOOK CONTENT

The content of ideological correctness has changed significantly with the shifts in China's political landscape over recent decades, and this has been reflected in the interpretation of history in school texts. Alisa Jones has shown how the Marxist terminology of class struggle has featured less and less prominently in textbooks during the period since the Cultural Revolution. Whereas considerable emphasis used to be placed on the role of peasant rebellions (*nongmin qiyi*) in shaping national history, discussion of these has been pared down in successive editions of the textbooks. What remains is, broadly speaking, an orthodox, triumphalist, nationalist narrative celebrating the glories of Chinese civilization from ancient times—a narrative in many respects very similar to that promulgated by history textbooks in Nationalist China before 1949, and for decades afterwards in Kuomintang-ruled Taiwan.[17]

Meanwhile, the newest textbooks give greater prominence than ever before to discussions of the role of "minority nationalities" in the national story. Patriotism has largely taken the place of Marxism in providing the ideological scaffolding around which the narrative is constructed; the downplaying of class struggle and socialist themes has left the "One China Principle" as the key moral and political message of the texts. Below I discuss the treatment of Mongolia, Tibet, Taiwan and Hong Kong in the latest mainland history textbooks, since although these occupy a relatively minor place in the overall narrative (in terms of the space devoted to them), they amply demonstrate the way in which nationalist priorities determine the vision of the past that is presented to secondary school students in the People's Republic.

THE MONGOLS—FROM HATED INVADERS
TO BROTHER CHINESE

Chinese history has always been and still remains very much the story of "great men" (women scarcely figure—nor, interestingly, does the practice of footbinding or its abolition rate a mention in school texts). The focus is on key figures, usually political leaders, who are presented as either positive or negative moral exemplars (the positive greatly outnumbering the negative). Great men hardly come greater than Genghis Khan, who in the latest (2001) edition of the junior secondary text appears just after a chapter concluding with the proud assertion that football was invented in Song Dynasty China "three or four hundred years before… English football."[18] Just as the authors claim football for the motherland, so they claim the Great Khan, whose record of rape and pillage across northern China is entirely overlooked as he is held up as a paragon of triumph against adversity, overcoming the hardships of his youth and the scheming of his rivals to unite the Mongolian grasslands and take his armies "as far as Europe's River Danube."[19]

The triumphalism with which Genghis Khan has been appropriated as a glorious Chinese hero is made breathtakingly apparent by the recent extension of his mausoleum in Inner Mongolia (the relevant chapter in the textbook opens with a picture and description of the old 1950s structure). The new additions feature massive bass-relief sculptures dominating the surrounding grasslands, on a scale calculated to make Albert Speer turn green with envy. The centerpiece is a huge concrete disk with a map of the world showing all the areas conquered by the Mongol armies. Similarly, in the textbooks, Mongolia is referred to as part of *Wo Guo* ("Our Country"), and the "achievements" of the Mongol Yuan Dynasty in promoting the "assimilation" of China's different nationalities are celebrated. Previous editions of the junior text briefly discussed the discriminatory treatment of the Han majority by the Yuan Dynasty's Mongol rulers, but this is not mentioned in the latest version. Thus, the traditional Chinese view of the Yuan Dynasty as a dark period of foreign oppression is turned on its head in the interests of contemporary inter-ethnic harmony, and, it seems, so that Han Chinese can take a share of macho pride in the Mongol conquests.

TIBETAN HISTORY AND SELECTIVE AMNESIA

Mongolia, Tibet and Xinjiang, present-day China's largest "autonomous regions," feature in the history texts only when episodes in their past can be convincingly related to developments involving China proper. This leaves some very large—and unexplained—gaps in the narrative regarding, for example, Tibet. In the latest junior secondary textbooks, half a chapter is devoted to an account of relations between the Tibetan Tubo Kingdom and the Tang Dynasty in the Seventh century, focusing on the marriage between the Tibetan King Songtsen Gampo, and the Tang Princess Wencheng. Such marriages were a tactic often deployed by ancient Chinese rulers to sooth the savage barbarian breast, and the textbook asserts that Songsten, who "admired the civilization of the central plains," several times sought a marriage alliance with the Tang. Eventually the Emperor Tang Taizong graciously condescended (so the text implies) to send him Princess Wencheng as a bride, and this alliance led to "closer economic and cultural contacts between the Tang and the Tubo, and strengthened the friendly relations between Han and Tibetans."[20] There follows a section in which Songtsen and his Chinese bride are both represented as hard-working and/or studious, upright and virtuous moral exemplars. What the text entirely fails to mention is that Songtsen actually had two wives—a Nepali wife by the name of Bhrikuti Devi, in addition to his Chinese consort. The king was setting a precedent to be followed by many of his successors in attempting to establish amicable and profitable relations with Tibet's powerful neighbors to the south in India/Nepal as well as to the east in China. However, this is entirely ignored by the Chinese textbook account, since it would undermine both the nationalist and also, perhaps, the moral import of the story (keeping multiple wives being officially frowned upon in twenty-first century China).

Tibet then almost entirely disappears from the textbook narrative for almost 1,000 years, until the seventeenth century. This is hardly surprising, since during that millennium the political ties between Tibet and China proper were in general fairly tenuous, with the notable exception of the Yuan Dynasty, when the Mongols intervened in Tibet's internal politics and subsequently adopted Tibetan Lamaism as their national religion. This highly significant episode in Mongol-Tibetan relations is only mentioned in passing, with the observation that "the Yuan government strengthened control over Tibet, and Tibet became a formal administrative unit under the Yuan dynasty."[21] What primarily concerns the authors is to demonstrate the closeness of relations between each of the different "minority nationalities" and the central Chinese state—not to discuss the nature of relations between the "minorities" themselves.

Tibet re-enters the narrative in the seventeenth century because this was the time of the "Great Fifth" Dalai Lama, who established his supremacy over the other lamas and their various sects. The textbook states that, after the Qing Dynasty was established (in the mid-seventeenth century), the Fifth Dalai Lama "personally entered the capital to offer his congratulations" to the Shunzhi Emperor.[22] The latter granted the Lama an audience, and "officially bestowed on him the title of 'Dalai Lama.'" Later, the Kangxi Emperor similarly honored the Panchen Lama. "From this time," declares the text, "the successive incarnations of the Dalai and Panchen Lamas were all required to receive the approval of [literally, 'enfeoffed by'] the central government." The text goes on to describe how the central government began to post high officials to Tibet from 1727.

> The Qing Government issued a proclamation declaring that the Mandarin [in Lhasa] represented the central government, and that he together with the Dalai and Panchen Lamas would manage Tibetan affairs. The identification of the successive incarnations of the Dalai and Panchen Lamas must be submitted to the central government for approval. Through the use of these methods, the Qing Government greatly increased the control of the central government over Tibetan affairs.[23]

There then follows an account of how the machinations of "British colonialists," aiming to "destroy the unity of China" and expand their influence into Tibet in the 18th century, were foiled by the steadfast refusal of the Panchen Lama to collaborate with them. According to the text, the Panchen told the British that "the whole of Tibet was under the sovereign control of the Chinese Emperor."

What is striking about this account is that no attention is given to developments within Tibet itself. As with the earlier treatment of Songtsen Gampo, the focus is almost exclusively on relations between Tibet's rulers and the "central government"—nothing else matters. The same is true of the treatment of the histories of Mongolia, the Uighur people of Xinjiang (who are discussed in the same textbook chapter as the "Great Fifth" Dalai Lama), and Taiwan. The only perspective that counts is that of the imperial court. It should be noted, however, that little or no information on alternative perspectives would be available to the writers of these textbooks, even if they were minded to look for it. The official interpretation of Tibet's history is overwhelmingly dominant within China, and is uncritically accepted by the vast majority of educated Chinese—very few of whom have ever visited "minority" areas such as Tibet or Xinjiang. Westerners who dispute this view are generally assumed to have been deluded by the distortions of the foreign media.

CORRECT VERDICTS AND THE PROMOTION OF CRITICAL THINKING

This crushing "One China" orthodoxy creates something of a quandary for textbook authors and editors when it comes to reconciling the traditional moralizing aims of history education with new aspirations to turn the subject into a vehicle for fostering skills of analytical reasoning and critical thinking. Education policymakers since the mid-1990s have adopted a new mantra of "quality education" (*suzhi jiaoyu*), that encompasses an even wider range of meaning than the equivalent term in English.[24] Influenced by recent developments in history teaching overseas, particularly in the Anglo-Saxon world, and concerned that China's schools need to do more to promote the creativity and critical faculties of their students if the country is to prosper in the new global "knowledge economy," history curriculum developers have attempted to introduce more challenging activities into textbooks. The latest texts for junior secondary level, for example, are peppered with boxes entitled "Use Your Brain!" (*dong nao jin*), but in almost every case there is still only one correct answer to the question posed—and this generally carries the same sort of crude political message as the main narrative. Thus, for example, accompanying the passage about the Panchen Lama's patriotic resistance to the overtures of British "colonialists" is a "Use Your Brain!" activity relating to the architecture of a temple built by the Qianlong Emperor to show his gratitude for the Panchen's loyalty. This temple, says the text, combined elements of Han and Tibetan architecture. "Think about it—what does the emergence of this fusion of Han and Tibetan temple architecture tell us?" asks the question in the activity box.[25] In theory, several answers might be possible, but in practice the text (and the political context) points to only one correct answer.

At the back of the same volume of the junior secondary textbook are several additional classroom activities, one of which is a "Historical Knowledge Contest." The nature of this activity indicates starkly the kind of approach to history education with which any aspirations to promote critical thinking must contend. The suggested topic for this is "Xinjiang, Tibet and Taiwan have been part of Chinese territory from time immemorial" (*Xinjiang, Xizang, Taiwan zi gu yi lai jiu shi Zhongguo de lingtu*). The contest involves setting a series of questions on the history of these regions, but the main point of the exercise is to instill in students a greater love of their motherland. This is illustrated by the short text introducing this appendix:

> I love the motherland, and I love the natural scenery of the motherland. I love not only the mountains, rivers and vast territory of the motherland, but also every tree and blade of grass, every flower and stone, every brick and tile—all these fill me with warm feelings, all these deserve my love and affection.

> I love the earth of our motherland! The wild winds have scoured her, hailstones have pounded her, thick snows have hemmed her in, great fires have scalded her, heavy rains have flooded her... but despite all these travails, she silently stands firm. As soon as Spring arrives, she reawakens, and with a confident heart bursts forth into overflowing life, and the contending hues of countless flowers.[26]

What this excerpt (from an essay entitled "I love My Motherland') has to do with history is unclear; its inclusion in the textbook is in fact a telling testimony to the ahistorical definition of "China" and "Chineseness" that informs the approach to the national past in these school texts. "The motherland" here is depicted in organic terms, as an inviolable living entity whose every blade of grass is sacrosanct. The incompatibility of this "blood-and-soil" vision of national identity with the kind of critical, reflective pedagogy that history curriculum developers in China nowadays claim to advocate explains the awkwardness and tokenism that characterizes attempts in these books to introduce a more "activity-based" approach to learning.

TAIWAN AND HONG KONG—CHINESE UNITY IN THE FACE OF IMPERIALIST AGGRESSION

Hong Kong and Taiwan, like Tibet, Xinjiang and Mongolia, lie on the margins of China, far from the historic centers of state power; hence they occupy a similarly peripheral place in what is an overwhelmingly state-centered textbook narrative. Taiwan warrants only the occasional mention in mainland textbooks, one exception being the section dealing with the Sino-Japanese War of 1894–1895. This war resulted in defeat for China—a defeat at the hands of a traditionally despised Asian neighbor that was felt, at the time and since, to be particularly humiliating. It officially ended in April 1895, with the signing of the Treaty of Shimonoseki, which amongst other "humiliations" ceded the island of Taiwan to Japan. "The signing of the Treaty of Shimonoseki," declares the senior secondary textbook, "aroused a national campaign against the humiliating peace negotiations and the Qing court for its surrender policy. In Taiwan, people from all walks of life protested vehemently against the cession of the island to Japan. All of the Taiwan people 'would rather die to lose the island than to live to cede it.'" (sic.)[27]

The text goes on to describe the brief armed struggle waged by "the patriotic leaders of Taiwan" and their followers against the "Japanese aggressors." It omits to mention that some members of the Taiwanese elite, realizing that they could expect no assistance, military or otherwise, from the Qing government on the mainland, took the step of declaring an independent "Republic of Taiwan" with the former Chinese governor as president. This episode has for obvious reasons been played up by pro-independence elements in contemporary Taiwan, and the same reasons account for the omission of any mention of the "Republic of Taiwan" in mainland texts. In fact, the declaration of independence was a measure of desperation on the part of Taiwanese opponents of the Japanese occupation, rather than a reflection of any highly developed sense of Taiwanese distinctiveness or any real desire for political separation from the mainland. However, the mainland school texts here, as elsewhere, seek to portray events in black and white terms, rather than in subtler shades of grey, and thus depict the Taiwanese as united in their resolve to defend China's unity to the last drop of blood. Foreign perfidy is therefore implicitly blamed for the eventual collapse of resistance: "In October, the British missionaries in Tainan led the Japanese aggressors into the city. The whole island fell into Japanese hands." The textbooks do not mention that, prior to this, the gates of Taipei had been opened to the Japanese by members of the Taiwanese gentry who were anxious to put a stop to looting by Chinese troops.[28] After a passage boasting that the Japanese suffered over 30,000 casualties in their campaign to pacify Taiwan (including "several princes and generals'), but giving no figures for Taiwanese casualties, the account of the island's cession ends thus:

> The Taiwan protection movement showed clearly that there was an enormous reservoir of anti-aggression sentiment among the broad masses in Taiwan. The movement itself was a new leaf in the Chinese history of anti-aggression. Actually, during Japan's 50 years of occupation of Taiwan, the broad masses on that land never ceased their anti-aggression struggle.[29]

It is interesting to note the use of the term "anti-aggression" in this account as a euphemism for "anti-Japanese." This reflects at least two preoccupations on the part of the Chinese educational authorities: a reluctance to be seen as condoning outright xenophobia, and a related concern to avoid the diplomatic repercussions that would result from the use of a term such as "anti-Japanese" in school textbooks. The repeated use of the term here and in later descriptions of the brutal Japanese invasion of China in the 1930s also represents a direct challenge to Japanese textbook accounts of these wars that have tended to avoid use of the term "aggression," preferring instead to talk about a Japanese "advance" into Chinese territory.[30] The media in China, Japan, Korea, Taiwan and Hong Kong constantly monitor the content of school textbooks in neighboring countries (or "regions') for signs of distortion or nationalist xenophobia, with China and Korea in particular seeking to occupy the moral high ground in relation to Japan on this issue.

The use of the term "anti-aggression" may additionally reflect the widespread belief amongst Chinese that their "race" is by nature non-aggressive, in stark contrast to the congenitally aggressive, militaristic Japanese. The assertion that "China has never invaded another country" is often heard on the lips of educated Chinese, and this belief is reflected and reinforced by the narrative of the national past contained in school textbooks, particularly the accounts of relations between the Han and the various "minority nationalities," or with surrounding states such as Korea, Vietnam and Japan (all of which have in fact been subject to invasion or attempted invasion by one or more of China's ruling dynasties).[31]

The message of China's historical victimhood is powerfully conveyed through textbook accounts of modern and contemporary history, which is especially emphasized in senior secondary courses (though it is also studied by all students as part of the junior secondary history curriculum). China's modern history is conventionally considered to have begun with the First Opium War of 1839–1842, whereby Britain forcibly commenced the "opening up" of the Middle Kingdom to foreign trade and imperialist influence. The senior secondary course, *A Modern and Contemporary History of China*, faithfully follows this conventional chronology, beginning with a narrative of the Opium Wars and a discussion of their impact. Part of this "impact" consisted of the cession of Hong Kong to Britain as one of the terms of the Treaty of Nanjing, the first of many so-called "Unequal Treaties" forced upon China by the imperialists during the 19th century. The cession of Hong Kong is listed as the first item of the "major content" of the Treaty, and the textbook includes a map showing Hong Kong Island shaded, along with pictures of Henry Pottinger, the first British governor, and of the seal of Hong Kong—and that is all.[32] The text at no point contains any discussion of internal developments within Hong Kong during the period of British administration, just as it includes no coverage whatsoever of the history of Taiwan under Japanese or Kuomintang rule.

MONGOLIA, TIBET AND THE SCHEMING IMPERIALISTS

Just as Hong Kong and Taiwan appear solely as bit-players in the drama of relations between the late-Qing state and the imperialist Powers, so too do Mongolia and Tibet. The senior secondary textbook devotes over two pages to a discussion of the secession of Outer Mongolia in 1911, depicting this as an outcome of the machinations of Russian imperialists.[33] "At the beginning of the twentieth century, Russia aggressively extended its forces towards the Mongolian areas, constantly sent spies into the Mongolian areas to collect intelligence, bought in, drew over and forced some princes, dukes and Living Buddhas, and instigated them to separate and betray their native country" (it is not clear here whether "native country" refers to Mongolia or China).[34] The text proceeds to discuss Mongolian independence in 1911, with scare quotes indicating the authors' refusal to accept the legitimacy of this move: "At the end of 1911, supported by the armed forces of Russia, Outer Mongolia declared "independence," established "the Great Country of Mongolia," and supported the Living Buddha as "Emperor."[35] It goes on to describe how the weak administration of Yuan

Shikai, President of the Republic of China, was bullied into accepting Russia's political control of the region. "Outer Mongolia," it asserts, "actually became a covert colony of Russia."[36] However, in contrast to the earlier discussion of Taiwanese resistance to Japanese "aggression," and the subsequent narrative of Tibetan "resistance" to British imperialism, the text has nothing to say about the feelings of the Mongolian people on the subject of independence. Having made the point that Mongolian independence was the result of an imperialist plot, the textbook falls silent on this subject—omitting any mention, for example, of the Mongolian Revolution of 1921, or of the reasons why, or even the fact that, the Chinese Communist Party eventually came to recognize the independence of Outer Mongolia.[37]

The narrative goes on to discuss the "invading activities of Britain in Tibet," claiming that soon after China's 1911 Revolution, "Britain took the chance to instigate elements who were on intimate terms with Britain in Tibet to stage an armed rebellion, to drive out the Sichuan army stationed in Lhasa and Rikeze, and to declare 'independence,' attempting to break Tibet from China."[38] The next sentence declares that "the rebellion in Tibet was strongly opposed by the people, the patriotic monks and priests, and the upper circles in Tibet," but the account then describes how Britain bullied the Chinese government into abandoning plans for an armed intervention. The Simla Accords of 1913 are dismissed as an "illegal" attempt by Britain to split Tibet from China, and the British are similarly attacked for "presumptuously" drawing the "illegal" McMahon Line demarcating the boundary between China (or Tibet) and India, "which incorporated 90,000 square kilometers of China's territory into British India."[39] This claim forms the basis of China's ongoing border dispute with India. What is missing here, as elsewhere in discussions of the histories of regions on China's periphery, is any acknowledgement of the perspective of the local inhabitants? For the writers of the textbooks, just as for the predominantly Han teachers and students who use them in the classroom, Tibetan history has significance only insofar as it can be related to the grand narrative of China's progress towards modernization and Great Power status. The attempt to establish Tibetan independence becomes just one more instance of imperialist interference in China's internal affairs—another obstacle to be overcome by the heroic Chinese people in their united and determined pursuit of prosperity, dignity and international respect.

ETHNIC SOLIDARITY AND THE UNIFICATION OF THE MOTHERLAND

The new textbooks for junior secondary level devote more space than their predecessors to ramming home the message of the amicable unity of all of

China's "nationalities." In this respect, the narrative traditionally culminated with the "peaceful liberation" of the minority nationality regions by the People's Liberation Army, and the subsequent setting up of "autonomous regions." Thus Tibet was "peacefully liberated" by the Chinese army in 1951 and, as the current textbook puts it, "the mainland was finally unified, and the people of every nationality achieved solidarity and brotherhood [a rough translation of the term *tuanjie*]."[40] When the army entered Lhasa, the soldiers received "a warm welcome from the government of the Tibetan region and local citizens'—an assertion illustrated by a contemporary picture of smiling monks greeting grinning Chinese soldiers.

With this, to borrow a phrase from *1066 and All That*, the history of Tibet is typically considered to have "come to a full stop," being henceforward definitively subsumed within the history of the Motherland as a whole. However, the more recent textbooks do not stop here, going on to devote a whole unit (Unit 4) to the topic of "ethnic solidarity and the unification of the motherland."[41] This brings the theme of the "solidarity" between the Han and the various "brother nationalities" (such as Tibetans, Uighurs and Mongols), together with the theme of the reunification of Hong Kong and Macau (accomplished in the late 1990s, and thus now part of the triumphant history of the People's Republic), and the issue of "cross-straits relations" (between the mainland and the yet-to-be-reunified province of Taiwan). History here thus merges into, or is replaced by, the explicit promotion of the government's current political agenda.

A section in the chapter on "solidarity among the nationalities" (*minzu tuanjie*) describing "the establishment of areas of [minority] nationality autonomy" (*minzu chuyu zizhi de shixing*), is immediately followed by a section celebrating "the collective progress/development of each nationality" (*ge minzu gongtong fazhan*).[42] "The living standards and cultural level (*sic.*) of members of minority nationalities have both been greatly improved," declares the text. Illustrations feature members of ethnic minorities (all attired quaintly in their national costumes): grinning Uighur children at Turfan's Grape Festival, monks praying at Lhasa's Jokhang Temple (the temple associated with Songtsen Gampo's Han bride, Princess Wencheng), a Tibetan farmer spraying his field with an advanced water-jet, female dancers in flowing robes performing at a song-and-dance festival to celebrate the 50th anniversary of the People's Republic, along with other pictures showing tea picking, a "Wa" women performing a traditional "drum dance," and a Korean girl doing the high jump.

The prominence typically accorded to colorfully dressed women and children (usually engaged in singing, dancing, traditional festivities or craft activities) in propaganda images of China's "minority nationalities" has also been noted by many observers.[43] Such images serve to project an image of these minorities as non-threatening, quaint and backward—gratefully dependent upon the Han "big brother" for technological progress and socioeconomic development. It is apt, therefore, that this chapter should end with a picture of a particularly famous child from a minority nationality: the Eleventh Panchen Lama. A "free reading card" (*ziyou yuedu ka*) describes the official process of selecting the eleventh incarnation of the Panchen, hailing this institution as "a great event related to the solidarity of the nationalities."[44] The card does not mention that another Tibetan boy identified by the Dalai Lama's government-in-exile as the Panchen Lama has been held in custody by the Chinese authorities for the past decade—his whereabouts remain unknown.

Treatment of the reunification of Hong Kong and Macau in the new textbooks is predictably celebratory, though once again the perspective is that of the central government, with particular prominence given to the declarations of Deng Xiaoping on these matters. The possibility that Hongkongers or Macanese themselves might have distinctive views of their own regarding reunification is not up for consideration here, as the opening of this chapter makes clear:

> The Hong Kong, Macau and Taiwan problems are all unfinished business bequeathed to us by history. The solution of these problems, and the realization of the reunification of the Motherland, is the determined resolve of the entire Chinese race, including Hong Kong, Macau and Taiwan compatriots, overseas Chinese and mainlanders.[45]

Alongside this text, a picture shows the celebrations that took place at midnight on June 30, 1997, in front of the huge digital clock set up on Tiananmen Square to count down the days, hours, minutes and seconds to Hong Kong's return to the Motherland. The caption below this describes the crowd counting down the seconds to midnight: "As the red digits on the Reunification Clock ticked over, the crowd rhythmically let out great shouts. Their shouts shook the whole of this Great Sacred Continent (*Shenzhou Dadi*) [i.e., China]. This was the Mother's heartbeat, the footfall of History."

Most of the text is devoted to descriptions of the Sino-British negotiations over Hong Kong's retrocession, with the stance of the Chinese government depicted as firm, resolute and uncompromising (as indeed it was). The symbolism of the entry of the People's Liberation Army into Hong Kong, and its establishment of a garrison there (a cause of great unease at the time to many Hong Kong people) is evoked with a picture and boxed text. The reaction of Hongkongers themselves is not discussed at all—except in the caption to a picture showing several middle-aged women letting off balloons: "Hong Kong people welcome the return to the Motherland."[46]

Far more attention is devoted to the feelings of the Taiwanese people, when in the following chapter the "daily-growing intimacy of relations" (*riyi miqie de jiaowang*) between the mainland and Taiwan are discussed.[47] The growth in contacts—personal and commercial—between Taiwan and the mainland since 1979 is noted, with pictures showing a tearful reunion between elderly relatives separated for decades by the travel ban in force until the late 1980s, a march in Taipei in favor of Beijing's Olympic bid in 2001, and happy Taiwanese tourists on the Great Wall. The text conveys the impression that all Taiwanese are longing for reunification with the Motherland, and that only the machinations of ill-intentioned foreign powers and Taiwan's self-serving political leaders are standing in the way of this outcome. Entirely glossing over the Cold War, the text reproduces certain key statements of Mao Zedong, Deng Xiaoping and Jiang Zemin regarding the importance of reunification with Taiwan, while noting the progress made in Cross-Straits relations during the late 1980s. The fact that reunification has still not occurred is explained as follows:

> Between the late 1980s and early 1990s, due to the changing international situation, foreign anti-China forces increasingly made use of the Taiwan problem in order to restrain and control China. [At the same time,] the Taiwanese authorities exploited the changing international climate in order to gradually abandon the One China Principle, unceasingly blow the "Two Chinas" trumpet, and deliberately plot the separation [of Taiwan from China]. The "Two Chinas" and "One China, One Taiwan" separatist agenda has destroyed the improving trend in cross-straits relations. The Chinese government and the Chinese people are using political, military and diplomatic means to pursue their determined struggle against separatism and "Taiwanese independence."[48]

CONCLUSION

The preceding discussion of the current content of history textbooks on the Chinese mainland demonstrates the emphasis placed by authors and curriculum developers on a state-centered, monolithic concept of nationhood in their coverage of regions and peoples that in fact exemplify the diversity and complexity of contemporary China. As noted at the start of this chapter, history textbooks in Taiwan nowadays portray Taiwanese and Chinese history in very different terms. Even in Hong Kong, the local educational authorities have pursued the controversial introduction of local history into the school curriculum, although the post-1997 politics of that Special Administrative Region have compelled them to adhere to the core precepts of the One China Principle, thus compromising some of the original aims of this initiative. Meanwhile, in independent "Outer" Mongolia, the legacy (and nationality) of Genghis Khan are viewed rather differently from their depiction in Chinese textbooks—though arguably with scarcely greater objectivity.

I have discussed recent curricular developments in Hong Kong and Taiwan at length elsewhere.[49] Here, having outlined the way these and other regions on China's periphery are treated in school textbooks on the mainland, and discussed some of the reasons for this, it remains to consider the potential implications for perceptions of these areas and peoples on the part of Chinese students. These implications include the prospects for the achievement of the kind of "ethnic solidarity" that the textbooks explicitly promote. They also involve perceptions among mainlanders of the historical realities (or the varying interpretations of these) underlying calls for Taiwanese independence, or discontent amongst Hongkongers with Beijing's policies towards that territory.

Students across China study the same curriculum for history, as for most other subjects, and they generally use the same textbooks. The books discussed above are, in addition to being studied by Han Chinese students in Beijing, Shanghai and Chongqing, also used by Tibetan, Uighur, and Mongol students in Lhasa, Urumqi and Hohhot.[50] Moreover, alternative resources for the teaching of Tibetan, Uighur and Mongol history are not available, nor is it usual for any provision to be made for the teaching of local history (except, perhaps, in a few exceptional elite schools in cities such as Beijing). The curriculum reflects the traditional Confucian view that history is, properly, the chronicle of the central state—therefore areas such as Tibet, Xinjiang and (Inner) Mongolia, not being (nor recognized as ever having been) states, have no distinct or separate histories of their own. What they have instead is culture—dances, songs, quaint folk customs and practices, and colorful costumes. Political sensitivities reinforce the lack of interest in teaching, researching or writing (and publishing) about the histories of these "minority" regions, so that on a recent visit to the main bookstore in Lhasa I was unable to find a single book on the modern history of Tibet; instead, the shelves were stacked with tourist guidebooks and volumes on religion, culture and customs, with titles such as *Tibet— Land of Mystery.*

The phrase "contemptuous museumification" has been aptly used to describe official policies towards ethnic minorities in mainland China,[51] but there is nothing uniquely Chinese about such an approach. Textbooks in British or French schools during the age of empire tended to be equally, if not more, dismissive of the histories of colonial peoples (though, as I have shown elsewhere, the same was not true of textbooks in a "post-imperial" anachronism such as late-twentieth-century Hong Kong).[52] Africans and Arabs were typically portrayed as backward, if picturesque, peoples, grateful to their colonizers for bestowing on them the benefits of progress and civilization.[53] The relations between the Russians and the peoples of Central Asia were depicted in very similar terms during the Soviet period. As we have seen, it is as the colorful but backward recipients of benefits bestowed that "minority nationalities" of Chinese Central Asia (Tibet, Xinjiang and Inner Mongolia) are still depicted in contemporary Chinese textbooks.

The material benefits that Chinese rule has brought to these areas—in terms of the development of infrastructure, modern health services, sanitation and education—cannot be dismissed, but this does not blind the "minorities" in question to the colonial nature of their relationship with the Han "big brother." The burgeoning domestic tourism industry has in recent years contributed to an upsurge of interest in Tibet and Xinjiang among educated Chinese middle-class youth—an interest reflected in the current fashion for decorating bars and cafes in Beijing with photographs of and objects from Tibet. However, many Tibetans are conscious that this interest seldom extends beyond a romantic fascination felt by urban Chinese sophisticates for the primitive, mysterious, remote and picturesque. At the same time, there is concern amongst older Tibetans and Uighurs that the school curriculum, while failing to provide Han Chinese with the basis of any real understanding of their communities, also denies their own children access to knowledge of their ancient and complex histories and cultures.[54] It is debatable whether such a state of affairs constitutes a sound basis for constructing relationships of mutual respect, let alone "solidarity," between Han and Tibetans, Uighurs, Mongols and others.

More alarming, perhaps, not least because of its potential implications for stability throughout the East Asian region, is the way in which young Chinese perceive the "Taiwan problem." The chances of finding a needle in a haystack are rather better than those of locating a mainland Chinese who is prepared to concede the legitimacy of any alternative to the standard textbook account of Taiwan's historical relationship with the Motherland. Here, as in other respects, the Communist regime may find itself the victim of the very success of its own propaganda, since the public conviction that Taiwan has always been and forever must remain an indivisible part of China is so strong as to severely limit the government's room for manoeuvre in any negotiations. The very legitimacy of the Communist Party is so dependent on its reputation for promoting and upholding national unity (premised on the "One China Principle'), that a radical compromise on the Taiwan issue might dangerously undermine the Party's grip on power on the mainland.

Blame for secessionist impulses in Taiwan, as in Tibet, Xinjiang and—historically—in (Outer) Mongolia, continues to be attributed, in textbooks as in the Chinese media, to the interference of foreign imperialists, rather than on the complexities of internal politics and inter-ethnic relationships within the Chinese Empire. At the same time, China is consistently portrayed throughout school history textbooks as a paragon of "non-aggression," frequently the victim but never the perpetrator of unjust wars with foreign nations. These twin beliefs help to explain the hysterical indignation with which perceived slights to China's national dignity from Japan and America have been received in recent years. They also mean that a Chinese government would face little difficulty in justifying to public opinion any decision to go to war—most likely with Japan and America—over Taiwan. Moreover, given that the legitimacy of Mongolian independence is implicitly rejected by the textbooks (and by many educated Chinese), a scenario whereby a Chinese government might seek to deflect attention from internal difficulties through a campaign to recover and pacify lost lands along the northern frontier is by no means inconceivable.[55] After all, China did fight brief border wars with both India and the Soviet Union during the 1960s.

This is not to suggest that any veering towards military adventurism on the part of the Chinese state is inevitable—far from it. However, the course of China's continued economic development is beset by potential threats to her political and social stability, not least the challenge of spreading the benefits of growth in an equitable fashion to backward and impoverished inland regions (including minority regions such as Tibet), managing the implications of massive internal migration, and dealing with the problems of large-scale under- and unemployment. The Communist regime has made the promotion of an uncritical, state-centered patriotism a key element in its strategy for containing threats to internal social cohesion—and the history curriculum for schools continues to be seen as perhaps the foremost vehicle for conveying patriotic messages. The problem is that a homogenous and totalizing vision of national identity leaves both government and people ill-equipped to either comprehend or deal with the evolving complexity of relations between the Han majority and the "minority nationalities," or between the central state and the inconveniently distinctive Han populations of Taiwan and Hong Kong (or, for that matter, Guangzhou). The solution may perhaps lie in a broader vision of "Chineseness'—less rigidly ethnocentric, and more pluralist, adaptable and inclusive; the kind of vision proposed by "Harvard Confucianists" such as Tu Wei-ming.[56] To date, however, there is no sign that the Communist authorities are even aware that such an alternative vision might exist, let alone that they are ready to embrace it.

NOTES

1. This was the "Anti-Confucius and Lin Biao" campaign of the early 1970s, which paired the ancient sage with Mao's disgraced former deputy.

2. One notable example is Zeng Guofan, one of the leaders of the late nineteenth-century "Self-strengthening" movement.

3. See Mei-Hui Liu, Li-Ching Hong and Edward Vickers, "Identity Issues in Taiwan's History Curriculum," and Stephane Corcuff, "Historiography, National Identity Politics and Ethnic Introspection in Taiwan," Chapters 3 and 4 in Edward Vickers and Alisa Jones ed. *History Education and National Identity in East Asia.* (New York: Routledge, 2005).

4. See Alisa Jones (2005), "Changing the Past to Serve the Present: History Education in Mainland China," Chapter 2 in ed. Vickers and Jones, op. cit.; also Barry Sautman, "Myths of Descent, Racial Nationalism and Ethnic Minorities," in *The Construction of Racial Identities in China and Japan,* ed. Dikotter, (Hong Kong: Hong Kong University Press, 1997),pp. 75–95.

5. In 2000 I mentioned this debate over the "Out of Africa" theory to two Hongkongese colleagues at the University of Hong Kong, and discovered that they were also reluctant to accept the idea that the ancestors of Chinese might have come from Africa (though they would have settled for Europe).

6. Chih-Yu Shih, "Ethnic Economy of Citizenship in China: Four Approaches to Identity Formation," in *Changing Meanings of Citizenship in Modern China* eds. Merle Goldman and Elizabeth J. Perry (Cambridge, MA.: Harvard University Press, 2002), pp. 232–254.

7. See Edward Vickers, *In Search of An Identity: The Politics of History as a School Subject in Hong Kong, 1960s–2002* (New York: Routledge, 2003), Chapter 2. Also the surveys carried out by the Hong Kong Transition Project, led by Michael DeGolyer at the Hong Kong Baptist University.

8. See Joseph Fewsmith, *China Since Tiananmen: The Politics of Transition* (Cambridge: Cambridge University Press, 2001).

9. Anthony Sweeting, *A Phoenix Transformed* (Hong Kong: Hong Kong University Press, 1995)

10. Fewsmith, op. cit. See also Suzanne Ogden, *Inklings of Democracy in China* (Cambridge, MA: Harvard University Asian Center, 2002).

11. Peter Hayes Gries, *China's New Nationalism* (Berkeley, CA: University of California Press, 2004)

12. See Gries, op. cit., Chapter 7.

13. On China's postmodernist/postcolonialist debates see Fewsmith, op. cit., Ogden, op. cit., and Wang Hui, *China's New Order: Society, Politics and Economy in Transition* (edited by Theodore Huters) (Cambridge, MA: Harvard University Press, 2003).

14. Quoted in Fewsmith, op. cit., 223.

15. Bob Adamson, *China's English: A History of English in Chinese Education* (Hong Kong: Hong Kong University Press, 2004).

16. Alisa Jones, Chapters 1 and 2 in eds. Vickers and Jones, op.cit.

17. Alisa Jones, Chapter 2 in eds. Vickers and Jones, op.cit.

18. *The People's Education Press* (PEP), Zhongguo Lishi (Chinese History), Year 7, Volume 2, 2001, p. 60.

19. Ibid., 62. The result might be expressed in footballing terms: China: 1–Europe: 0.

20. Ibid.,p. 21.

21. Ibid., p. 63.

22. Ibid., p. 99.

23. Ibid., p. 100.

24. Alisa Jones, "Changing the Past to Serve the Present," Chapter 2 in eds. Vickers and Jones op.cit., pp. 91–93.

25. PEP (2001) op.cit., p. 100.

26. Ibid., p. 121.

27. PEP, A Modern and Contemporary History of China, Vol. 1. (English-language version of the history textbook for senior secondary level), 2002, p. 76.

28. These gentry were led by Koo Hsien-jung, the father of Koo Cheng-fu, who during the 1990s became Taiwan's chief negotiator with the mainland Chinese government. On the coverage of this episode in Taiwanese textbooks of the late-1990s, see Stephane Corcuff (2005), Chapter 4 in eds. Vickers and Jones, op. cit., p. 140.

29. PEP, A Modern and Contemporary History of China, Vol 1, 2002, p. 78.

30. See Julian Dierkes, "The Stability of Postwar Japanese History Education Amid Global Changes" 2005, Chapter 8, and Yoshiko Nozaki, "Japanese Politics and the History Textbook Controversy," 2005, Chapter 9, eds. in Vickers and Jones, op. cit.

31. For example, the Japanese term *kamikaze*, meaning "divine wind," was originally coined to describe the storms that in 1281 wrecked the invasion fleet dispatched by China's (Mongol) Yuan dynasty Emperor Kublai Khan (Kublai is referred to in the texts by his Chinese reign title, Yuan Shizu). This episode is nowhere mentioned in the junior secondary history textbooks, though it is noted that the Yuan dynasty "strengthened control over the Liu Qiu [islands—i.e., Okinawa]." China's historic claims to overlordship over Okinawa are linked to the continuing territorial dispute with Japan concerning sovereignty over the Diaoyutai/Senkakuji Islands.

32. PEP, A Modern and Contemporary History of China, Vol. 1, 2002, pp. 8–9.

33. Ibid., pp. 161–164.

34. Ibid., p. 163.

35. Ibid., p. 163.

36. Ibid., pp. 163–164.

37. This eventually came as the result of Soviet pressure on the CCP.

38. Ibid., p. 164.

39. Ibid., p. 165.

40. PEP, Zhongguo Lishi, Year 8, Vol. 2. 4, 2002.

41. Ibid., pp. 54–69.

42. Ibid., pp. 56–57.

43. Notably Uradyn E. Bulag, *The Mongols at China's Edge: History and the Politics of National Unity* (Lanham, MD: Rowman and Littlefield, 2002).

44. PEP (2002), Zhongguo Lishi, Year 8, pp. 59.

45. Ibid., p. 60.
46. Ibid., p. 61.
47. Ibid., pp. 66–67.
48. Ibid., p. 66.
49. See Chapters 3 and 5 on Taiwan and Hong Kong in eds. Vickers and Jones, op. cit.
50. And all students—including those from ethnic minorities—study history through the medium of Chinese. However, People's Education Press has recently published English-language versions of its senior secondary history textbooks, as part of a strategy to allow students in some elite schools to improve their English by studying some subjects through the medium of English.
51. *Edward Friedman, Paranoia, Polarisation and Suicide: Unexpected Consequences of Taiwan's 2004 Presidential Election.* Annual SOAS Taiwan Lecture, presented at SOAS, London, June 24, 2004.
52. Vickers, op. cit., 2003.
53. See *"Benefits bestowed"? Education and British Imperialism,* ed. J.A. Mangan,(Manchester, UK: St. Martin's Press, 1988).
54. I base these observations on personal conversations with Tibetans and Uighurs in Beijing, Xinjiang and Tibet during 2003 and 2004.
55. Within the Chinese Academy of Social Sciences there is a special group devoted to the task of researching China's various claims to land currently ruled by Russia, Mongolia, India and various Central Asian states, as well as Chinese claims to various islets and atolls in the Sea of Japan and the South China Sea.
56. Tu Wei-ming (ed.), *The Living Tree: The Changing Meaning of Being Chinese Today* (Stanford: Stanford University Press, 1994).

CHAPTER 2

CULTURE WARS: JAPANESE HISTORY TEXTBOOKS AND THE CONSTRUCTION OF OFFICIAL MEMORY[1]

Keith Crawford

INTRODUCTION

The collective memories of nations are scarred by their past and what they decide to celebrate or forget about their history says much about how they wish to be seen by themselves and others. For the British important defining moments have been the London Blitz and the Battle of Britain, events burnt deeply into the British psyche that in some elements of popular culture create and maintain definitions of what it means to be British. For the Germans the experiences of National Socialism and the horrors of the Holocaust have been pivotal in shaping the social, moral and political reconstruction of post-war Germany (see Pingel, this volume). In addition, the dropping of the atomic bombs has enabled Japan to present Hiroshima as a site of national victim-hood.[2] But while the defeat of Nazi Germany resulted in the creation of a new political culture that underpinned the

What Shall We Tell the Children?, pages 49–68
Copyright © 2006 by Information Age Publishing

construction of a new nation, post-war Japanese society has found it difficult to fully embrace such a process (see Nicolls, this volume). In Tokyo the Yasukuni Shrine, where the Japanese show respect to their war dead, includes among those honored individuals executed for war crimes. For Paris "It is as though a memorial to Germany's top Nazis still sat at the center of Berlin."[3] Adjacent to the shrine is a war museum containing artefacts such as military uniforms, letters, poetry, wartime newsreels of Japanese military actions, a full-size Japanese Zero and as you leave the museum over 6,000 black and white photographs of Japanese servicemen who lost their lives in war. Visitors are not offered analysis or interpretation that explores Japan's wartime activities in anything approaching a critical fashion. Since 1990, several senior government officials have visited the shrine.[4]

An important cultural and political context is provided by the fact that contemporary Japan has been accused, by its critics, of not fully coming to terms with its imperialistic role during the 1930s and 1940s. The activities of Unit 731, responsible for bacteriological warfare in Harbin, China[5] the experiences of Chinese and Korean "comfort woman," sexual slaves used by Japanese soldiers, and the Nanjing Massacre in 1937, which saw thousands of Chinese civilians and soldiers killed are events that have been a powerful feature of Japan's political relationships with its Asian neighbors. Claim and counter-claim regarding authenticity, alleged fabrication and responsibility generate fierce debate and conflict within Japan's political culture. Hein and Selden have pointed out that "The stories chosen or invented about the national past are invariably prescriptive—instructing people how to think and act as national subjects and how to view relations with outsiders."[6] This is the case inside Japan and since the 1980s these debates have been powerfully acted out in arguments over the content of school history textbooks which have generated long running court cases, violent demonstrations, death threats and the resurgence of a growing and influential cadre of Japanese neo-nationalists.

The aim of this chapter is to explore the way in which the social construction of Japanese history textbooks illustrates tensions inside Japan concerning images of national identity. The next section briefly describes the bureaucratic process through which Japanese textbook knowledge is officially sanctioned. This is followed by a critical analysis of the history textbook controversies that have raged in Japan and, in particular, the recent conflicts surrounding the authorization of a new generation of history textbooks for school use in 2004. This is contextualized by an analysis that places the cultural wars fought over Japanese national identity within a framework of a resurgent conservative nationalism that has profound implications for Japanese domestic politics and international relations.

THE BUREAUCRACY OF TEXTBOOK SELECTION

The intensity of conflict over the construction of official knowledge inside Japan is partly the product of the way in which textbooks very nearly assume the role of semi-official government documents providing authoritative statements of control and the manner in which they can be seen to reflect national policy imperatives. Japanese textbooks are nationalized and standardized.[7] All school texts must be screened and approved by a textbook screening committee made up of Ministry of Education civil servants, appointed teachers and scholars who ensure that texts meet ministry guidelines determining content and vocabulary. Japanese teachers must choose texts from an officially sanctioned list of six to eight history textbooks. However, because the Japanese national curriculum prescribes the subject matter, and because each textbook must deliver this content, the texts are very similar.

A framework written by the Ministry contains criteria to be used in writing textbooks. These criteria are sent to publishing companies who contract professional historians and teachers to write drafts that are presented for approval. Writing in 1988, on the way in which history textbooks are controlled by the Ministry, Horio claimed that the "inspectors have been uncompromising in their desire to constrain the freedom of authors with regard to a number of important issues ... Moreover, the Ministry has been quite meddlesome with regard to ...Japan's repeated war-making."[8] While attempts have been made since 1990s to liberalize the textbook screening process, to simplify it and make it more transparent, final authority to decide content remains with the Ministry of Education.[9]

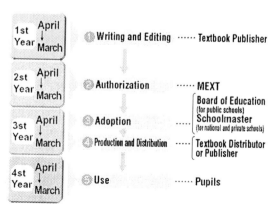

Figure 2.1.   Overview of Elementary and Secondary Education Ministry of Education, Sports, Science, and Technology. Available at: http://www.mext.go.jp/english/org/formal/16.htm

WARTIME ACTIONS AND THE POLITICS
OF NATIONAL MEMORY

After capturing Shanghai on December 9, 1937, the Imperial army attacked Nanjing, the then capital of China, and on the 13th December entered the city. During the next six weeks it is alleged that Japanese troops engaged in a program of atrocities during which they looted and burned, raped, tortured, and murdered Chinese civilians and soldiers.[10] American journalists wrote that "Wholesale looting, the violation of women, the murder of civilians, the eviction of Chinese from their homes, mass executions of war prisoners and the impressing of able-bodied men turned Nanjing into a city of terror."[11] The correspondent of the *Chicago Daily News* called the siege and capture of Nanking "Four Days of Hell" in his dispatch on December 15, 1937. On December 14, the reporter from the Tokyo *Asahi Shimbun* newspaper wrote, "At one time, after Nanjing was captured, more than 30,000 Chinese were driven to the foot of the city wall. Machine guns then swept the crowd and grenades were thrown from atop the wall ... 30,000 people were all killed, most of them were women, children, and elderly."[12]

Despite these, and since then, numerous eye witness accounts from victims, perpetrators and media observers, photographic evidence and academic accounts, for decades official reaction inside Japan was to question, and in some cases deny, the reliability of the evidence of what became known as the Nanjing massacre.[13] Writing in 1991 Buruma has claimed, only partially accurately, that through official evasions the event had been "...killed by silence."[14] Those who have marginalized and denied the Nanjing Massacre and have fought to ensure that accounts either do not appear in history textbooks, or are highly sanitized, include powerful political figures and social commentators who cannot be lightly dismissed.

As well as university academics, they number among their members and supporters executives from companies such as Mitsubishi, Mazda, Toshiba, Fujitsu, Canon and national banking organizations as well as newspaper owners and TV executives.[15] Lobbying, appeals, and petitions to the Ministry of Education and local curriculum committees have also been part of their strategy. Political support has come from ministry of education officials. In November 2004, Education Minister Nariaki Nakayama told a news conference "Every country's history has light and shadow. While we must reflect on bad deeds, we must not conduct education on the basis of a self-torturing historical perspective that everything that has been done was bad"[16] and that "It is good that references to "comfort women" and abduction from occupied territories are decreasing." Within hours Nakayama was forced to play down his remarks by claiming that they were based on his personal beliefs and that he should not have made such comments in public stating that "I should have refrained from speaking from my individual standpoint."[17]

The political and ideological context of the cultural wars over the construction of official memory in Japan lies in the resurgence of conservative nationalism during the 1990s. Like many technically advanced capitalist nations Japanese society in the 1980s and 1990s suffered from a crisis of confidence generated in large part by challenges to the idea of the nation-state posited by economic globalization. Socioeconomic crisis threatened to undermine the social hegemony of dominant interest groups and led to a fundamental questioning of core values. Economic crisis saw the power of the nation-state weakening and, for conservatives in particular, to a "sense of loss."[18]

Also of significance was the impact that the end of the Cold War had upon Japan's political position, the destruction of an East-West binary undermined Japan's position as a democratic bulwark against the threats of Communist expansionism in the East. One outcome has been that "Grievances once swept under the rug by expensive American brooms in the name of anti-Communist unity were exposed to public view again."[19] A significant problem for Japan in the post-cold war climate is that it is caught between promoting a form of Asian federalism requiring greater socioeconomic and political unity with Korea and China, its most important trading partners in the region, or to continue to support its close relationship with the west, and with the United States in particular as the involvement of the Japanese Self Defence Force in Iraq testifies. There has been in some sectors of Japanese political culture a tendency to retreat into a nationalism that seeks to hold on to old certainties. In addition, the apathy and delinquency of Japanese youth, their disaffection and alienation from Japanese society and their support of American culture are seen as important threats to Japanese national identity.[20]

The political culture of Japan is dominated by the Liberal Democratic Party (LDP) that, in various coalitions, has controlled Japanese politics for decades in support of a conservative political ideology. A consistent theme of LDP education policy has been that national pride and patriotism ought to be essential elements of the school curriculum.[21] The ideology of Japanese conservatism emphasizes the importance of a strong state and regards custom and tradition as vital properties in an established order. Japanese conservatives have seen cultural changes and shifts in patterns of socioeconomic and political relationships as dangerous to traditional forms of life. Within this context schools become vitally important cultural sites responsible for articulating, reproducing and maintaining clearly defined sets of knowledge and values.

CREATING "OFFICIAL" HISTORY

Given this context, what has been the role of official screeners inside the Ministry of Education in shaping national memory? Japanese textbooks do not ignore the Nanjing massacre and other atrocities.[22] But there have been and remain attempts by politicians and pressure groups to remove, censor or to marginalize accounts to promote a particular view of Japanese national identity. The civil law suits brought by Professor Saburo Ienaga, who fought against textbook screening claiming that it violated freedom of expression and was unconstitutional, provide the most well known illustration of Japan's textbook wars.[23] In 1982, Ienaga forced the Japanese government to acknowledge that the word "advance," used in history textbooks, was a euphemism for Japan's invasion of Asia, and to accept that it amounted to "aggression."[24] In 1993, Ienaga challenged a Ministry ruling that eight sections of his book concerning the activities of Unit 731 be removed or adapted.

The Ministry had ordered content to be deleted or revised from a 1983 version arguing that the existence of the unit was open to discussion and that the content showed Japan in a negative light.[25] The High Court agreed that Ienaga could include details of Unit 731, and asked the Ministry to adopt a more liberal approach in its screening process. The court rejected claims by Ienaga that seven other sections of his book had been illegally censored, including a section about comfort woman. The court upheld the Ministry's right to screen textbooks and to remove passages considered objectionable or inappropriate including references to war crimes.[26] The manner in which Professor Ienaga's textbooks were subject to screening is illustrated in Table 2.1. [27]

More recently, Okamoto has argued that the climate of textbook censorship was transformed in the 1990s by the rapid internationalization of Japanese society and criticism of post-war Japanese nationalism by other nations in the region.[28] Okamoto's frame of analysis was the "long-lived textbook" used in Fitzgerald's study on American history textbooks that linked alterations in content to social change.[29] Okamoto claims that in response to social changes in the 1990s the Ministry took a more objective standpoint in granting approval to history textbooks. Okamoto claims that this change influenced descriptions of the Nanjing massacre by comparing a 1983 version of a history textbook with a 1994 version, yet the differences in this example are, at best, marginal (See Table 2.2).

Table 2.1.   The Censoring of Ienaga's Textbooks

Ienaga's textbook	Comment made by the Ministry of Education	Ienaga's Response
Describing the Nanking Massacre		
Immediately after the occupation of Nanking, the Japanese army killed numerous Chinese soldiers and citizens. This incident came to be known as the Nanking Massacre.	Readers might interpret this description as meaning that the Japanese Army unilaterally massacred Chinese immediately after the occupation. This passage should be revised so that it is not interpreted in such a way.	The facts of the Nanking Massacre by the Japanese military forces were made known through news reports just after the incident and through documents submitted during the Tokyo War Crimes Trials. Since then, more detailed facts have become widely known among the Japanese people.
The Activities of Unit 731		
A unit specializing in bacteriological warfare called the 731 Unit was stationed on the outskirts of Harbin and until the Soviet Union entered the war, this unit engaged in such atrocious acts as murdering several thousand Chinese and non-Japanese by using them in biological experiments.	Delete entire passage. No credible scholarly research exists concerning Unit 731. It is still premature, therefore, to take up this matter in a school textbook.	The historical facts concerning Unit 731 have been collaborated by innumerable records and documents. By demanding the deletion of this passage the government is trying to conceal, in academic studies, the truth about criminal activities.

CREATING NATIONAL MEMORY: CONTINUITY OR CHANGE?

Okamoto's claims are over-optimistic; evidence does not suggest a move towards liberalizing the textbook screening process. Barnard, in analyzing the content of 88 high school history textbooks issued in 1995, writes that the discourse of presentation was deliberately designed to protect Japanese face. Barnard writes that the language of the textbooks "… not only protects the negative face of the Japanese state, but also defers to its positive face…"[30] Barnard concluded that, "What I think the textbook data that I have examined clearly shows is that the present day Ministry of Education identifies itself closely with the Japanese state of 1945, and the power structures within that state."[31] Barnard's analysis becomes more credible given the conflicts that have dominated revisions of history textbooks during the past five years.

Table 2.2.   Changes in Japanese History Textbooks

1983	(page 317)...Because Japan undervalued such a situation, and the military aimed at the rule of the northern part of China, its aggression had been expanded taking the opportunity of the Lu Gou Qiao Incident in July, 1937. Therefore, the second co-operation of the Kuomintang and the communist army was formally approved in September, and both Japan and China began the full-scale war (*the Japan–China War*).[1] **Though Japan occupied the important places in the northern part of China and the Nanking area by the end of 1937,**[2] the unity of the Chinese side kept, moving their government from Nanking to Wu Han and to Chungking to continue resistance. Though Japan occupied Wu Han and Kuangchou in October, 1938, only important cities and the traffic lines which had connected the cities were secured, and its rule did not extend to wide rural areas. The pro-Japanese regime of Wang Zhao-Ming (1883–1944), which Japan had established in 1940 in order to oppose to the Chungking Government, did not have much power. (1) *At that time, the Japanese Government called this war the "China Incident."* **(2) In occupying Nanking, the Japanese military slaughtered a lot of Chinese, and invited criticism from the world** (*the Nanking Massacre*).
1994	(Page 310) The Japanese military had expanded its aggression taking the opportunity of the Lu Gou Qiao Incident in July, 1937, aiming at invasion to the northern part of China. On the other hand, the second co-operation of the Kuomintang and the communist army was approved in September in China, and both Japan and China began the full-scale war (the Japan–China War). **Japan occupied the important places in the northern part of China and Nanking by the end of 1937. Especially in occupying Nanking, they slaughtered a lot of Chinese and invited criticism from the world** (*the Nanking Massacre*). The Chinese side kept undertaking support from Great Britain, the United States, and the Soviet Union, moving their government from Nanking to Wu Han and to Chungking to continue resistance. Though Japan occupied Wu Han and Kuangchou in October, 1938, only important cities and the traffic lines which had connected with cities were secured, and its rule did not extend to wide rural areas. Japan hoisted the construction of the East Asian New Order in 1940, opposed the Chungking Government, and built the pro-Japanese regime of Wang Zhao-Ming (1883–1944) in Nanking. However, Japan could not receive wide support, and there was no knowing how the war would develop.

The "imagined community"[32] is powerfully institutionalized in Japan and images of myth and legend remain at the heart of Japanese national identity at the beginning of the 21st century. Olsen has suggested that "Textbooks, like religious ritual, are devices for putting ideas and beliefs above suspicion"[33] a claim which illustrates the position occupied by a powerful conservative attack upon liberalizing the content of history textbooks. The intensification of textbook wars and the role of ultra-conservative nationalism gathered pace in the mid-1990s within a context where the Japanese government began to publicly express regret for the Imperial army's wartime behavior. On August 23, 1993, Prime Minister Hosokawa Morihiro expressed "profound remorse and apologies" for Japan's wartime actions. On August 15, 1995, Prime Minister Murayama Tomiichi

expressed feelings of "deep remorse" and "heartfelt apology." These conciliatory gestures provoked intense challenges from Japanese conservatives
and ultra-nationalists.[34] In August 1995, Prime Minister Tomiichi issued a
public apology after, the Education Minister Yoshinobu Shimamura, said
that Japan had no need to apologize further for its wartime activities.[35]

Tensions were further heightened in 1997, when the publication of *The
Rape of Nanking: The Forgotten Holocaust of World War II* by the late Iris Chang
created a storm of controversy. What is now generally agreed to be a deeply
and seriously flawed work generated a similar impact to that of Daniel
Goldhagen's book *Hitler's Willing Executioners: Ordinary Persons and the Holocaust* (1996). Chang was unequivocal in her condemnation of Japan; in an
interview with the *South China Morning Post* she claimed that:

> The Japanese have for decades systematically purged references to the
> Nanking massacre from their textbooks. They have removed photographs of
> the Nanking massacre from museums, tampered with original source mate-
> rial, and excised from popular culture any mention of the massacre. Even
> respected history professors in Japan have joined right-wing forces to do
> what they perceive to be their national duty: discredit reports of a Nanking
> massacre.[36]

Chang's book generated intense hostility in Japan and fuelled the anxieties of ultra-nationalist conservatives. The book was, and still is, criticized as
inaccurate, shoddy scholarship containing mediocre analysis. Japan's ambas-
sador in Washington, Kunihiko Saito, described it as "...one-sided and filled
with historical inaccuracies."[37] Japanese nationalists threatened action ranging from lawsuits to assassination.[38] So intense was opposition that the book's
publication in Japan was dropped after threats of violence from right-wing
extremists forced the Japanese publisher to withdraw. Chang and her U.S.
publisher had objected to the planned removal of photographs and to
include in the book a section correcting claimed inaccuracies.[39]

Controversy over events such as the Nanjing Massacre and comfort
women have been used as political weapons to create a context within
which debates over national identity were articulated. In January 1995, Professor of Education at Tokyo University, Nobukatsu Fujioka and his supporters co-founded the *Association for the Advancement of A Liberalist View of
History* and in December 1996, the *Reform Society for Creating New History
Textbooks*, aiming to revise what he dubbed Japan's "masochistic education"
in history. Fujioka and his supporters are implacably opposed to the politics of apology. Their objective is to "...inculcate a sense of pride in the history of our nation."[40] They are deeply uneasy about the economic and
political rise of China and Korea which, against a background of Japanese
economic decline, has bred an insecurity which has led ultra-conservative

nationalists to construct an argument that sees Japan at war, economically, with the rest of Asia.[41]

The groups are particularly opposed to texts approved in 1997, that refer to comfort women and to accounts of the Nanjing massacre that, they argue, contribute to the manufacture of an anti-Japanese ideology and are the product of an international conspiracy aimed at undermining Japan. Conservative opposition played a prominent role in the process of authorizing versions of history textbooks to be used in Japanese elementary and junior high schools from September 2004. In October 2000, eight Japanese publishing houses submitted proposals and an analysis of the changes made between the 1997 and 2002 versions reveals interesting continuities and changes. In the 1997, descriptions of the Nanjing Massacre (See Table 2.3) six of the eight textbooks in current use state that hundreds of thousands died, and four refer to Chinese claims of 300,000 victims. In new editions only two publishers mention the number of victims, and none refer to the Chinese claim, the remainder state that "a lot of people" or "many" were killed.[42] While there is continuity in describing the Nanjing massacre as a mass slaughter of prisoners of war, women and children, six out of the eight texts for 2002 absolve the Japanese people from any culpability by stating that they knew nothing of the massacre until after the war had ended, only two out of the 1997 textbooks adopt this stance.

As one of the new texts the *Society for History Textbook Reform* drafted *The History of a Nation,* Fujioka claimed that 250,000 advance copies of the book had been ordered.[43] Presented for screening by the *Fuso Publishing Company,* the book questioned the historical authenticity of the Nanjing massacre and ignored the experiences of comfort women or the work of Unit 731.[44] The authors of the text were asked to make 137 revisions, five times the average number of amendments asked for in the seven other texts and 43% of the total number of changes requested.[45]

The events at Nanjing, referred to as "the Nanjing Incident" of 1937,[46] are discussed in the briefest of terms, the texts notes that "there were many casualties among the civilians [inflicted] by the Japanese force."[47] What is more forcefully discussed is the claim that doubts have been expressed as to the extent of deaths and the events of the incident and that it has generated much different opinion, although readers are not provided with any reference as to what those doubts are or who has expressed them. In a section discussing the International Military Tribunal for the Far East doubts are expressed by the authors as to the veracity of the Nanjing incident and the legitimacy of the tribunal and its findings. The text recognize that the tribunal acknowledged the massacre of Chinese civilians at Nanjing but also states "To be sure, regarding the reality of the incident, points of doubt have been raised in terms of the data, and various views exist, so the controversy still continues today."[48]

Despite changes the book was criticized by some for being too national-istic, overtly ideological and for ignoring the sensitivities of other Asian nations.[49] The *China Daily* accused the textbook of altering or removing important historical facts related to Japan's wartime activities in Asia. The Chinese accused the Reform Group's textbook of portraying Japan's impe-rialism as a force for good in helping to free Asian countries from colonial rule. The state-run *Renmin Ribao* (*People's Daily*) has carried a number of articles criticizing the adoption of the textbook. The paper quotes a For-eign Office official as stating that, "The nature of the problem regarding the textbooks in Japan is whether the Japanese side can correctly handle their history of invasion. The Japanese side should take concrete action to honor its commitment on the issue and educate Japanese young people with the correct view of history."[50] Japan is accused of "dodging reality," and failing to "treat history as it is"; here the claim is made that "the Japa-nese Rightist forces are attempting to tamper with and delete this part of their bloody history of invasion."[51] While acknowledging that protest in Japan was significant[52] and concerns profound, the *People's Daily* also notes the political power of the Reform Society commenting that, "The new his-tory textbook … distorts history, publicizes a 'Japanese Empire History Viewpoint' and beautifies the aggressive war. The adoption of the textbook no doubt brings harm to inexperienced youngsters" and "will turn young people into 'tools of extra-right politicians.'"[53]

It is difficult to appreciate the depth and intensity of the anger felt by South Koreans and the Chinese with both complaining that the book dis-torted history and justified Japan's wartime aggression in Asia. South Korean President Kim Dae Jung urged Japan to have a "correct" under-standing of its history and Chinese President Jiang Zemin said that Japan should pay "special consideration" to the textbook and handle the issue "so as not to damage the friendship between the two countries."[54]

It is not only the *Fuso* Book that has attempted to marginalize Japan's wartime activities, the issue of how to report the experiences of comfort women remains highly controversial. In February 1996, a report for the Human Rights Committee of the United Nations described the comfort women as sex slaves and their treatment as a crime against humanity. The report called upon Japan to punish those responsible, compensate victims and ensure that discussion of the event was included in the school curricu-lum. Table 2.4 illustrates that new drafts from only three of the publishing houses mention comfort women, against seven out of the eight books authorized for use in 1997. As in the 1997 textbooks, there is some inc[?]sistency in the approach in these texts with each emphasizing diff[?] issues e.g. appeals for compensation, the forced nature of conscript[?] the fact that Korean, Taiwanese *and* Japanese women were conscr[?]

Table 2.3. Descriptions of the Nanking Massacre in High School History Textbooks

Publishing House	Current Textbooks (1997)	New Editions
The Nippon Shoseki	Japanese troops invaded northern China and occupied Shanghai and Nanking and killed many Chinese people. The Japanese troops slaughtered at least 150,000– 200,000 people including women, children and POWs in the middle of February) the Nanking Incident).	Japanese troops occupied the capital city Nanking and killed about 200,000 people including POWs, plundered and behaved violently. This provoked international criticism (the Nanking Incident). Most Japanese did not know about this incident until the end of the war.
The Shimizu Shoin	Japan took part in cruel acts in parts of China. They killed many people including soldiers, the old, women and children without distinction especially in the Nanking occupation. The numbers of the dead are said to be more than several hundred thousands, in China it is said more than 300,000 died. Other countries criticised the mass slaughter at Nanking strongly but the Japanese people knew nothing.	Japanese soldiers killed people including soldiers, the old, women and children without distinction especially in the Nanking occupation. Other counties criticised the mass slaughter but the Japanese people knew nothing. It is assumed that the dead were hundreds of thousands or more than 300,000.
The Teikoku Shoin	Japanese troops occupied the capital city of Nanking. In Nanking Japanese troops killed a lot of people including woman and children. For this other countries criticised "the Japanese barbarous act" (the mass slaughter of Nanking).	Japanese troops occupied the capital city of Nanking. In Nanking Japanese troops killed not only soldiers but a lost of Chinese people including woman and children and were criticised for commiting "barbarous acts" (the mass slaughter of Nanking). But the Japanese people knew nothing of this.
The Kyoiku Shuppan	Japanese troops occupied the capital city Nanking and killed a lot of Chinese people. Including soldiers, women and children and they plundered and behaved violently (the incident of the Nanking slaughter). It is said that there were 200,000 victims but in China more than 300,000.	Japanese troops occupied the capital city of Nanking and killed a lot of Chinese people including POWs, children and women and behaved violently (the incident was called the Nanking slaughter).

Table 2.3. Descriptions of the Nanking Massacre in High School History Textbooks

Publishing House	Current Textbooks (1997)	New Editions
The Osaka Shoseki	The Japanese troops were resisted and slaughtered 200,000 people in Nanking, they have been criticised by other countries but the Japanese people knew nothing. This incident is called the mass slaughter of the Nanking incident. China estimates that there were more than 300,000 victims.	The Japanese troops were resisted and killed many Chinese people including women and children. For this Japan was criticised by other countries (the Nanking incident). The Japanese people knew nothing until the situation was revealed at the Eastern international military trial.
The Tokyo Shoseki	Japanese troops occupied Nanking at the end of the year. In Nanking they killed about 200,000 people including women and children (the mass slaughter of Nanking).	Japanese troops occupied Nanking at the end of the year. During the process Japanese troops killed a lot of Chinese people, including women and children (the Nanking Incident). This incident was criticised as the mass slaughter of Nanking but the Japanese people knew nothing.
The Nippon Bunkyo Shuppan	In the Nanking occupation a lot of people were killed but the Japanese people were not informed. It is assumed that there were hundreds of thousands of victims including POWs. At the Eastern international military trial 200,000 victims were suggested, in China the number is 300,000	The Japanese troops killed a lot of Chinese people at Nanking but the Japanese people knew nothing (the slaughter of the Nanking incident). There is no established theory about the numbers of the victims of this incident.
The Fuso Company		The Japanese troops occupied Nanking (there was a lot of death and wounding caused by the Japanese army; it was called the Nanking incident). The Tokyo Tribunal recognised that the Imperial Japanese Army killed a large number of Chinese when it occupied Nanking in 1937. Meanwhile, there are documents indicating doubts about the incident. There are various views and the discussions are still ongoing.

Table 2.4.   Descriptions of Comfort Women in Junior High School History Textbooks

Publishing House	Current Textbooks (1997)	New Editions
The Nippon Shoseki	Women were taken as comfort women and treated badly.	Young women from Korea and other Asian countries were collected and sent to the front as comfort women. The people were taken forcibly. Ex-comfort women and the victims of the Nanking incident have asked the Japanese government for compensation and an apology.
The Shimizu Shoin	Some Korean and Taiwanese women were forced to work in comfort institutions at the battlefront.	In non-human institutions there were not only Japanese but also Korean and Taiwanese women.
The Teikoku Shoin	In the war men forced to work as soldiers and women as comfort women suffered unbearable hardships. There were a lot of victims in Korea and Taiwan. Some of them used to be comfort women...).	The issue of compensation for Korean and Taiwanese who were taken to comfort institutions and forced to work as soldiers during the war has been brought to light in trials.
The Kyoiku Shuppan	Many Korean women were sent to the battlefront as comfort women (illustration of women seeking compensation)	No description
The Osaka Shoseki	Young Korean women were sent to the front as comfort women (illustration of women seeking compensation)	No description
The Tokyo Shoseki	Many young women were sent against their will to the battlefront as comfort women	No description.
The Nippon Bunkyo Shuppan	Some women were forced to accompany the army as comfort women	No description
The Fuso Company		No description

An unnamed textbook editor claimed his company's decision to omit a reference to comfort women in the latest edition of their book was based on editorial discussions not on pressure from the government or any other party. In addition, he claimed that "We also considered some teachers" remarks that it is difficult to teach junior high students what the comfort women were"[55] But while mention of the Nanjing massacre and comfort women appear in history textbooks, descriptions are characterized by blandness in the sense that they do not directly confront the issue and do not offer explicit evaluation. Instead ambiguity is locked into the discourse in a way that offers teachers room to explore the events or to manoeuvre away from them and even to cast doubt upon their importance and the validity of the evidence-base.

CONCLUSION

Different views of the past are more than ever the origins of conflicts between nations and ethnic groups and what has been interpreted by some of its neighbors as at best ambivalence and at worst denial has caused Japan acute embarrassment and has adversely affected its relationship with China and with Korea. China is worried by the economic and military links between Japan and the United States that it fears could be used to strengthen the position of nationalist Taiwan. For many Chinese, Japan's economic power arouses strong memories of 1930s imperialism. Many Chinese are reared on tales of Japanese atrocities during the 1937–1945 occupation and at the age of eight, schoolchildren are shown their first photographs of Japanese troops, allegedly, bayoneting and beheading Chinese in Nanking.

In creating national identity the borders in people's minds are more powerful than those drawn on maps as Japan's attitudes towards the form of official knowledge sanctioned in history textbooks suggests. The analysis in this paper highlights just as strongly the condition of contemporary Japan as it does the problem of wartime behavior. At the beginning of the 21st century ideological and political control of textbook content can be seen as one response to socioeconomic disruption, global recession and conservative resurgence. The history curriculum in Japan is an intense site of friction and antagonism that has national and international implications for the evolution of Japanese nationality and nationhood. The outcome of constructing social representation, historical memory and identity in this fashion is that it produces cultural silences. What is often absent is a plurality of discourses and narratives which might emerge from oppositional histories or what Apple calls "mentioning" where "limited and isolated elements of the history and culture of less powerful groups are included in the texts.[56] While socioeconomic and political influences continue to shape Japan's attitudes to the manufacture of official historical knowledge, the concept of "face" is highly significant in understanding the ethical and moral dimension of Japan's approach to publicly acknowledging wartime atrocities either through formal political action or through the curriculum. Silence or reticence is not a way of avoiding guilt but of avoiding public shame and humiliation. Since 1945, many Japanese have acknowledged the wartime atrocities of the Imperial army, but inwardly.

Central in this debate is the need to ensure continuity between past and present, to maintain the cohesiveness of society and order based upon traditional social, political and ethical mores. Japanese textbook censorship is about creating a cultural congruence based upon a mythology of the past characterized by inclusivity. Japanese conservatives see their role as the construction of a past that can be accepted approvingly together with the neutralization of an unacceptable past that might provoke criticism and rejection. Institutional memory is powerfully supported within Japan and is an integral element of the structure of governmental and bureaucratic power. State control over textbook content remains a key means of transmitting hegemonic and ideological control and is, therefore, an important site of political struggle. It is through controlling textbook content that government can legitimize a particular set of values that provides people with an intellectual and moral sense of direction that seeks to unite them in the face of a fracturing social cohesion. At the heart of this endeavor remains the complex question of what it meant to be Japanese at the beginning of the 21st century.

NOTES

1. I would like to thank the University of Nagoya, Japan for providing me with a six month research scholarship in 2004–2005 that enabled me to re-visit the analysis of an earlier paper on Japanese history textbooks, bring the story up to date and conduct further research into Chinese history textbooks. In particular I want to thank Shen Jingjing for her friendship, support and for looking after me when I needed it most; Professor Masahiro Chikada; Professor Kotaro Kuroda; Professor Tomoko Torii; Professor Tatsuya Natsume; Professor Mohammad Sarif and Professor Masami Matoba for their companionship and enthusiasm. My thanks are also due to Sachiko Matsui for producing English translations of parts of Japanese history textbooks, for translating articles from the Japanese newspaper media.

2. I. Buruma, *Wages of Guilt: Memories of War in Germany and Japan*, (New York: Farrar Strauss, 1994).

3. E. Paris, *Long Shadows: truth, lies and history*, (London, Bloomsbury, 2001), p. 125.

4. In July 1996, the Japanese Royal Family and Prime Minister Hashimoto visited the Yasukuni Shrine to pay their respects. The LDP decided that cabinet ministers should officially visit the shrine and in November 1996 the Japan Foreign Affairs Committee approved a motion asking all visiting Heads of State to visit the shrine. On August 15, 2000 nine members of Prime Minister Yoshiro Mori's Cabinet visited Yasukuni although Mori stayed away. In April 2001 Junichiro Koizumi became Prime Minister and pledged to visit the shrine which he has done each year (see *The Japan Times*, 11th May, 2001).

5. H. Gold, *Unit 731 Testimony* (Yen Books, Singapore, 2000, 2nd edition); S.H. Harris, *Factories of Death: Japanese Biological Warfare, 1932–45 and the American Cover-Up*, (London, Routledge, 2001).

6. L. Hein and M. Selden, eds. *Censoring History: Citizenship and Memory in Japan, Germany, and the United States*, (New York: M.E. Sharpe Inc, 2000).

7. T. Seddon, "Politics and Curriculum: A case study of the Japanese history textbook dispute, 1982," *British Journal of Sociology of Education*, Volume 8, No.2, 1987, 213–225.

8. T. Horio, *Educational Thought and Ideology in Modern Japan: state authority and intellectual freedom*, (S. Plantzer, trans. and ed.), (Tokyo, University of Tokyo Press, 1988) p. 175.

9. L.J. Schoppa, Education *Reform in Japan*, (London, Routledge, 1993).

10. There are numerous internet-based resources on the Nanjing massacre. Some provide sources of genuine merit, others devote themselves to anti-Japanese and anti-Chinese rhetoric that is in itself interesting but needs to be treated with caution. One of the better sites is http://www.arts.cuhk.edu.hk/NanjingMassacre/NM.html based at the Hong Kong Chinese University, while it has some useful links it does not appear to have been updated since the late 1990s. Masato Kajimoto's website contains some excellent material although unfortunately the video links do not work; see http://www.geocities.com/nankingatrocities/index.htm. A number of books have been written about the Nanjing massacre apart from Chang's work. These include J. Yin, and S. Young, *The Rape of Nanking: An Undeniable History in Photographs*, (Chicago: Innovative Publishing House, 1996); J.A. Fogel and C.S. Maier, *The Nanjing Massacre in History and Historiography*, (California: University of California Press, 2000); T. Brook, ed. *Documents on the Rape of Nanking*, (Michigan: University of Michigan Press, 1999); J. Rabe, *The Good Man of Nanking: The Diaries of John Rabe*, (Vintage Books, 2000); K. Honda, (translated by F. Gribney, and K. Sandness) *The Nanjing Massacre: A Japanese Journalist Confronts Japan's National Shame*, (East Gate Books, 1999). From a very different viewpoint that calls into question whether the Nanjing massacre happened, mitigates what happened or denies the event see T. Takemoto and Y. Ohara, *The Alleged "Nanking Massacre": Japan's rebuttal to China's forged claims*, (Tokyo: Meisei-sha, Inc, 2000); T. Masaaki, *What Really Happened in Nanking, The Refutation of a Common Myth*, (Tokyo: Sekai Shuppan, 2000) and M. Yamamoto, *Nanking: Anatomy of an Atrocity*, (Praeger: Westport, Conn, 2000).

11. *New York Times*, December 17, 1937.

12. *Asahi Shimbun*, December 14, 1937.

13. The photographs appear on numerous internet-based sites and in many books on the Nanjing Massacre and are also a central feature of the exhibition in the museum at the Memorial to the Victims of the Nanjing Massacre in Nanjing. Recent scholarship has called their authenticity into question and they have been dismissed, by some Japanese writers, as fakes or as being unconnected with events in Nanking. For a Japanese conservative view see the website for *The Association for the Advancement of Liberalist View of History (http://www.jiyuu-shikan.org/e/)* that includes a critical account of the Nanking photographs. See http://www.jiyuu-shikan.org/e/fujioka/index.html.

14. Buruma, Ibid., p. 114.

15. Y. Tawara (1999). "Recent trends in tampering with history by ultra-conservative groups: What's going on with the Society for New History Textbooks). *Senso sekinin kenkyu kikan (War Responsibility Research Quarterly)* 25, pp. 62–71. Tokyo.

16.   *Japan Times*, November 28, 2004, p. 2.

17.   *Japan Times*, December 1, 2004, p. 2.

18.   M.W.Apple *Official Knowledge: Democratic Education in a Conservative Age*, (London: Routledge, 1993)

19.   Hein and Selden, Ibid, p. 15.

20.   A. Gerow, "Consuming Asia, Consuming Japan: The New Neonationalistic Revisionism in Japan," in *Censoring History: Citizenship and Memory in Japan, Germany, and the United States*, eds. L. Hein and M. Selden, (New York: M.E. Sharpe Inc., 2000).

21.   M. Yamazumi, "State control and the evolution of ultra nationalistic textbooks" in *The Rape of Nanking: An Undeniable History in Photographs*, J. Yin and S. Young, (Chicago: Innovative Publishing House, 1996).

22.   In 1997 accounts were included in each of the authorized history textbooks for junior high schools, in 14 out of the 18 world history textbooks for high schools and in 14 out of the 19 textbooks for high schools. Accounts of comfort women have been included in junior high school textbooks in since 1996 and in 16 out of the 19 history textbooks for senior high schools from 1998. See C. Barnard, "Isolating Knowledge of the Unpleasant: the Rape of Nanking in Japanese high-school textbooks," *British Journal of Sociology of Education*, Volume 22, Issue 4, pp. 519–530, 2001 and, for an excellent analysis of recent scholarship, D. Askew "The Nanjing Incident, Recent Research and Trends," *Electronic Journal of Contemporary Japanese Studies* at http://www.japanesestudies.org.uk/articles/Askew.html, 2002.

23.   N. Yoshiko and I. Hiromitsu "Japanese Education, Nationalism and Ienaga Saburo's Textbook Lawsuits" in *Censoring History: citizenship and memory in Japan, Germany and the United States*, eds. L. Hein and M. Selden (London: M.E.Sharpe, 2000).

24.   *The Times*, August 30, 1997.

25.   *Economist*, September 6, 1997; *Telegraph*, August 30, 1997.

26.   *The Times*, August 30, 1997.

27.   Adapted from *Truth in Textbooks, Freedom in Education and Peace for Children* published by the National League for Support of the School Textbook Screening Suite at http//:www.ne.jp/asahi/

28.   T. Okamoto, *The Distortion and the Revision of History in Post-war Japanese Textbooks, 1945–1998*, unpublished MA Thesis, (Queens College, City University: New York, 1998).

29.   F. Fitzgerald, *America Revised: History Schoolbooks in the Twentieth Century*, (New York: Vintage Press, 1979).

30.   C. Barnard, "Protecting the Face of the State: Japanese high school history textbooks and 1945," *Functions of Language*, Volume 7, No.1, 2000 p. 10; see also C. Barnard, *Language, Ideology and Japanese History Textbooks* (London: Routledge Curzon, 2003).

31.   Ibid, p. 28. In a talk to the Foreign Correspondent's Club, Barnard, argued that the textbooks are phrased in such a way as to cover up the facts about Japan's wartime actions. He claimed that almost none of the 1995 authorized textbooks examined referred to Japanese "people" or "soldiers" involved in the Nanjing Massacre. Individuals are lumped into an anony-

mous group, "the Japanese army," while Chinese and other nationalities are referred to as "people" (The *Japan Times*, April 22, 1999).

32.   B. Anderson, *Imagined Communities: Reflections on the Origin and Spread of Nationalism*, (London: Verso, 1971).

33.   D.R.Olsen, "On the Language and Authority of Textbooks" In *Language, Authority and Criticism: Readings on the School Textbook*, eds. S. de Castell, A. Luke, and C. Luke, (London: Falmer Press, 1989), p. 241.

34.   In 1995, on the 50th anniversary of the end of the war, Japan considered and proposed a "No War Resolution." It was rejected by the Diet mainly because it contained a formal official apology for wartime atrocities. In September 1997 Prime Minister Ryutaro Hashimoto repeated the apology, again it was not approved by parliament. On May 9th 1998 the acting secretary general of the LDP, Hiromu Nonaka, became the first Japanese leader to visit the memorial to the victims in Nanking. For an excellent analysis of the politics of apology in Japan see Kishimoto Kyoko "Apologies for Atrocities," *American Studies International*, Volume 42, Issue 2/3, pp. 17–51, 2004.

35.   *Voice of America*, August 10, 1995.

36.   *South China Morning Post*, December 13, 1997. While on its publication it received considerable praise from the U.S. and Chinese media Chang's book has since been subjected to intense, and critical, review including accusations of shoddy scholarship, bias and the inaccurate and partial use of sources. For two critical reviews written shortly after publication see D. Kennedy, "The Horror," *The Atlantic Monthly* (April 1998); J. Fogel, "Review of The Rape of Nanking," *The Journal of Asian Studies*, Volume 57, Number 3 (August, 1998), pp. 818–20.

37.   *Tokyo Time*, May 11, 1998, p. 16; *Newsweek*, July 20, 1998, p. 19.

38.   Such threats are not made idly. In 1989, Hitoshi Motoshima, the Mayor of Nagasaki, was shot and badly injured for suggesting that Emperor Hirohito bore some responsibility for World War II.

39.   *The Times*, February 20, 1999.

40.   Cited in T. Otake, "Row Over Denial of Sex Slaves Rages," *Japan Times*, December 28, 1996, p. 12.

41.   The group's work is actively promoted by the national newspaper *Sankei shinbun* and the manga of Yoshinori Kobayashi. Kobayashi is one of Japan's most widely read and controversial manga authors, his work sells in huge numbers. *On War (Sensoren)*, published in 1998 in which Kobayashi denies the Nanjing massacre and the fate of comfort women, sold over 500,000 copies in is first year of publication. A later magna, *On Taiwan*, (2000) in which he again denies the existence of sexual slaves, sold 250,000 in six weeks. Kobayashi's right-wing political views are well known in Japan and he was a founding member of the *Japanese Society for Historical Textbook Reform*. Lying at the heart of Kobayashi's work are powerful elements of Japanese patriotism, nationalism and xenophobia.

42.   *The Sankei Shimbun*, April 4, 2001.

43.   Over seventy descriptions were rejected as being "difficult to understand or likely to cause misunderstanding." In other cases it was determined that the editors had "adopted one-sided views without due consideration." The original text contained, as one censor put it, "many self-righteous descriptions" that would not have helped children "develop an ability to consider histori-

cal facts from various angles."(*The Japan Times*, April 19, 2001). In May 2001 the South Korean government demanded that Japan make twenty five revisions to the textbook and ten additional alterations to the seven other junior high school texts. South Korean Foreign Minister Han Seung Soo explained his government's position."Distortions in some of the textbooks reopen old wounds in the minds of (South) Korean people," he said, "and harm the (South) Korea-Japan friendship that is set to grow stronger in the future" (*The Japan Times*, June 28, 2001).

44. *The Yomiuri Shimbun*, April 4, 2001.

45. *The Asahi Shimbun*, April 4, 2001.

46. K. Nishio et al. *New History Textbook* (Tokyo: Fusosha, 2001), p. 270.

47. K. Nishio, Ibid., p. 278.

48. K. Nishio, op.cit., p. 294.

49. *The Asahi Shimbun*, April 4, 2001.

50. *People's Daily*, August 27, 2004.

51. *Peoples Daily*, September 26, 2004.

52. See Y. Nozaki, "Japanese politics and the history textbook controversy," 1982–2001, *International Journal of Educational Research* Volume 37, Issues 6–7, 2002, pp. 603–622.

53. *People's Daily* August 30, 2004; see also *People's Daily*, August 29, 2004.

54. *The Japan Times*, March 9, 2001. The Japanese government treats the concerns of its regional neighbors over the content of textbooks very seriously. The Ministry of Foreign Affairs has a department which houses dual language versions of commonly used textbooks, has a library of older textbooks and provides an international audience with information regarding Japanese education. The unit also collects foreign textbooks about Japan and has a collection of textbooks used in former colonies.

55. *The Japan Times*, April 4, 2001.

56. Apple, Ibid., p. 56.

CHAPTER 3

A GENDERED NATIONAL IDENTITY

An Analysis of North and South Korean Textbooks[1]

Misook Kim

INTRODUCTION

It is claimed that the process of globalization will lead to a gradual collapse in the concept of nationhood. However, complex debates concerning the nation and national identity continue to occur in several parts of the world including for example, Israel, Palestine, within the former states of the Soviet Union and the Balkans. The concept of nationalism is very influential in the Korean peninsula. Korean politicians claim, regardless of political persuasion, that they are nationalists in a context where the stigma of being accused of "anti-nationalism" critically damages reputations. Korean attachments to nationalism stems from the belief that both Koreas can only survive by emphasizing the "national" during times of socioeconomic conflict such as the failure of independent industrialization; the impact of the Japanese colonial period; the Korean War and the partition of the Korean peninsula.[2]

What Shall We Tell the Children?, pages 69–87
Copyright © 2006 by Information Age Publishing

What does it mean to be a Korean? Is there an instinct or fixed attribute of being one and the same nation? Currently, this is not a tenable position, in the case of Koreans their identities vary among South Koreans and North Koreans in a way that indicates that national identity modifies with historical circumstance. If this is true, how do individuals identify themselves as members of a national community? What are the determining factors that make a nation a community? How has national identity been formed in similar, or alternative, ways within the very different political systems of South and North Korea? In order to answer these questions, an attempt is made here to analyze the differences and similarities between national discourses on national identity in South and North Korean elementary school textbooks.

National identity is not the natural outcome of a common culture of long antiquity. National identity includes active sociopolitical practices to unify groups across social divisions, organizing and re-organizing elements of ethnicity, territory, language, tradition, experiences and memory based on specific principles. Amalgamating differences through national unity is a project of social integration achieved through the exercise of sociocultural power that is dependent upon historical context.[3] Schooling, a crucial ideological endeavor, promotes national identity through the transmission of official knowledge. In this process school knowledge creates and establishes social boundaries between "us" and "them" and stresses "we-ness," defining who is a qualified, or disqualified, national subject. This process is often gendered and violent. Thus, school knowledge is determined through a selective tradition and impacts upon people's subjectivities and social relations in quite specific ways.[4]

Comparative studies of North and South Korean education began after the Joint Declaration of South and North Korea was made in 1992; however, notwithstanding some excellent results, these studies are problematic. First, many are empirically weak due to the difficulty of gathering material and data from North Korea. Second, although schooling undergoes continuous change caused by modifying power structures and social relations, not many studies have dealt with how South and North Korean education has developed throughout the years. Third, most studies tend to ignore gender relations in their analysis or assume that it is a marginal issue.[5] Gender relations, along with class relations, are an important organizing principle in Korean society. This is not simply a problem of differentiating between male and female, but is an issue in how biological sexual differences develop into a hierarchy of sexuality in educational contexts and how this process affects the social structure of the two Koreas and the formation of identity.

RESEARCH METHOD

Elementary school textbooks were selected in order to analyze representations of national identity and gender. The reason for this focus stems from the fact that textbooks in Korea are regarded as important weapons in the internalization of a ruling ideology. I elected to analyze ethics textbooks that, I assumed, would reveal the dominant culture of each country. For the North Korean textbook, *Ethics of Communism* published in 1972, and again in 1995, and used at the 4th grade of elementary school, was chosen together with *Korean*, published in 1987 and in 1997. The two South Korean textbooks selected were *Ethics*, published in 1979, 1987 and 1996, and *Korean*, published in 1976, and in 1987. To investigate how the official knowledge of the two Koreas has developed historically I classified the textbook content into three periods: the 1970s; the late 1980s and the 1990s. In Korea the 1970s was a period strained by the Cold War and severe ideological confrontation. I examined how interpretations of nation and gender described in textbooks changed as the Cold War paradigm was weakened during the 1980s and the similarities and differences between the recent editions published in the 1990s. The analytical tools employed were based upon theories regarding nationalism, feminism, and the critical sociology of education.

First, emblems and characteristics that symbolized the nation were examined. Various social and cultural practices are made in building a nation-community and to identify individuals as members of a national community. Above all, it is important to realize the nation as a particular community, distinguished from other communities. Thus, the common emblems of the two Koreas that differentiated the national community from others and led to individual cohesiveness and attachment to the national state were examined. Furthermore, analysis of the context in which the emblems were created was conducted. The supposition was made that ideal national subjects in textbooks provide vital clues in revealing social relations and their characteristics in a specific period. In this research, instead of experientially judging whether interpretations of national identity could be seen to be true, I attempted to analyze the discourse presented in order to understand how specific persons were presented as national heroes, and how gender relations influenced these depictions. Second, one of the most important factors in the process of representing national identity is the setting of social boundaries between the "us" and "them" and establishing the "we." How "others" (internally or externally) are created, and how relationships are represented was also analyzed. The third element of the research dealt with chronological changes in national discourse. Finally, I consider the value of national discourse in the period of inter-Korean reconciliation, and provide suggestions concerning unification education in Korea.

EMBLEMS OF NATIONAL STATES

For the analysis of representative emblems of national states I considered differentiation, attachment, and unity to constitute the community of a national state.[6] Furthermore, I wanted to consider which were handed down from the past enabling people to identify with the national state as natural and taken for granted. The emblems selected were the family; land; the national anthem; the national flag; language and custom. For the purposes of this chapter I have chosen to analyze the concepts of family and land.

FAMILY

The family metaphor is one of the most frequent and important in shaping national identity in Korea. For instance, the nation/state is represented as the "homeland"; the "motherland"; in terms of "ancestors"; "the same lineage"; "Dangun's[7] descendants"; the "North Korean brotherhood"; "brotherhood" and "compatriots" in the textbooks of South Korea. The South Korean textbooks also designate the nation/state by using vocabulary such as "homeland"; the "North Korean "brotherhood" and "descendants with the same lineage." Of course, other societies also represent people and the nation as a brotherhood or family, but the lineage denominator is especially emphasized on the Korean peninsula. Emphasis on pure lineage is a characteristic found in nomadic tribes, who have vague boundaries as a nation, but it is rare to find agricultural tribes stressing pure lineage.[8]

Finding evidence to prove that the Korean nation is a community descended from the same blood origins is not an easy task. Physical characteristics can support this claim but these are common among Northeast Asians including the Mongol tribe, and other characteristics can be reasonably understood as products of life and cultural surroundings. Yet it is very hard to trace the blood of people who do not belong to the family.[9] Using family trees is problematic since they are based on noble class males. This is not consistent with the principal concept of the nation in which all members of the society, beyond the feudal and hierarchical order, are equally qualified as national subjects.

Therefore, what is the meaning of family expressions consistently used in Korean society? The family, in most societies, is a basic and continuous social community that stipulates individual identities and social relationships. This is common in Korean society due to the deep entrenchment of Confucianism and its emphasis on the family and historical experience. In this respect, the pure lineage expression emphasizes an essential community with one, unavoidable, destiny.

The following examples from a North Korean textbook clearly show the unification of individuals through a primitive sense of family ties:

> After my father had been to Pyongyang through the family visit program, all of us were missing our grandmother... Why can't we see her?[10]

> Just as a separated family should get together, so should separated nations.[11]

> American imperialists separated our nation into South and North, and, therefore, our people have to live separately. Accordingly, our relatives cannot see or write to each other... Why should the same nation live separately?[12]

In people's family experiences and memories there are conflicts between couples, parents and children. However, family discourses in the textbooks of the two Koreas selectively stress unity and a strong emotional community. This kind of family discourse contributes to the maintenance of asymmetrical gender relations in the nation state as females are subordinated to males, and children to adults in a traditional patriarchy.[13] The following examples from South Korean and North Korean textbooks respectively vividly demonstrate patriarchal characteristics:

> Sung-gyu, what do you think is the best legacy of our ancestors?... Great King Sejong's Korean alphabets, the pluviometer, General Yi Sunshin's Turtle ship.... In the old days, our ancestors created an excellent culture and enjoyed a high cultural level, and introduced it to Japan, some of it was even handed over to China.... I feel ashamed recalling that when I was a student, I was very reluctant to sweep Chosun Dynasty's kings' tombs near my school.[14]

> While attending Chang-duk school, our Leader, Kim Il-sung honored his father, Kim Hyung-jik, whose instruction was to understand the circumstances of our country and people by studying Korean and our history, and he studied very hard ... He made a resolution to defeat the Japanese imperialists in order to retake our country.[15]

The first example shows that the tradition of the nation should be managed by sons, as families are managed. The example from the North Korean textbook shows the process through which Kim Il-sung realized the historical responsibility of retaking his country by studying Korea and Korean history. These examples recognize a relationship with a remote non-individual force (history, tradition, culture, etc.), and achieve a sense of the nation-community.[16] These repeated discourses linking individuals and an abstract community lead them to become bearers of the national community.[17] Here, national continuity is built by a patriarchy: ancestors, father and son.

It is noteworthy that Kim Il-sung is consistently emphasized as the head of the North Korean state family:

> While singing, I always take our father the Leader and the beloved leader's deep love into my heart, and will be a good daughter who is loyal to him.[18]
> Our Leader, who is renowned in the world,
> is not my own father.
> He who retook our country,
> keeps our country, with all of us in his arms,
> He is our benevolent father.[19]

Whereas the family discourse of the nation is used to unite social members, the difference between the private family and the public national state is simultaneously emphasized. The family discourse of the national state employs a symbolic power, the sense of family community, but differentiates the national state as being more important than the private family. Children in North Korea are cut off from an emotional attachment to their private family and parents and are converted into members of Kim Il-sung's national family; they are also educated to believe that this process is honorable and important for the North Korean socialist state.[20]

The traditional family discourse of nationalism in the Korean peninsula causes family love to be a basic standard in judging who is a qualified national subject:

> The spy, who piloted an airplane, was a person from Sokcho, Kangwon Province, and also had a family. We can realize how terrible and vicious communists are through his behavior in that he did not say anything to his family, and gave up his family and nation.[21]
>
> Many South Korean children were exported to European countries, such as France, Italy, Sweden and Denmark. This misery happened because of scoundrels building a nest in South Korea.... How can they sell their consanguineous children? South Koreans are sons-of-bitches, far from human beings and worse than beasts![22]

According to the above citation, attachment to the family is a fundamental feeling and a moral principle. The member of the national community who gives up his family becomes a vicious and terrible beast. Similar counterparts can be found in North Korean textbooks because care for children is a fundamental human value, people who export their "consanguineous children" are "sons-of-bitches, far from human beings and worse than beasts."

LAND

The land is an important metaphor of the nation. Textbooks in the two Koreas represent their national states as "the Korean peninsula"; "the land of our ancestors' graves"; the "southern land"; "our territory" and "our country, our land." The national community has a clearly fixed geographical space and is territorially distinguished from other countries. However, the land is also a symbolic space, collectively calling its people and their experiences, memories and emotions. For instance, in Korea we often see political refugees or people taking a handful of soil. Some political leaders kiss the ground or smell it when returning to their home country. Bodies, buried in foreign countries are sometimes moved to the "mother land."[23] Textbooks from the two Koreas interpret the national state through the land:

> My country! Our ancestors lived from generation to generation, and my descendants will live for a long time in this land, my country! We love this land...[24]

> I heard so many stories about Mt. Kungang from my grandmother....Mt. Kunkang is a beautiful place to visit, which has a traditional story, a woodcutter and a fairy...[25]

> Shouldn't we live in our own country and in our own land, making ourselves comfortable and happy? Let us hurry to get rid of Japanese imperialists, land owners and capitalists, and establish the country of the people....When will I return to this country, where I grew up and our ancestors are buried?[26]

The meaning of a fixed and actual space, or a hometown, is weakened due to advances in transport information technology, and rapid globalization. Yet, many people still place special emphasis upon the land. For sedentary agricultural people the land is the root of their existence.[27] The tendency to link people to place leads some to regard Koreans abroad and refugees as having lost their homeland:

> In the Pusan Civic Center, there was a meeting for Vietnamese refugees, leaving for a new life....I had to wander without nationality. Now I have no homeland to devote myself to. I have no national flag. I have no national anthem....There is no land for us to stand in.[28]

> These days, so many children in countries where socialism has collapsed and capitalism is revived are wandering for food without any education. Marana is a little student in the capital of a country where socialism has collapsed....Her situation is very different from that of previous years....Her classmates became cigarette sellers or car cleaners after they were expelled due to tuition problems....[29]

Here, refugees and children of a country converted to capitalism are those who do not live in their own land. They are rootless people who are lacking morality and emotion.[30]

Drawing clear boundaries between people who live in a fixed space, the Korean peninsula, and others make the idea of national identity for overseas Koreans confusing. For example, people often think that overseas Koreans living in China or other countries "have a hard time." Another problem is that we strongly push overseas Koreans towards "our" arbitrary national characteristics that include the Korean language, songs, and memorial services or we would not admit their different national identity. This tendency restrains the development of a more flexible and inclusive national identity necessary to understand the differences of Korean residents abroad and refugees more properly.

QUALIFIED/DISQUALIFIED NATION SUBJECTS: WARRIORS AND MOTHERS

South Korean Textbooks

Desirable national subjects are historical products, and provide clues to specific power relations in time and space. In the 1979 South Korean textbook national heroes are General Kim Yu-sin; Wonsool; General Kwak Je-woo, called the red-garment general, General Yi Sun-shin and General Kim Jwa-jin. Patriotic warriors frequently appeared in textbooks published in 1979, but have gradually disappeared. Chief of the loyal troops, Jo Hun and his 700 soldiers, and nameless soldiers of the Korean War, were introduced in 1987 and, in 1997, nationalists in the field of education and music, who were against Japanese colonization, were also presented.

Changes in national subjects in the North Korean textbooks were closely related to the nature of the government. Following a military coup, in the Park Jung-hee regime 1979 textbooks presented desirable Korean images as soldiers who fought against enemies to save the country or who died in the war. Lack of legitimacy for the military regime was identified with national crises such as the Japanese invasion of 1592 or the Japanese colonial period. The regime emphasized that people should unite under the great leader as the central figure to overcome national crises and that the country should be powerful enough not to suffer from disgraceful colonialism or invasions from other powers.[31] National discourse, initiated by an authoritarian regime, contributed to the presentation of worthwhile national subjects as male soldiers and served to enlarge and strengthen a hierarchical and totalitarian military culture. In this discourse, females or old people who could not fight in the war became second-class people, who should be obedient to male warriors.[32]

The South Korean textbooks of 1979 contained a most important female, Mrs. Shin Saimdang, as a national subject. She has been regarded as the ideal woman, the wise mother and good wife. However, Shin Saimdang was not a typical woman in the Chosun dynasty. She actively displayed her talents as an outstanding female artist. She lived in her parents' home taking up the duties of an absent son. When she had trouble with her husband because of a concubine he kept, she left to meditate on Mt. Kumgang. In this manner, she was not obedient but independent despite social restrictions. As her son, Yulgok, wrote in his Sunbihangjang, she was not eager to educate her children or support her husband, but she was not a bad mother.

Even though there were many outstanding mothers in history, Shin Saimdang was defined as the representative woman. It is not because she independently displayed her talents, but because she brought up Yulgok, who was a great politician and scholar. Under military government, Yulgok was regarded as an ideal scholar and politician. Indeed most of the section of "Saimdang and Yulgok" was taken up by a description of Yulgok's loyalty and filial duty. In the 1970s the introduction of Shin Saimdang as a great woman was interpreted as meaning that women should put aside their own problems, such as unequal social participation and household duties, and instead follow the patriarchal order by spreading the gospel of the mythical female subject who was faithful to the ethics of patriarchy, despite her own talents.

Textbooks of North Korea

In North Korea, which gives importance to resistant nationalism, textbooks present anti-Japanese and anti-American fighters as desirable national subjects. Kim Il-sung is a representative character that receives significant attention in textbooks:

> While marching, our commando group realized that many "punitive forces" were chasing after it. Our Great Leader, Kim Il-sung decided to seduce and kill those scoundrels.... In combat, our commando group killed 140, and captured 30 of the punitive group...[33]

It is interesting to find that Kim Il-sung was described as an active and aggressive commander in combat, while at the same time he demonstrated consideration for his subordinates, people, and children. For instance, he apparently put straw into a man's loose shoes; shared his food with his men in the middle of dangerous combat and took good care of children and orphans as if he were their father. This representation is very different from some Western or Southern Korean hegemonic narratives where caring is oppressed or denied in heroes because of its "feminine" nature. This emphasis on the leader's caring ways leads people to a spontaneous obedience to the regime by mobilizing feelings of respect, gratitude, moral duty and affection. Values such as fostering or intimacy are not allowed in other leaders, but this is a virtue in Kim Il-sung or Kim Jung-il both powerful symbols of the nation state.[34]

Desirable subjects, other than Kim Il-sung and his son, were, for example, anti-American fighter Lee, Soo-bok and anti-Japanese fighter Choe, Hee-sook. Lee, Soo-bok appeared in poems in several textbooks. However, the female fighter, Choe Hee-sook, only appeared in the *Ethics of Communism* (1972). Instead a fictional character, Gum-soon, appeared in *Ethics of Communism* in 1995 and *Korean* in 1997. According to the textbooks, she was a child liaison soldier who was arrested and tortured to death by Japanese policemen; although she was a young child she refused to betray her colleagues in the anti-Japanese guerrilla units. In the 1990s a female fighter no longer made a physical attack on male imperialists since that could be a serious threat to Korean masculinity, instead she was a preserver of purity and of revolutionary spirit. The female military body was only "invited" by men according to the needs of the system.[35]

After independence and until the post-war restoration period, women were pushed to contribute to society, to participate in production. However, this view changed after the restoration in 1961, when Kim Il-sung quelled internal conflict within the party and his regime was firmly established. North Korean women were required to take part in the 7-Year People's Economy Plan, and to become mothers. As Kim Il-Sung was idolized, women's freedom and rights were only considered to be granted by his mercy, not through their struggle. The mothers of the two leaders were stressed as ideal women who served their husbands and sacrificed themselves for their children. At the beginning of North Korea's independent history women who had previously been required to be aggressive and revolutionary, were now expected to be "...the passive, domestic, and supportive mother" and to support males (Yun, Mi-ryang, 1991). Qualified male subjects in both Koreas' textbooks focused on their abilities as warriors or as leaders, but in the case of females, the role of the mother as the bearer of great national warriors or leaders was emphasized. Female heroines in textbooks were not independent subjects of the national state. Women were visible only through marriage with men or through the family.[36]

THE RELATION BETWEEN THE "US" AND THE "THEM"

In forming national identities one of the most important factors is to make, fix, and substantiate social boundaries between the "us" and the "them" in a specific way. This section examines how the "us" and the "them" are represented as different communities in textbooks. The first two examples are taken from South Korean textbooks of 1979 and 1987; the third appeared in a North Korean textbook published in 1972.

> It was during the Korean War. One day, a communist visited your grandfather to offer him a well paid job ... The well paid job was a lie. He was locked up in a public warehouse, and was taken to war ... Soo-nam ... drew something on a paper. ... In the drawing, a wolf was eating a little rabbit, under which it was clearly written. We should not be cheated by communists' lies.[37]

> North Korea teaches children songs with a context filled with hatred of our country and friendly nations. Its textbooks employ many military words like "capturing the enemy's hill," "a shock troop," "and suicide corps." Moreover, mathematics textbooks ask questions in the form of the number of soldiers on our side that the People's Army has killed.[38]

> South Korea, where American imperialists are building a nest, is a Dark World in which foolish landowners and capitalists live, but farmers cannot live. It has nothing to wear, to eat, and to work. They are not allowed to go to school without money, and there is no cure for diseases in the Death Land ... We should fight together in order to build a good world where all the people can study and cure diseases without money.[39]

In the examples above, South Korea's main opponent is North Korea, and vice versa; loyalty towards a national regime is promoted by putting stress on hostility and misery, as well as the superiority of a particular national system. The two Koreas take advantage of the ideological coexistence of the division and the threat of war. They do not allow the proper understanding of the "other side," and thus maximize the role of ideology in maintaining their ruling systems.[40]

However, the setting of the 1990s weakened this tendency. This is shown in the analysis of units in textbooks.[41] The 1979 South Korean textbooks contain 23 units of which six (26%) are designed to inspire anti-communism or hostility toward North Korea. However, later textbooks reduced this content to two units (16.7%) out of 12, and one unit (8.3%) on unification education was added. The 1996 textbooks consist of nine units, none of them inspiring anti-communism, and includes one unit (11.1%) dealing with unification education. 1996 textbooks deal with the grief of separated families, emphasizing that the two Koreas need to strengthen mutual exchanges because they share similar culture and customs regardless of their political and ideological differences.

North Korean textbooks also reflect this change. In the *Ethics of Commu-nism* published in 1972, only four units (8.9%) out of 45 are related to pub-lic order, the rest (91.1%) contain content idolizing Kim Il-sung; hostility towards U.S. and Japanese imperialism, and the social and economic prob-lems of South Korea. However, 1995 textbooks mark a contrast. Whereas 18 units (60%) out of 30 deal with public order, only 12 units (40%) idolize Kim Il-sung, present hostile attitudes towards the U.S. or Japan or discuss the inferior life style of South Korea. In the two North Korean textbooks, published in 1987 and 1997 respectively, six to seven per cent emphasize class consciousness; the inferiority of South Korea, or hostility toward American and Japanese imperialism.

There are noticeable changes between the two North Korean text-books. In the 1975 version all poems idolize the Kim Il-sung family, but significantly in the 1995 version a poem *45 Minutes*, which is not about them but about saving time was included. Furthermore, no historical heroes other than anti-American and Japanese fighters are mentioned but General Ulmil, Han Suk-bong's mother, and Edison, a foreigner surpris-ingly enough, are introduced for the first time in 1997. Textbooks of the two Koreas show remarkable changes late into the 1990s. South Korean textbooks of 1996 do not contain any expressions of hostility towards North Korea. However, North Korean textbooks still show hostility towards South Korea, probably because North Korea continues to strengthen its national defensive strategy in the light of the collapse of socialist countries in Eastern Europe.

EXTERNAL OTHERS: HISTORICAL SCARS AND GLORY

In order to form a strong national identity in a post-colonial country one of the most important opponents is imperialism or the politics and ideol-ogy of nations considered to be imperialistic. After independence, politi-cal leaders and the intelligentsia in nations attempting to develop a new sense of national identity tend to devote themselves to the active reorgani-zation of their history and traditions. Emphasis is put on past history, not as one of suffering and subordination, but as a brave struggle for preserv-ing national independence. In addition, the population are encouraged to work for the development of the national economy under the premise that, although the lead of more economically advanced countries, they still maintain a culture that is in many respects superior to that of more affluent nations.

SOUTH KOREAN TEXTBOOKS

The most important external "other" in South Korean textbooks is Japanese imperialism. This can be clearly understood by the fact that more than half of the historical heroes in textbooks are fighters against Japanese imperialism. It is especially true in the textbooks of 1979, which reflect the politics of the period. After the military coup of 1962, Park Jung-hee's view of national history was that "our" history was a retrogressive one, and "our" tradition was an obstacle to industrialization as demonstrated in *Our Future*. This view is changed in *Our National Strength*, published in 1971. Here he states that our nation is independent, democratic, and peace loving, and that our history is a proud one that has created an excellent national culture in spite of many difficulties.[12] This is well demonstrated in textbooks of the period:

> Our land is rather small. What is worse, it is divided into the South and North. We are a proud nation. It is clearly understood by seeing our 5000-year history and its remarkable culture. We are an outstanding and patient people.[43]

According to government discourse of the time, our society accepted Western values and culture without consideration and as a result, social confusion and disorder became prevalent, weakening national consciousness. In order to restore a unified national consciousness, freedom and equality of democratic values were not seen as appropriate; instead, traditional filial duty and loyalty are emphasized as an ideology of the authoritarian military regime.

Government discourse of the 1980s is also actively represented in that even though it is claimed that the nation should follow the example of advanced capitalist countries, it is superior to Western imperialism:

> At an old books fair held in France, books of our ancestors metalography were displayed to surprise world historians, demonstrating that we invented metal before the West.... In the old days, our ancestors created an excellent culture, and introduced it to Japan. At that time, the Japanese learned from us drawing, architecture, ceramic techniques, and letters and so on.[44]

Subordinate experiences under Japanese colonialism or national suffering are displaced with national superiority in that "our" culture was more advanced than the Japanese culture and "we" educated the Japanese.[45] The emphasis on General Yi Sun-shin as a national hero was designed to recover national authority. It is an effort in reorganizing history as a brave struggle to protect national independence, not as a difficult and disgraceful one. It is Korean males who restore a national authority wounded by colonialists.

NORTH KOREAN TEXTBOOKS

In a similar vein, the most important external other in North Korean text-books is Japanese imperialism. Accordingly, North Korean society justifies itself through a discourse that reminds people of their miserable life style, the sorrows of a colonial nation, and infernal deeds:

> Workers were forced to work for construction under Japanese whips; farmers were deprived of all of their rice after an arduous harvest by Japanese imperi-alists and landowners, and had to leave their homes with a back bundle....
> Our Great Leader Kim Il-Sung bore flaming hatred towards the Japanese invaders...[46]

Resistant nationalism against Japan before independence has continued in the form of a resistant consciousness and hostility towards American imperialism after independence. As the Korean War, which is viewed as a revolution against anti-imperialism and feudalism, failed due to American intervention, the North Korean ruling class converted hostility towards Japanese imperialism into hostility towards American imperialism. By way of justifying its regime, North Korea expresses the Japanese as the "Japanese bastard"; the "enemy"; and the "Japanese militarists" and Americans as the "American bastard"; the "American invaders"; the "American jackals" and the "enemy." This expression has continued to the late 1990s:

> In 1866, when American fellows arrived in the Daedong River by the pirate ship, Sharmen, they killed people, set fire to houses, and stole things.... Being crazy about gold, American jackals developed gold mines and forced people to work just like cows or horses. Moreover, they deprived us of a lot of valuable treasures, forcing people to work more than 16 hours in dangerous mines.... On June 25, 1950; they started a war to occupy the northern part of our republic.[47]

> Since American forceful occupation of South Korea, they have slaughtered children, women, and old people everyday.[48]

Following the logic of the text, as American imperialism is more terrible than Japanese imperialism, South Korea is oppressed and starving. By con-trast the text stresses that North Korea has defeated imperialism and has high levels of material wealth. However, due to warlike South Korean and American imperialists, North Korea must continually prepare for war. The texts stimulate loyalty by placing previous suffering, current enemies, and the horror of the enemy together.[49] Textbooks of the late 1990s continue to focus upon the anti-American and Japanese struggle or the Kim Il-Sung family and support the strategy of mobilizing colonial memories and war and routinizing crisis as a way of maintaining the ruling system.

Many illustrations in North Korean textbooks show brave struggles against imperialism:

> When American imperialists sneaked into Yung-Gyu's village ... boy partisans quickly approached the tent with guns and hand grenades.... They realized that Americans would kill party members and people would be locked in a warehouse.... That night, the boys killed the American jackals and liberated the village in cooperation with the People's Commando Group...[50]

This example emphasizes a history that is not characterized by suffering and disgrace, but by a brave struggle to preserve national independence. However, in making "glorious" history, men such as Kim Il-Sung or other males are the heroes.[51] As claimed by Cynthia Enloe, national discourse in textbooks is based upon men's memory, shame, frustration, and hope.[52]

CONCLUSION

This study has shown how national discourse, which is one of the governing ideologies of the Korean peninsula, is represented in textbooks. It analyzed what emblems of the nation state appeared, how boundaries of the "us" and "them" were established and how qualified and disqualified national subjects were represented, and how they differed over time. It discussed the social meanings of the family and land as representative emblems of the nation in the textbooks of the two Koreas. Expressions for the nation conveyed continuity, collectivity, and strong emotional attachment to the family. However, in national family discourse, women in traditional families were in charge of reproduction and stayed subordinate to males. The national family discourse of patriarchy with Kim Il-Sung, was emphasized consistently in North Korean textbooks. The traditional family discourse of the nation caused family love or responsibility to be a standard to judge who was a qualified national member. Another significant metaphor of the nation state was the land, not only in terms of geographic boundaries, but also in terms of symbolic spaces for the life and emotion of the national population. The discourse of uniting people, places and lives, interfered with the development of the national identities of overseas Koreans, refugees and foreigners by developing nationalism centered on a specific space, the Korean peninsula.

The justification of both regimes is based upon national efforts to mobilize national unity around an unstable past. Passing through the Japanese colonial period and the separation of the two Koreas, the two different political systems required loyalty and unity, while attacking enemies of the past and present. In this process, the two Koreas represented male warriors as heroes, especially in the 1970s. Women were invisible entities in making glorious history, or were merely assistants or reproducers. The North Korean view of women changed from revolutionaries to mothers of revolutionaries.

While South Korean textbooks frequently displayed Japanese imperialism as a national enemy, North Korean textbooks emphasized hostility towards Japanese imperialism and American imperialism. This tendency was very clear in the 1970s, but expressing hostility towards each other in textbooks weakened in the late 1990s. However, compared to South Korea, North Korea continues to pursue a defensive strategy; mainly due to the collapse of the socialist countries and its economic difficulties. Meanwhile, textbooks resisted the existing colonial discourse by reorganizing it in a way that national existence and history was glorious in spite of obvious suffering.

Textbooks from the two Koreas ignore social differences within the nation, instead they consistently emphasize equal fraternal love and national unity. National discourse in textbooks stresses the production of national subjects who are loyal to the nation state, rather than the production of critical national subjects. In South Korea, it is aggressively claimed that we need to emphasize similarities between the two peoples as a precursor to unification. However, similarities of national discourse have serious limitations. This is particularly evident given the complexity of stressing uniformity, ignoring the differences of various groups or individuals, unity based on blood relations, patriarchal tendencies and a national discourse that supports hostility to different nations and peoples.

Given this, should national discourse in Korean society be abolished? The removal of national discourse, which has powerfully contributed to the constitution of societies and the national identities of the two Koreas, is no easy task. In this respect there is a need to devote attention to the progressive reorganization of national discourse and identities. It is necessary to acknowledge, tolerate and respect internal differences and diversity inside the nation. Textbooks urging unification should not be limited to unification based on the unity of blood relations or an obscure return to tradition. This is especially true with respect to South Korea's descriptions of North Korea. Not only should the peoples of the two Koreas make efforts to understand one another but also the policies of the two Koreas should be ones with a cultural basis that shares the vision of a democratic society whose national subjects are both critical and respect social difference.

NOTES

1. This paper is a revision one of which was first published in South Korea. See M. Kim (2002), "National identity represented by N. and S. Korean textbooks," *Korean Journal of Sociology of Education*, 12(1): 43–65.

2. J. Yim, "Review on the understanding "the nation" by the Korean history researchers" *Criticism of History*, Autumn, 1994, 114–137, pp. 114–115

3. S. Hall, "The question of cultural identity" in *Modernity and its Futures* eds. S. Hall, *et al.*, (Cambridge: Polity, 1996); P. Schlesinger, "On national identity: some conceptions and misconceptions criticized." *Social Science Information.* Number 26, Volume 2, 1987, pp. 219–64; E. Balibar, (1996). "The Nation form: history and ideology." in *Becoming National: a reader* eds. G. Eley, and R. Grigor Suny, (New York and Oxford: Oxford University Press, 1996)

4. Schlesinger, Ibid; Balibar, Ibid.; M.W. Apple, *Official Knowledge.* (New York: Routledge, 1993); F. Anthias and N. Yuval-Davis in "Woman-nation-state" in eds. G. Eley and R. Grigor Suny, Ibid; G. Eley and R. Grigor Suny, "Introduction: from the moment of social history to the work of cultural representation." in eds. G. Eley and R. Grigor Suny, op. cit.

5. Regarding gender studies on North Korean textbooks, see B. Kim et al. "Women education and femininity in North Korea: on the view of womanhood in Textbook and Chosun women," *Research on Unification Policies*, Volume 9, Number 2, 2001, pp. 173–209; M. Min and J. Ahn, *Research on Woman Education in North Korea.* (Seoul: Korean Woman's Development Institute, 2001).

6. Balibar, 1996, Ibid.

7. Dangun, as a mythical character, refers to the progenitor of Korean.

8. It is after the modern age that 'brotherhood', meaning the offspring of a mother or brother, became generally used. See M. Min and J. Ahn, Ibid.

9. T. Noh "Examination on the era of building Korean nation," *Criticism of History.* Winter, 1992, pp. 16–25.

10. *Ethics* of South Korea, 1987, pp. 137–138.

11. *Ethics* of South Korea, 1996, p. 81.

12. *Ethics of Communism of North Korea,* 1972, pp. 196–197.

13. A. Mclintock, "No longer in a future heaven: nationalism, gender, and race." in eds. G. Eley and R. Grigor Suny, op.cit.

14. *Ethics* of South Korea, 1979, p. 93.

15. *Ethics of Communism of North Korea,* 1972, pp. 4–5.

16. C. Callahan, "Nationalism and ethnicity" in *Nationalism: critical concepts in political science,* eds. J. Hutchinson and A. Smith, (London and New York: Routledge, 1999).

17. Balibar, Ibid.

18. *Korean* of North Korea, 1987, p. 12.

19. *Korean* of North Korea, 1997, p. 68.

20. M. Kim, "A feminist analysis of nation state discourses of North Korean textbooks," *Korean Journal of Sociology of Education*, Volume 11, Number 2, 2001, pp. 29–52.

21. *Ethics* of South Korea, 1976, p. 36.

22. *Ethics of Communism* of North Korea, 1995, pp. 36–38.

23. L. Malkki, "National geographic: the rooting of peoples and the territorization of national identity among scholars and refugees." In G. Eley and R.Grigor Suny (eds) op.cit, 1996.

24. *Ethics* of South Korea, 1979, pp. 131–132.

25. *Ethics* of South Korea, 1997, p. 76.

26. *Ethics of Communism of North Korea*, 1972, pp. 60–61.

27. Malkki, 1996, Ibid.

28. *Ethics* of South Korea, 1979, p. 129.

29. *Ethics of communism* of North Korea, 1995, p. 16–19.

30. Malkki, 1996, op.cit.

31. H. Jun, *Comparison of political discourse in the two Koreas: on the basis of the communicative structure and language strategy*, Ph. D. Dissertation (Yonsei University, 1997); J. Kim, *Research on nationalism in government discourse in South Korea and North Korea: historical development and the formation of similarities/differences*. Ph. D. Dissertation (Yonsei University, 1999).

32. S. Moon, "Begetting the nation: the androcentric discourse of national history and tradition in South Korea," in *Dangerous Women: gender and Korean nationalism*, eds. E.H. Kim and C. Choi (New York, Routledge, 1998).

33. *Ethics of communism* of North Korea, 1972, p. 96–99.

34. M. Kim, "National identity represented by North and South Korean textbooks," *Korean Journal of Sociology of Education*. Volume12, Number 1, 2002, 43–65.

35. Mclintock, Ibid., p. 269.

36. Anthias and Yuval-Davis, Ibid.

37. *Ethics* of South Korea, 1979, pp. 28–31.

38. *Ethics* of South Korea, 1987, pp. 97–99.

39. *Ethics of Communism* of North Korea, 1972,pp. 49–53.

40. Lee, Ho-yung. "The formation of "national identity" in the two Koreas after Independence: sociology of "others'," *Social and Cultural Changes of the two Koreas and Korean Impression in the 21st century*, (Seoul: The Academy of Korean Studies, 2001), pp. 569–570.

41. Because each unit includes several themes, each needs to be carefully analysed. However, I believe that it is meaningful to study the tendencies of themes in each unit published in different periods.

42. S. Jun, "Meaning of the image of South and North Korean women in the education" B. Lee, (ed). *Meaning of the Image of South and North Korean Women before Unification*. Seoul, (Korean Women's Institute: Ewha Woman's University, 1997, pp. 143–152.

43. *Ethics*, 1979, pp. 125–127.

44. *Ethics*, 1987, p. 93.

45. However, resistant descriptions about Japanese colonization were weakened in textbooks in 1996, and the expression "Japanese enemy" of 1979 and 1987 was changed to "Japan" in textbooks of 1996.

46. *Ethics of Communism*, 1972, pp. 60–61.

47. *Ethics of Communism*, 1972, p. 179.

48.   *Ethics of Communism,* 1995, p. 85.
49.   Kim, Jung-hoon, Ibid; Lee, Ho-yung, Ibid.
50.   *Ethics of Communism,* 1972, pp. 64–65.
51.   *Korean,* 1987, pp. 90–93.
52.   McClintock, op.cit.

NORTH KOREAN TEXTBOOKS

Kim Myung-Nam et al (1987), *Korean, 4th grade, Elementary school,* Pyeong-yang: Gyo-yook Publishing Company.

Lee Gwang-Seop et al (1997), *Korean. 4th grade, Elementary school,* Pyeong-yang: Gyo-yook Publishing Company.

Gyo-yook Publishing Company (1972), *Ethics of Communism, 4th grade, Elementary school,* Pyeong-yang: Gyo-yook Publishing Company.

Gyo-yook Publishing Company (1995), *Ethics of Communism, 4th grade, Elementary school,* Pyeong-yang: Gyo-yook Publishing Company.

SOUTH KOREAN TEXTBOOKS

The Ministry of Education (1979), *Ethics, 4th grade, Elementary school,* Seoul: The National Textbook Corporation.

The Ministry of Education (1987), *Ethics, 4th grade, Elementary school,* Seoul: The National Textbook Corporation.

The Ministry of Education (1996), *Ethics, 4th grade, Elementary school,* Seoul: The National Textbook Corporation.

The Ministry of Education (1976), *Korean, 4th grade, Elementary school,* Seoul: The National Textbook Corporation.

The Ministry of Education (1987), *Korean, 4th grade, Elementary school,* Seoul: The National Textbook Corporation.

CHAPTER 4

BEYOND THE NATIONAL AND THE TRANSNATIONAL

Perspectives of WWII in U.S.A, Italian, Swedish, Japanese, and English School History Textbooks

Jason Nicholls

As a uniquely pan-global historical experience it is not surprising that World War II is a popular topic in secondary school history in many countries. Why then do history textbook portrayals of the conflict tell us such different stories? Is the war playing itself out in some way? Surely, the role played by different nation states during the war and the final outcome of the conflict has been crucial in shaping the politics of the present as well as portrayals of the past. In her pioneering study, *Identity and Transnationalization in German School Textbooks*, Yasemin Soysal identifies the connection between Germany's aggressive nationalist past and its pacifist transnational-oriented present as portrayed in school history textbooks. Thus:

What Shall We Tell the Children?, pages 89–112
Copyright © 2006 by Information Age Publishing
All rights of reproduction in any form reserved.

> Unlike its Asian counterparts and more so than other European countries, Germany displays a prudence in representations of national identity in its social science textbooks. Rather than asserting national myths and presenting irredentist narratives as the core components of nationhood, the textbooks focus on the representation of a more globalized and diversified world and the place of a relativized German identity in that world. This departure from the traditional representations of national identity should no doubt be understood vis-à-vis the critical juncture of the Holocaust and World War II.[1]

Soysal notes that virtually all German textbooks "...reflect a consensus over the condemnation of the Nazi past."[2] In other words, the transnational perspective adopted in German textbooks today, pacifist and committed to peace, positing all nations as equals, engages with the aggressive excesses of a nationalist past by denouncing that past. In turn, this condemnation demarcates a clear distance between past and present; a message to all that Germany has come a long way since 1945 and that Germany is a nation to be trusted.

This transnationalized perspective bares a close resemblance to positions developed by supranational cultural and humanitarian organizations such as UNESCO and the Council of Europe.[3] Since the late 1940s, these bodies have suggested transnational oriented approaches that accentuate common values as a means to counter national excess in history education, a response by the world to past acts of inhumanity in the world to improve the world. An example of a textbook attempting to present history from a transnational perspective would be *Illustrated History of Europe*.[4] In this book, authors from numerous European countries came together to write a common history in an attempt to transcend national biases and stereotypes. Translated into several languages, the book has proved popular in many European countries and several editions have been published. However, while similar, Germany's journey to the transnationalized present represents, among other things, an attempt to salvage the position of the German nation in the world. Indeed, in light of "...its harrowing nationalist and militarist past," writes Soysal, "Germany had no choice but to anchor its identity within the prospect of an integrated Europe and a transnational context."[5] Past and present, present and past are thus inextricably bound; Germany's transnationalized present embedded as much in national self-interest as in the politics of peace. Given the response to World War II identified by Soysal in Germany and German school textbooks, it becomes fascinating to probe how and with what perspectives other nations portray the conflict.

Japan and Italy, Nazi Germany's principal wartime allies, share considerable responsibility for the propagation of World War II. Yet the post-war actions and responses of these two countries have contrasted strongly with those of Germany.[6] In her study, Soysal acknowledges how the transnationalization of post-war identity sets "Germany apart from the…[case]…of Japan…in which the national dimension still plays a visibly larger role in matters of defining identities through education."[7] The situation with history textbooks in Italy is far more elusive. Indeed, while contemporary historians like R. J. B. Bosworth have done much to elucidate how the historiography of World War II in Italy has developed and changed since 1945, exactly how the war is dealt with in school textbooks remains a largely uncharted area. The portrayal of the war in Japanese and Italian school textbooks thus raises poignant questions. How, if at all, is responsibility for the war dealt with in textbooks from these countries? And if the wartime past is not criticized from a transnational perspective, as is the case in Germany, how is it dealt with?

The perspectives adopted in the textbooks of wartime victors, such as the United States and England, is equally intriguing not least because the pressure to transnationalize, as experienced by Germany, has been sharply absent. To date, several studies have been conducted comparing portrayals of aspects of the war in textbooks from both nations.[8] On the whole, United States textbooks have been found to portray the war from nationalist perspectives. This being said, several studies suggest nationalist bias in English textbooks.[9] The question is perhaps, to what extent do English and United States textbooks, celebrating the defeat of nationalist dictatorial regimes during World War II, lapse into their own forms of nationalistic self-adulation?

Finally, there are the perspectives adopted in the textbooks of neutral countries such as Sweden. In recent years understandings of Sweden's role during World War II have become more complex and controversial.[10] Whereas until the 1980s, Sweden's neutrality was perceived largely in moral terms in recent years it has come to be understood in increasingly political terms; more "non-belligerent" than neutral.[11] Debates are now concerned with the moral price of remaining outside the conflict. This has led to much soul searching and re-evaluation in Sweden. No longer is it possible to question the war *per se* from an outside position of moral and national superiority, yet clearly the Swedish nation was not involved in the fighting. In what way are perspectives of the war in Swedish textbooks affected by contemporary national controversies?

From one setting to the next, textbooks may be used in different ways and to perform different functions. This means that in comparative studies such as this, involving the analysis of textbook samples from no less than five countries, an absolute parity can never be established. Nevertheless, as previously pointed out with Stuart Foster, virtually "…all nations use textbooks to some extent as a means to tell stories or narratives about their national pasts."[12] Similarly, they have "an amplified significance," writes Soysal, since they are "representative of officially selected, organized, and transmitted knowledge" and "indispensable to the explication of public representations of national collectivities and identities."[13] Others make similar claims.[14] School textbooks are key gatekeepers to particular forms of knowledge, organized and presented in a particular way, and enmeshed in dynamic inter-relationships with power. Indeed, they present us with what Stanner likens to "...a view from a window which has been carefully placed to exclude a whole quadrant of the landscape."[15] Comparing views seen through different windows we come to behold the world as it appears to others.

In this study, contemporary textbooks from the United States, Italy, Sweden, Japan and England were subjected to rigorous analysis. The aim was to assess what perspectives on World War II are currently adopted in textbooks from the five countries and why. The adoption of transnational perspectives in German textbooks, as identified in the work of Soysal, is clearly a response to the aggressive and militaristic excesses of the Nazi period. It also corresponds to Germany's location as a self-interested nation within the international politics of the present. From what perspectives do textbooks from other nations respond to the war? How do responses correspond to each nation's place and interests in the international politics of the present? Finally, how is it possible to recommend alternative perspectives and how will these relate to our comprehension of history as a discipline and to our understandings of the subject?

THEORY AND METHOD

Epistemology

Epistemology underpins research. That is to say, research is driven and directed by particular understandings of what constitutes knowledge and, simultaneously, of what does not. Curiously, however, epistemological issues tend rarely to be acknowledged by scholars involved in textbook research.[16] Commenting on the state of educational research in general, Scott and Usher point out how epistemological and ontological questions often appear "...unnecessary in relation to the immediate practical task of getting research going."[17] This, they claim, is a mistake. On the contrary, "philosophical issues are *integral* to the research process and cannot be ignored until after the event."[18] Yet the established epistemological positions are fundamentally problematic. In this study, however, I adopt a theoretical framework that allows for the sensitive acknowledgement of differences in textbooks across cultures and yet facilitates and indeed justifies critique. This framework is grounded in a "modern" reading of Foucault.

Advocated contra positivism, critical theory and relativism, Foucault's contribution is reconceived as a practical framework "...of thought that…[is]…not irrationalistic, …and that moreover…[is]…not reducible to Marxist dogmatism."[19] According to this reading, history, truth and the subject are neither relativized nor essentialized but relationally constituted and dynamic, unidentifiable outside of an essential and ongoing relation to *otherness*. While on the one hand Foucault's ideas are seen to be rooted in universal *forms* that ground his entire enterprise—history, truth, power, knowledge, genealogy—the identity of *form* is constituted only through the acknowledgement of a dynamic reciprocal relationship to an *other*, to other *forms*, and essentially to *content*: multiple histories, specific effects of power, particular knowledges. In this way history and truth are neither given nor denied. Rather they become comprehensible as the expression of dynamic relationships: between form and content, between power and knowledge, between subject and object and so on.

Within this framework, relationally constituted subjects—the researcher, the teacher, the student—are not stripped of agency since truth and progress are at their disposal providing a much-needed sense of meaning and purpose to the task at hand. However, due to the fact that these concepts are always relationally constituted their potential excesses are kept in check. The position and motivations of the subject, the comparative textbook researcher, for example, are thus re-conceptualized. Neither driven by pretensions to discover the whole "truth" at the expense of an oppressed other, nor trapped within an irrational anti-epistemology, where all movements become those of a lost subject without identity and purpose, the subject is conceived "in action," an agent constantly re-negotiating the road ahead.

Critical orientation

Epistemology and critical orientation are intimately connected.[20] What, how, and why it is possible to assess and make critical recommendations on the socio-political level are bound to definitions of truth and subjectivity on the epistemological level. This study involves the comparison of perspectives of World War II in the school textbooks of five countries. While I am sensitive to the reasons why different perspectives of the war have been adopted, that textbooks are located amidst relations of power and knowledge that are configured differently from one national setting to the next, this research is not simply an attempt to describe nationally specific differences. In other words, this is essentially a critical study based on the assumption that current perspectives of World War II found in school history textbooks are not simply given nor beyond critique, but open to further interpretations and recommendations within limits and boundaries.

Essential to this study is the idea that neither the transnational nor the national need be conceptualized as narrowly exclusive positions. On the contrary, the very identity of the transnational is understood as relationally constituted, bound to the national, the regional, the local, the individual and *vice versa*. Similarly, it could be argued, to portray World War II from either a singularly national perspective or a singularly transnational perspective is narrowly conceived. World War II was a multidimensional conflict with multidimensional effects. It follows, therefore, that when students are encouraged to interpret World War II from a multiplicity of perspectives they are enabled to construct interpretations of the conflict beyond the national and the transnational that, in turn, may offer new, alternative and potentially positive perspectives. Exactly how students are encouraged to interpret perspectives (or are not as the case may be) will always be related to understandings of the nature of history as a discipline: not simply as alluded to in textbooks but in general across cultural settings.[21]

The relationship between perspectives in history textbooks and the nature of history as a discipline is illustrated in Figure 4.1. At one extreme, retention-oriented history requires students to memorize textbook content. Here the textbook contains only a single perspective, either national or transnational, and acts as the core syllabus tool. In history classes the teacher teaches extensively "from the textbook," corresponding examinations based on students' knowledge of textbook content. In contrast,

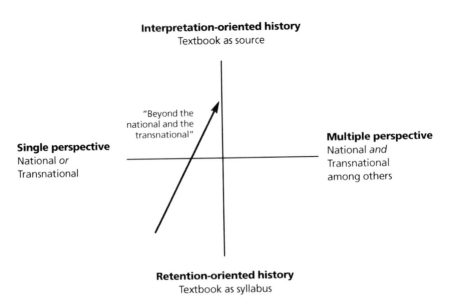

Figure 4.1.   Model to illustrate the relationship between perspectives in history textbooks and the nature of history as a discipline.

interpretation-oriented history might incorporate the textbook into lessons only very occasionally. Here the textbook provides a source of perspectives that students are encouraged to engage with but not as the sole source. Other sources such as film, TV documentaries, slides, software packages, alternative textbooks, personal accounts, and literature, may be used just as frequently in lessons as the textbook. Ideally, the critical interpretation of sources and evidence become the basis for historical study, the teacher's role to facilitate this end. Crucially, this is not the same as saying anything goes.

On the contrary, the critical interpretation of perspectives requires students, like researchers, to interpret as well as to describe differences. To move beyond the national and the transnational, therefore, is to critique the reduction of history to either a single national or transnational perspective, yet it is not synonymous with the relativization of all perspectives. As indicated by the arrow in Figure 4.1, there must be some knowledge retention, there cannot be only interpretation without the retention of knowledge, and there must be some sense that single perspectives exist in contrast to multiple perspectives, plurality has no identity outside of relations to its *other.* singularity. Most important of all, perhaps, to argue that "anything goes" is, at the same time, to limit the potential for critique to zero, stripping the subject—student, teacher, textbook researcher—of intent and purpose. Simply replacing single perspectives with multiple, without stipulating the grounds upon which critique is justified, mocks the very idea of going "beyond" the national and the transnational.

Perspectives of World War II discovered in United States, Italian, Swedish, Japanese and English textbooks are summarized in the results section of this study, the relationship between perspectives and disciplinary tendencies in each country is critically evaluated in the final discussion.

Method

The Textbook Sample

Tightly defined samples of upper secondary level textbooks were selected for analysis. This included three texts from each of the five countries, all published within the last ten years. All the United States texts were listed as commonly adopted books by the American Textbook Council. Italian, English and Swedish textbooks were produced by major publishers. This is also the case for the textbooks in the Japanese sample, claimed by Kaya Michiko, Executive Director of the *International Society for Educational Information,* to constitute at least 60% of the entire Japanese market.[22] Swedish and Italian textbooks were translated into English for the purposes of this study, Japanese textbooks were available, translated, from the *International Society for*

Educational Information in Tokyo. Copies of the United States, Italian and Swedish textbooks were obtained at the Georg Eckert Institute for International Textbook Research in Braunschweig, Germany. The English textbooks were obtained from libraries at the University of Oxford. Japanese textbooks were obtained from the Japanese Embassy Library, London. The entire textbook sample is listed in Appendix A.[23]

Analysis

The analytical framework applied across the textbook sample consisted of sub-questions developed around a single guiding theme: *Perspectives of WWII in U.S., Italian, Swedish, Japanese and English textbooks.* Sub-questions were developed to analyze textbook content, story lines, narrative tone and author perspective. Questions were formulated following previous studies in which the author has been involved as well as the work of Stradling.[24]

Examples of sub-questions used:

- To what extent is World War II conceived as a clash of transnational ideologies rather than simply a clash of nations?
- To what extent is the conflict portrayed as a national campaign rather than a global war?
- How are contributions made by nations in Africa, Asia, the Caribbean and Australasia covered, if at all?
- How are local and individual perspectives of the war acknowledged? Is the conflict portrayed as a total war?
- From what perspective is the Holocaust portrayed?

RESULTS

United States Textbooks

In United States textbooks, international peace, human rights, freedom and democracy are valorized as the ideals of the American nation, rather than the severely contested transnational ideals of humanity as a whole. As the "…arsenal of democracy" (US1, p. 401), it is therefore the United States that is depicted as the natural and pseudo-unilateral defender of the world, crushing authoritarian dictatorships, liberating the oppressed and making reluctant concessions to the Soviets. In this way, World War II becomes the story of how America responded to tyrannical regimes in the world, the American nation winning the day for humanity.

Across all the textbooks, the American people and its leadership are positively and righteously portrayed as "…turning the tide of the war" (US3, p. 506). Even controversial national policies such as racial discrimination within the military and the use of the atom bomb are effectively sub-sumed and overcome within the broader story of national triumph and necessity. Confirming previous findings, coverage of major battles and turning points is dominated by those arenas in which U.S. forces were involved with little attention paid to crucial Soviet contributions and the Eastern Front.[25] Individual accounts and perspectives are incorporated fairly frequently but again tend to be subsumed into the all-pervasive national narrative, personal and emotive stories of heroism on the road to U.S. victory. Although there are few references to the total nature of the war, the Holocaust is covered across the entire sample, at times in depth, the result "...of Hitler's fanatical hatred of the Jews"(US1, p. 414). Yet no connections are made between Hitler's racist policies and those that divided significant sections of U.S. society.

In U.S. textbooks World War II is depicted as a clean-cut affair, an epic tale of good versus evil with its own heroes and villains. In this tale it is the American nation that triumphs over deadly regimes threatening to domi-nate the world. Through constant references to "we" and "our," authors cre-ate a sense of there being little distance between past and present. In fact, portrayals of unilaterally bestowed United States benevolence are made to appear so universal as to seem timeless, an essential offering, the struggle for peace, justice, equality and democracy reliant on the intervention of the American nation alone and never the preserve of transnational bodies or alliances. According to this perspective, World War II, the routing of the Italian, German and Japanese regimes, one after the next, appears as merely one example of United States goodwill among several others.

Italian Textbooks

The portrayal of World War II as a transnational ideological struggle between "Fascism...democracy and communism" is central to perspectives found in Italian textbooks (I3, p. 407). Similarly, the global and total nature of the conflict is unanimously recognized. Major battles and turn-ing points, in the Atlantic, on the Eastern Front, in North Africa, the Pacific, at Normandy, as well as the embroilment of civilian populations and the Holocaust, are discussed in all textbooks, at times in depth. Like-wise, the roles played by Canadian, Gaullist Free-French, Chinese, Finnish, Rumanian and Hungarian forces are all acknowledged. Significantly, local perspectives as well as those of individuals are noticeably absent.

Taking the moral high ground, Italian textbook authors condemn the propagation of the war as a catastrophe of the highest order. Moreover, with "...democracy and international peace as their idealistic emblem"(I1, p. 460), it is the wartime Allies, particularly the Anglo-Americans, who are resoundingly celebrated. Yet responsibility for World War II is placed firmly with "… the policy of aggression and conquest of Nazi Germany"(I2, p. 1471) and to a lesser extent with the actions of the Japanese, the Italians—with the exception of Mussolini—portrayed overwhelmingly as guiltless junior partners. Frequently, Mussolini is portrayed as a deluded leader out of touch with the hearts and minds of the Italian people. Stories of Italian military blunders, losses, miscalculations, strategic errors and general incompetence abound, giving the overwhelming impression that, in spite of Mussolini's military ambitions, the wartime populace made neither good soldiers nor good fascists. Only with the occupation of Central and Northern Italy by the Nazis (post-1943) do Italy's misunderstood subjects become competent partisan fighters: anti-Mussolini, anti-German occupation and anti-fascist.

In Italian textbooks, the spawning of war and Italy's alliance with the Axis are portrayed as a universal disaster both for Italy and humanity as a whole. Yet behind the moral denunciation we find that by placing blame for Italian involvement on the "fascist degenerate" Mussolini, the Italian people are cleared of responsibility. Likewise, by focusing only on Italy's military blunders readers are distracted from the fact that Italian fascist forces committed wartime atrocities—e.g., in the Balkans. On the whole, therefore, textbooks from Italy depict fundamentally good Italians embroiled in a fundamentally bad war. This gives rise to an intriguing dual perspective in which it is the antifascist resistance, the partisans, literally Mussolini's executioners, who are most emphatically portrayed fighting heartily on the side of righteousness in defense of national honor.

Swedish Textbooks

Even though Sweden was officially neutral during World War II, perspectives in Swedish textbooks do not express a pacifist condemnation of the belligerent nations from a position of moral authority. If anything, Swedish portrayals are tied up with the contradictory nature of wartime neutrality. On the one hand, Sweden is depicted attempting to secure its neutral status on terms acceptable to Nazi Germany. Here Sweden is depicted engaging politically. On the other hand, Swedish textbooks give a strong sense of the war as something completely *other.* Here Sweden is depicted detached, a spectator. As with the Italian textbooks this gives rise to a peculiar dual perspective.

Threatened from the south and from the east, Sweden's neutrality is invariably portrayed in the context of the geo-political struggle endured by the Nordic countries at the hands of more powerful states. After the signing of the Hitler-Stalin pact, for example, the attack on neighboring Finland by the USSR is covered in some depth across all the Swedish texts. Then Denmark and Norway are described as being occupied by Nazi forces in April 1940. However, even though "...it seemed that defenseless Southern Sweden would be next...Sweden was not occupied" (S1, p. 302). This is put down to Germany's desperation to "...control the transportation of Swedish iron ore via Norway"(S2, p. 64). Indeed, it is Germany that is depicted allowing Sweden to remain neutral. Only in *Living History 9* are students invited to question "...what a country must do to claim that it is neutral" (S1, p. 303).

Having established the reasons for Sweden's neutrality, Swedish textbooks then devote coverage to the fighting of the war. As the only country in this study considered neutral, it is perhaps not surprising that perspectives of the conflict are underpinned by a sense of detachment. For, even though Sweden's wartime position is commonly conceived today as merely non-belligerent rather than neutral, and Sweden's fate would be decided by the outcome of the war, World War II was fought by nations other than Sweden. Perspectives of World War II appear thus as perspectives of something *other*, in which Sweden is never anything more than a disengaged onlooker. In light of depictions of the Swedish nation engaging politically with Nazi Germany to consolidate its neutrality, this gives rise to an eerie sense of identity crisis and uncertainty, the connection between the shipment of iron ore and German aggression in the wider war never alluded to.

This sense of detachment is not to suggest that the view of the conflict in Swedish books is undiscriminating, unaffected by geo-political concerns. Confirming prior observations, the war in Europe tends to dominate Swedish textbook portrayals, the Pacific arena portrayed as a distant secondary affair.[26] However, although the Holocaust is described in detail in two of the texts, there is no sense of the transnational ideological struggle between liberalism, fascism, and communism. Sweden was the liberal democracy that stood watching from the sidelines. Similarly, there are few examples of individual or local perspectives, Sweden the nation with few examples of its own. Perhaps not surprisingly, attempts to valorize the role of the nation and its people in the conflict are sharply absent across Swedish textbooks. Instead, the perspective is one of a small country in the far north of Europe, wishing to remain neutral but forced to be non-belligerent in a conflict that was in no way of its own making.

Japanese Textbooks

Japanese textbooks portray World War II from an overwhelmingly national perspective (see Crawford, this volume), the transnational ideological struggle between fascism, liberalism and communism receiving only secondary attention. Despite descriptions of the emerging tripartite alliance with Germany and Italy, Japan tends to be depicted fighting alone, first against China and then the United States. Confirming observations made in a previous study, the involvement of other Allied nations such as Britain and the Soviet Union receives little coverage, while the contributions of forces from India, Canada, Australia, New Zealand, Kenya, Jamaica and Free France are never mentioned.[27] Similarly, although the invasion and occupation of China and the subsequent resistance by Chinese forces is provided in some depth, the gravity and seriousness of the almost decade long occupation is discussed more often than not from a Japanese perspective. Thus, "…the prolongation of the war with China" was "contrary to Japanese expectations"; leading to a "shortage of materials" and to increased "military expenditure" (J2, pp. 323–324). Atrocities committed by Japanese forces moving through China are only briefly mentioned, commonly relegated to footnotes.

Responsibility for the controversial attack on Pearl Harbour tends to be downplayed in Japanese textbooks giving rise to a distinctly national perspective on the origins, perpetration and outcome of the Pacific War, again confirming prior findings.[28] In sharp contrast to textbooks from other nations, the outbreak of hostilities with the United States is portrayed as inescapable, Japan's response to economic sanctions that placed the security and well being of the Japanese nation at risk. Indeed, by September 1941, two months prior to the attacks, we find the U.S. depicted as having already "…decided on war" (J1.p. 330). Fighting in the Asia-Pacific region dominates coverage in the Japanese textbooks; key battle arenas in the Soviet Union and in North Africa scarcely portrayed. Finally, it is not Japan that loses the war, nor is it the Japanese leadership or the people who fail. On the contrary, it is the United States, with its "…enormous military might," that is portrayed as the indestructible victor (J3, p. 279).

In sharp contrast to the unanimous condemnation of the nationalist past identified in German textbooks by Soysal, the global significance of Japan's wartime actions are downplayed in Japanese textbooks. Although it is recognized in footnotes that "…hostilities enveloped the whole world" (J2, p. 327), Japan's war is cast as anything but a transnational historical experience, portrayals dominated primarily by national geo-political concerns. The perspectives of other powers, nations and peoples are covered only with extreme brevity while local and individual perspectives are completely absent. Perhaps most significantly, there is little sense of Japan's involvement in, let alone responsibility for, the humanitarian tragedy of the conflict. The Nanjing Massacre, for example, is never openly condemned. Described as "…an episode that was to incur international criticism" (J2, p. 323), that "…after the war, became a major question at the Tokyo trials" (J1, p. 324), Japanese responsibility for the massacre is made to appear more the opinion of others. Similarly, in spite of its alliance with Nazi Germany, Japan is in no way portrayed as a complicit partner in the perpetration of wartime atrocities. Perhaps this explains why the Holocaust is depicted with such extreme brevity; the consequences of Japan's key support of international fascism alluded to in only the narrowest terms.

English Textbooks

A wide variety of perspectives are adopted in English textbook portrayals of World War II. Thus, while the transnational ideological struggle between liberal, fascist and communist visions of the world are acknowledged, so too is the intensely political power struggle between the nation states themselves. What is more, local and individual perspectives are included, often in the form of numerous sources, purposely offering contradictory points of view on particular events. As for regional perspectives, major battle arenas on the Eastern Front, in the Pacific and in Western Europe are covered in roughly equal measure across the sample with, somewhat surprisingly, less attention devoted to events in North Africa.

Britain's experience of the war is depicted from a mixture of perspectives. In Rees's *The Modern World*, for example, although after the fall of France it is acknowledged that "...Britain and the Commonwealth had stood alone against Hitler" (E3, p. 166) the rescue of troops from Dunkirk is portrayed not as a great moment in British history, as some suggest, but rather "...a tremendous defeat" (E3.p. 165). Similarly, while the importance of the Battle of Britain is affirmed, it is not valorized. Indeed, victory tends to be put down to impatience and miscalculation on the part of Hitler who "...did not realize how near the RAF were to defeat" (E3, p. 166). Nevertheless, Britain is portrayed playing a major role in the war alongside its partners. Thus it is the events of 1940/1941 that "...set an example to the rest of the world and showed that the British people were not prepared to give in" (E2, p. 84) and it is "...the British [that] held up the Japanese advance in the jungles of Burma" (E2, p. 85) and "British, Canadian and U.S. forces" that "...landed in Normandy on June 6, 1944" (E2, p. 84). Despite wider coverage of the Soviet and Pacific arenas, Britain is portrayed as a worthy ally.

English textbooks give a strong sense that the war is open to interpretation. On one level, this should be welcomed since it offers a platform for high levels of critical engagement and analysis. On another level, it is not difficult to see how this pluralism may slide into a kind of relativism, particularly where students are not positioned to critically engage (for whatever reason) with perspectives. In addition, the incorporation of such a wide range of perspectives may in fact serve to elevate Britain's role as a member of the Allies in the conflict, from third of the big three to a relative equal. Yet by presenting a multiplicity of perspectives on World War II, the English textbooks appear to offer readers something that is neither purely national nor transnational, regional nor local.

DISCUSSION

Accounting for Differences

On a purely descriptive level, the results of this study reveal how different perspectives of World War II have been adopted in textbooks from different nations. How can these differences be accounted for? As has been argued throughout this chapter, World War II continues to cast long shadows over the international politics of the present that in turn affect subsequent perspectives of the past.

Emerging from World War II as the world's richest and most powerful nation, the reach of United States political, economic and military power has increased exponentially. The situation has been further consolidated with the collapse of the Soviet Union, America's only post-war rival. In recent years, United States foreign policy has become increasingly assertive, unilateral interventions legitimized in the name of freedom, democracy, peace and the protection of human rights, symbols of the American nation. In this way, Allies have become junior partners—their contributions the equivalent to compliance with American directives. Likewise, the enemy continues to be identified in purely moral terms—"the Axis of Evil" and "rogue states." In sharp contrast, the position of the United Nations, with its emphasis on multilateral solutions, has been progressively eroded; the actions of the United States and its junior allies calling the legitimacy of the organization increasingly into question; its ideals, that peace and freedom should be the preserve of humanity, sidelined and ignored. Portrayals of United States forces toppling dictators in World War II bare an uncanny resemblance to recent coverage of the ousting of regimes in Afghanistan and Iraq, as does the prevailing stress on the moral righteousness of American actions. Perspectives of World War II in United States textbooks appear anchored in the international politics of the present.

After World War II Italy lay impoverished and without a political voice. The least powerful of the main Axis nations, Italy was the first to surrender to the Allied powers, actively changing sides and fighting against Nazi Germany from 1943 onwards. After World War II, Italian politics and identity came to be rooted both in the discourse of anti-fascism and in aspirations to be seated as an equal at the top table of a prosperous, stable and united

Europe.[29] These trends are mirrored in perspectives of World War II identified in Italian history textbooks. Indeed, even though Italy's wartime anti-fascism has come under intense criticism, exposed as a myth by forces in the Italian academy, the perspective—that responsibility for World War II rests with Mussolini not the Italian people—remained strongly in evidence across the school textbooks surveyed in this study.[30] Likewise, as is the case with Germany after World War II, Italy has gained a political voice through the wider transnational platform of an integrated Europe. A strong humanist/transnational perspective—that the war propagated by the Axis was a catastrophe for Europe the effects of which can only be overcome through peaceful cooperation—shines through in the condemnation of World War II across the Italian texts.

Perspectives in Swedish textbooks reflect controversies affecting a number of countries that were either occupied or neutral during the war. Where wartime neutrality was once idealized as pacifist and anti-war, it has come to be understood more recently in political terms, that is in terms of levels of complicity with the belligerent power, in Sweden's case Nazi Germany. While Swedish textbooks concede that Sweden negotiated its neutrality with the Nazis, the relationship between what was exchanged—iron ore and the free movement of German troops and arms through Swedish territory—and the wider "world war" are never made explicit. As such, World War II is portrayed overwhelmingly from the perspective of an isolated spectator. The contradiction between this and the reality of Sweden's complicity creates an unsettling feeling of identity crisis. With the realities of Swedish neutrality now out in the open, coinciding with the collapse of its famous welfare state in the early 1990s, and the late membership of the EU in 1995, Sweden has to come to question its role in the world. This anxiety is reflected in perspectives of World War II found in Swedish school history textbooks.

By the end of World War II, Japan lay in ruins, discredited and totally defeated. Although a key Axis member, Japan had fought in East Asia and the Pacific largely unassisted. After World War II, with the eight-year U.S. military occupation and the emerging cold war, Japan remained firmly within the American political and military orbit. The Marshall Plan ensured that Japan had the financial support to rebuild its economy. By the early 1970s, having paid all outstanding debts, Japan emerged as an economic powerhouse, exporting its goods around the globe. In many ways Japan's post-war economic fortunes mirror those of the former West Germany. Yet there are important differences. On the political level, Japan's relationship with neighboring countries continues to be affected by distrust and, in North East Asia, no initiative remotely similar to that of the EU has existed. There are numerous reasons for this, too many to be listed here. Nevertheless, where Germany has been able to overcome the past through the transnational and uniting project of European integration, assisted by a self-interested and politically ambitious France, Japan has remained isolated, its agenda dominated by bilateral relations with the U.S. Perspectives of World War II in Japanese history textbooks thus appear strongly tied to the international politics of the present. Moreover, the Japanese people continue to be essentialized in textbooks from Japan. This contrasts sharply with the German case identified by Soysal. Indeed, the overall impression is that little distance exists between the Japan of World War II and Japan today. Sanitized coverage of Japan's war in East Asia and then with the invincible U.S. dominates textbooks, the Japanese portrayed alone, distinct, perhaps misunderstood, fighting hard, working hard, toiling away then as now.

Britain has lost political power and influence in the years since World War II, the post-war alliance with the U.S. and the half-hearted embrace with European integration reflecting an overly inflated self-image that has been slow to dissipate. To be fair, Britain emerged from the Second World War as a nation between things. The last and largest of the European imperial powers the proximity of Empire was still close enough to affect notions of Britain's place in the world. Moreover, Britain had fought on the side of the victorious Allies and had secured a place as a permanent member on the UN Security Council. The combination of these things made Britain's situation different from that of other big European countries. Nonetheless, the world had changed dramatically. The U.S. and the Soviet Union had now emerged as the world's uncontested super powers and, by the late 1950s several Western European states had begun moving towards economic integration. In the meantime the Empire became a commonwealth and, relative to other European economies, Britain showed signs of chronic industrial decline. Since the late 1970s attempts have been made to resurrect a sense of Britain's essential role in the world: the libertarian/nationalist "Thatcher Revolution" followed by the Blairite "third way." Yet the results have not always been convincing, British governments clinging ever more desperately to the so-called "special-relationship" with the U.S. In English textbooks, due in part to the reliance on multiple perspectives, in which sources from many aspects of the war are incorporated, concessions are made to the supremacy of U.S. and especially Soviet contributions and, at times, to the luck that an enemy's mistakes may bring. However, this same emphasis on multiple perspectives can also appear to relativize and equalize differences, all things being open to interpretation Britain's essential wartime contribution becomes neither greater nor lesser than the contributions of others.

Critical Alternatives and Possibilities

Across the textbook sample used in this study, national differences have been identified, described and accounted for. What should be done next?

Are the differences, clearly entangled with the politics of the present, so overwhelmingly particular that they should be conceived as exotic "curiosities," five national patterns to add to the collection?[31] Is it at all possible to offer something that is more than a description of differences, something closer to a tentative critique that may form the basis for recommendations? The textbook researcher, as a relationally constituted subject, will always be bound to a location, socially, politically and culturally enmeshed in relations of power and of knowledge. Accordingly, the researcher can never assume a neutral position outside of relations to the objects being researched. To acknowledge this is to set necessary limits on the possibilities of criticism. Yet to recognize limits is not to contend that critical speculations positing alternatives are not possible.

As discussed above, exactly how students are encouraged to engage with perspectives—single and/or multiple; national and/or transnational or beyond—will always be related to understandings of the nature of history as a discipline in given settings, not only as alluded to in the textbooks themselves but in general. Moreover, according to this researcher, to move beyond the straight jacket of either the national or the transnational requires a particular disciplinary orientation in which students develop the means to critically engage with plurality. This orientation bares a close resemblance to ideas forwarded by Bob Stradling and P. C. Jager.[32] How might students in the United States, Italy, Sweden, Japan and England be encouraged to grapple with the perspectives identified above? This will depend on disciplinary tendencies in school history education in each of the five nations, briefly outlined below.

High school history in the United States is dominated by courses that survey "civilization," often from ancient times to the present day. Having to cover a wide range of time periods, often in the space of one or two semesters, course objectives tend to emphasize breadth of knowledge over depth of analysis. With the need to cover such an extensive range of content, and with no national curriculum guidelines, teachers often teach from a single textbook. Students are internally assessed, examinations tending to test the ability of students to retain and memorize facts and information. Textbooks routinely are large, often over 1000 pages long, and "all encompassing" in terms of content. Typically, they are dominated by a single narrative with sources used overwhelmingly to bolster, rather than question, story lines. Questions are incorporated at the end of sections and chapters, although rarely to ask students to critically engage with narrative.

History education in Italy continues to be knowledge intensive.[33] Following loose curriculum guidelines, the textbook plays a central role in the teaching and organization of Italian history classes, where students tend to be assessed based on the knowledge they have retained. Assessment is predominantly internal. Italian textbooks frequently are dominated by a single narrative with sources, pictures and charts used to enhance story lines. End of chapter questions that require students to "regurgitate the facts" are common. In Sweden, 20th Century history is taught in the final year of compulsory education following extremely loose curriculum guidelines. Moreover, recent reforms stipulate that a variety of dimensions and perspectives—global, European, Nordic, Swedish, local—should be incorporated into history classes.[34] Accordingly, with students being internally assessed, the use of textbooks and other resources varies widely. Nevertheless, Swedish textbooks tend not to offer multiple perspectives, dominated instead by narrative, sources incorporated to support the central story line. Textbooks often are fairly small, geared towards specific year groups, "complimentary" rather than "all encompassing." Some questions at the end of sections and chapters test memory, others interpretation skills.

History education in Japan is geared overwhelmingly towards passing university entrance examinations and is definitively retention-oriented, requiring students to memorize enormous amounts of knowledge. The textbook forms the basis of the history syllabus, the teacher's role to teach the textbook. Other resources are rarely used. While Japanese teachers may choose freely from a wide range of textbooks available on the market, these books will all have been censored by *Monbusho*, the Japanese Ministry of Education. Textbooks are narrative-based, offering a single perspective on events. Multiple perspectives are never used, sources incorporated only to support story lines. Questions at the end of sections and chapters are rarely if ever featured.

School history education in England is located within parameters set by the National Curriculum and the external examination syllabi. In contrast to the sweeping survey courses found in the U.S. and Japan, historical studies are typically based around themes and topics. Qualifications are based on results through continual assessment as well as examinations. In particular, course objectives routinely emphasize the importance of interpretation as well as knowledge retention. Since curriculum and syllabi are relatively prescribed, textbooks are commonly conceived as a resource only, used less frequently than in many other countries. The textbook market is liberal and competitive. Publishers, however, are forced to produce textbooks that compliment the National Curriculum and/or examination syllabi. Textbooks tend to include a multiplicity of perspectives and numerous sources with a relatively minimal narrative component. Assignments and questions are usually oriented around the comparison and interpretation of evidence as opposed to the retention of knowledge.

Guided by the model illustrated in Figure 4.1, perspectives of World War II can be located in relation to disciplinary tendencies. In American and Japanese textbooks, for example, we find portrayals of the Second World War to be anchored in single national perspectives in disciplinary contexts that are strongly retention-oriented and in which the textbook performs the role of syllabus. In Italian textbooks, however, World War II is portrayed from a more complex dual perspective in which a single national and a single transnational perspective are cast together, again in a disciplinary context that is retention-oriented and textbook based. The Swedish textbooks share a similarly split perspective, reflecting the uncertain role that Sweden, like Italy, played during the war. Yet the Swedish disciplinary context is more flexible, history tending to be more interpretation oriented, the textbook playing a complimentary rather than central role. Finally, in the English textbooks, perspectives of World War II are multiple and varied in a disciplinary context that often is more interpretation-oriented and in which the textbook is conceived not as syllabus but as source.

Taking a critical stance, it is possible to say that a flexible disciplinary dimension is essential to the construction of alternative perspectives. Clearly, in the American and Japanese cases there is less space for critical engagement with the national perspective offered. Rather, students are passive receivers with virtually no chance to grapple with perspectives. Italian textbooks were also found to portray the war inflexibly. In recent years, however, efforts have been made to incorporate more perspectives into textbooks and to develop a freer, more interpretive learning culture.[35] The Swedish case is somewhat different. Although multiple perspectives are not offered in textbooks, it is possible that students will engage with alternative perspectives in the course of other classroom activities. The English case with its emphasis on multiple perspectives and interpretation, appears closest to "beyond the national and transnational" binary. But appearances can be deceptive. With school history based around topics and themes, and with textbooks that can give a sense of "source overkill," it is not inconceivable that some students may feel lost amidst the perspectives, so relativized that difference has no value and that all things appear equal.

Since perspectives in textbooks and disciplinary context are clearly tied to locality, it is impossible to offer overarching quick-fix recommendations. There are strong reasons why certain arrangements exist in certain places. As such, replacing the various perspectives of World War II discovered in this study with a single "correct" perspective, as aspired to in Delouche's *Illustrated History of Europe*, or perhaps by Marxists, emphasizing the universal effects of economy and class-conflict, may well have the effect of negating essential differences. Nevertheless, it would be defeatist to conceive differences as simply relative or, for that matter, arbitrary, a random cluster of positions. Yes there are many histories of World War II, a plurality, and yet each history is defined, by the fact that, like the others, it is a history of World War II. To recognize this fact—this *truth*—is to place specific limits on the field of study, on the number of perspectives available to the researcher, the student, and the teacher; contesting the notion that "anything goes."

Critical engagement with multiple perspectives in history education should be clearly defined, not only in terms of an intrinsic suspicion of singular "catch all" perspectives, national or transnational, but also in contrast to the relativist notion that all perspectives are valid. Above all, critical engagement requires the student to evaluate and assess, and to make judgments, in addition to simply describing differences. Grounded in a particular definition of the subject and with it, the extent and limits of agency, the essential question becomes not what is the "correct" perspective to adopt, to learn or to teach, but rather: How is it possible to engage with plurality meaningfully and critically? Ideally, without falling prey to an arbitrary relativism, the relationally constituted subject—researcher, student, or teacher—constructs dynamic platforms from which to proceed with the conceptual tools necessary to perform critique at its disposal.[36] In some national contexts the space for this kind of critical engagement is certainly more accessible than in others.

At the present time textbooks continue to be important resources in history lessons in many countries, their production, distribution and usage tied to major economic, political and ideological interests. In addition, World War II continues to be a popular topic of study. In this research, perspectives of the conflict in textbooks from five liberal democracies, the United States, Italy, Sweden, Japan and England, were found to be clearly entangled with the international politics of the present, portrayals and representations of the war baring a clear relationship to current national and geo-political concerns. Could there be a better reason for students to explore, to compare, to unravel, and to critically engage? The answer is, probably not. Nevertheless, the results of this research indicate that, in most cases, students are expected to passively memorize rather than critique the perspectives they are offered. Likewise, transnational alternatives, while offering a radically different single perspective on events, negate the notion that students may engage critically with a plurality of perspectives. But that's not all. As argued above, to go beyond singularly national and transnational perspectives require more than a simple transition to multiple perspectives. Plurality alone is not a solution. On the contrary, it is through *critical engagement* with multiple perspectives that new and alternative positions may be achieved. Only then will students, teachers and researchers alike develop the means to grapple meaningfully with plurality, to develop critical understandings, assessments and evaluations of the conflict.

NOTES

1. Y. Soysal, "Identity and Transnationalization in German School Textbooks": pp. 128–129, in *Censoring History—Citizenship and Memory in Japan, Germany, and the United States*, eds. L. Hein and M. Seldon, (Armonk and London: East Gate Books, 2000).

2. Ibid., p. 129.

3. See G. Allardyce "Towards World History," in *Journal of World History*, Vol. 1, No. 1, 1990 and J. Slater, *Teaching History in the New Europe*, (London and New York: Council of Europe, 1995).

4. F.Delouche, *Illustrated History of Europe—A Unique Portrait of Europe's Common History*, (London: Cassell, 2001).

5. Soysal, Ibid.

6. See R.J.B. Bosworth *Explaining Auschwitz and Hiroshima—History Writing and the Second World War 1945—1990*, (London and New York: Routledge, 1994) and R.J.B. Bosworth and P. Dogliani, *Italian Fascism—History, Memory and Representation*, (Basingstoke and London: Macmillan, 1999).

7. Soysal, Ibid., p. 139.

8. See S.J. Foster and J. Morris, "Arsenal of Righteousness?—Treatment of the Atomic Bombing of Hiroshima in English and U.S. History Textbooks," in *Curriculum*, Volume 15, Number 3, 1994; J. Nicholls, "The portrayal of the atomic bombing of Nagasaki in U.S. and English school history textbooks," in *International Textbook Research*, Vol. 25, Issue 1, 2003; S.J. Foster and J. Nicholls, "Portrayal of America's Role During World War II: An Analysis of School History Textbooks from England, Japan, Sweden and the USA," (paper presented at the annual AERA conference, Chicago, USA, 2003); and J. Nicholls and S.J. Foster, "Portrayal of the Soviet Role in World War II: An Analysis of School History Textbooks from England and the USA," (paper presented at the International School Textbook and Educational Media Conference, Edge Hill College of Higher Education, England, 2003).

9. See P. Coman, "Reading about the enemy: School textbook representation of Germany's role in the war with Britain during the period from April 1940 to May 1941," in *British Journal of the Sociology of Education*, Vol. 17 (1996); A. Kallis, "Coping with the uncomfortable past: a comparative analysis of the teaching of World War 2 and the role of historical education in the construction of a European identity," in *Young citizens in Europe—Proceedings of the first conference of the Children's Identity and Citizenship in Europe Thematic Network*. (London: CiCe publication, 1999); and K.A. Crawford, "Constructing national memory: The 1940/41 Blitz in British History textbooks," in *Internationale Schulbuchforschung*, Verlag Hahnsche Buchhandlung, Hannover, Vol. 1, 2000.

10. A. Johansson, "Neutrality and Modernity: The Second World War and Sweden's National Identity," in *War Experience, Self Image and National Identity: The Second World War as Myth and History*, eds. S. Ekman and N. Edling, (Soedertaelje: Fingraf tryckeri, 1997).

11. P. Levine, "Swedish neutrality during the Second World War: tactical success or moral compromise?," in *European Neutrals and Non-Belligerents During the Second World War*, ed. N. Wylie (Cambridge: Cambridge University Press, 2002).

12. Foster and Nicholls, Ibid., p. 1.

13. Soysal, Ibid., p. 130.

14. See Crawford, Ibid.; J. van der Leeuw-Roord, "Working with history: national identity as a focal point in European history education," in *International Journal of Historical Learning, Teaching and Research*, Vol. 1, No. 1, 2000; and M. Apple and L. Christian-Smith (eds.), *The Politics of the Textbook*, (New York: Routledge, 1991).

15. W.E.H. Stanner in J.A. LaSpina "Designing diversity: globalization, textbooks, and the story of nations," *Journal of Curriculum Studies*, Volume 35, Number 6, 2003.

16. J. Nicholls, "Comparing the portrayal of World War II in school history textbooks beyond describing: epistemological and methodological issues in comparative textbook research," (paper presented at the annual Comparative Education Society of Hong Kong Conference, China, 2004).

17. D. Scott, D. and R. Usher, *Researching Education—Data, Methods and Theory in Educational Enquiry*, p. 9. (London: Cassell, 1999).

18. Ibid., p. 10.

19. M. Foucault, *Remarks on Marx*, p. 94, (New York: Semiotext(e), 1991).

20. J. Nicholls, "Methods in School Textbook Research," in *International Journal of Historical Learning, Teaching and Research*, Volume 3, Number 2, 2003. Published online at http://www.ex.ac.uk/education/historyresource/journalstart.htm.

21. See Foster and Nicholls, Ibid; R. Stradling, *Teaching 20th century European history*, (Strasbourg: Council of Europe Publishing, 2001); and P.C. Jager, "Is a common textbook in Europe desirable? A comparison of two approaches towards a European history education," in *EUROCLIO Bulletin*. Nr 18, 2003.

22. K. Michiko, *Japan in Modern History*, Volume 1, p. 8, (Tokyo: International Society for Educational Information, 1995).

23. Each textbook was ascribed a code (e.g., US1, S3, I2). Textbooks and their corresponding code are listed in Appendix A. Individual textbooks are represented in the results section by the code indicated in brackets.

24. See J. Nicholls, "The portrayal of the atomic bombing of Nagasaki in U.S. and English school history textbooks," Ibid; Foster and Nicholls, Ibid; Nicholls and Foster, Ibid; and Stradling, Ibid.

25. Foster and Nicholls, Ibid; Nicholls and Foster, Ibid.

26. Ibid.

27. S.J. Foster and J. Nicholls, "Portrayal of America's Role During World War II: An Analysis of School History Textbooks from England, Japan, Sweden and the USA," (paper presented at the annual AERA conference, Chicago, USA, 2003)

28. Ibid.

29. See Bosworth, Ibid.

30. Ibid.

31. P. Bourdieu, *Practical Reason—On the Theory of Action*, pp. 1–3, (Cambridge: Polity, 1998).

32. See Stradling, Ibid; Jager, Ibid.

33. See L. Cajani, "A World History Curriculum for the Italian school," in the *World History Bulletin*. Available at: www.thewha.org, Vol. XVIII No. 2, 2002.

34. See S. Salin and C. Waterman "Sweden," in *Education in a Single Europe*, eds. C. Brock and W. Tulasiewicz (London and New York: Routledge, 2000).

35. See Cajani, Ibid.

36. See Stradling, Ibid.

APPENDIX

U.S. Textbooks

G. Nash, *American Odyssey: The United States in the 20th Century*, New York: Glencoe McGraw Hill, 1994. (US1)

D.J. Boorstin and B.M. Kelly, *A History of the United States*, Needham: Prentice Hall, 1999. (US2)

A. Cayton, E. Perry and A.M. Winkler, *America: Pathways to the Present*, Needham: Prentice Hall, 1998. (US3)

Italian Textbooks

M.L. Salvadori, *The Contemporary Age*, Milan: Loescher Editore, 1998 (I1)

A. Giardina, G. Sabbatucci, and V. Vidotto, *History 1900 to the Present Day*, Rome: Editori Laterza, 1998. (I2)

G. Gentile, L. Ronga and A. Salassa, *Contemporary History and its Roots*, Brescia: Editrice La Scuola, 1997. (I3)

Swedish Textbooks

L. Hildingson and K. Hildingson, *Living History 7–9*, Orebro: Natur och Kultur, 1997. (S1)

K. Sjoebeck and B. Melen, *History: Life in Transformation*, Malmo: Interskol, 1995. (S2)

H. Almgren, B. Almgren and S. Wiken, et al., *History*, Orebro: Gleerups, 1995. (S3)

Japanese Textbooks

I. Susumu, K. Kazuo, K. Kota and S. Haruo, et al., *Comprehensive Japanese History (B)*. Tokyo: Yamakawa Shuppan, 1994. (J1)

N. Kojiro, et al., *Japanese History B*, Tokyo: Jikkyo Shuppan, 1994. (J2)

T. Kawata, M. Bito and H. Tanabe, et al., *New Social Studies: History*, Tokyo: Tokyo Shoseki, 1994. (J3)

English Textbooks

B. Walsh, *GCSE Modern World History*, London: John Murray, 1996. (E1)

R. Chandler and M. Wright, *Modern World History for Edexcel*, Oxford: Heinemann, 1999. (E2)

R. Rees, *The Modern World*, Oxford: Heinemann 1996. (E3)

CHAPTER 5

THE CONSTRUCTION
OF EUROPEAN IDENTITY
1945–PRESENT

Yasemin Soysal

LOCATING EUROPE[1]

The gradual advance of the European Union as a transnational political entity has stimulated a growing interest in Europeanness and its constituent characteristics. The reference to a vocabulary of European identity in popular and political discourses is almost routine and inadvertent, whether the matter is the expansion of Europe to include new members or the policy actions of member states in fields as diverse as economy, migration, environmental protection, and education. For the potential member states, Europeanness serves as a test of their compatibility for convergence and stipulates measures as inscribed in the nondescript question of "who belongs." For the existing member states, European identity is taken to signify a step closer to European unity. From a scholarly perspective, considering that the last two decades in social scientific production has been marked by a preoccupation with identity, a concern with Europeanness is not only inevitable but at the same time requires intervention.

What Shall We Tell the Children?, pages 113–130
Copyright © 2006 by Information Age Publishing
All rights of reproduction in any form reserved.

In essence, the underlying concern with European identity lies in the plausibility and requisiteness of Europe as a "demos."[2] The implicit assumption about European integration is that Europe requires its demos. A demos (the peoplehood, public of the polity) is seen essentially as the basis for legitimate polity-formation, the exercise of citizenship, and governance at the European level, all of which are projected to be inextricably linked with a shared identity and culture.[3] Europe requires Europeans. The problem of identity and legitimacy constantly surfaces in debates over Europe and European integration.[4]

WHAT DOES "EUROPEAN DEMOS" IMPLY?

In the discussions on identity and demos, we encounter three modes of constituting Europe: cultural collectivity; individual subjectivity and institutional unity. Each operates at a different level of analysis and commands different forms of enactment. Nonetheless, their overarching trajectory is the unified demos.

Europe as a cultural collectivity: Europe is postulated, and attempted, as a supranational community, members of which are bonded and bounded with culture that is rooted in the past of Europe and naturally evolving, despite unfortunate and at times, catastrophic breaks in continuity. The projected collectivity of Europe is encompassing and culture is its constitutive seal. For their part, the European Union elites, predominantly the Commission, busy themselves with building European collectivity. Since the late 1980s several communications and reports issued by the EU have recognized culture and identity as key dimensions of European integration—hence, the inordinate number of initiatives, either to create awareness among people about their European identity or to construct one.

At the locus of the theory and practice of Europe as a cultural collectivity are concerns about achieving social cohesion and solidarity. It is an organic community project, requiring, in Smith's vision, Europeans who share a common heritage, myths, history and cultural values.[5] Thereby the project has to draw upon generic assumptions as to Europe's common past, civilizational heritage, and distinct cultural values. The Greek and Roman legacy, Renaissance humanism and enlightenment, parliamentary democracy, and the Christian past are readily offered as the common European patrimony. This patrimony is presumed to be what naturally unites and makes Europeans and what distinguishes them from others.[6]

Europe as a category of subjectivity: Europe is charged with affording subjectivities and emotions conducive to political allegiance and a shared fate. Consequently, as a state of personhood, European is envisioned to be a subject position, embodying desires and sentiments, civic constitution, loyalties, and a distinctly "European" sense and sensibility of self.[7] European subjectivity as such is sought in the responses individuals confer to the signs and ideals of Europe. *Eurobarometer* surveys and analyses of electoral behavior come in handy as the most common, and taken-for-granted, methods of measuring subject positions and degrees of Europeanness.

Europe as an institutional unity: A much debated issue, perhaps to the point of excess, is Europe's prospects vis-à-vis the existing nation-states, variously articulated in such polarized tendencies and contestations as the "widening versus deepening"[8] of Europe or advocating a "Europe of nations" against the "nation of Europe" (or vice versa).[9] Whether expressed in the form of apprehension or anticipation, the concern lies with the political identification of the demos with a European authority structure, as opposed to identification with a particular nation-state. The prospective institutional unity of the imagined Europe is expected to summon stability, coordination, interdependence and mutual social responsibility, and binding values and principles—hence the community "we-feeling."[10]

Their differences notwithstanding, these modes of constituting European demos proceed from an implicit overlap between communities, cultures and publics. In that, the nation-state appears as both an attractive and convincing model whereby achievement of a culturally defined community is posited as a prerequisite to facilitate publics and communication. This view is clearly represented in the following:

> The nation-state represents a stable equilibrium capable of uniting large populations. Such a community guarantees a communicative capacity that enables deliberation and generates a sufficiently strong we-feeling that can carry the weight of effective and democratic governance.[11]

The *modus operandi* of such we-community is recognizable through which individuals can communicate better with each other and bond in solidarities.

Calhoun provides an excellent critique of the tacit affinity between community, cultures, and publics prevalent in popular and academic thinking, and warns us against analytically conflating them.[12] The literature on European demos and identity errs exactly on this front. I concur with Calhoun's suggestion as an analytical strategy and furthermore argue in this chapter that the presumed link between such constructs as identities, cultures and communities is neither tenable nor empirically becoming in the European case.

More importantly, I assert that absent from the debate are the questions: What kind of an identity is being built or envisioned in European public spheres? What kind of a common public space does Europe need and can Europe afford? How much does a shared political identity and culture constitute the basis of this common public space? These questions should focus our sociological attention to the empirical patterns of Europeanization.

In this chapter, I attempt to locate the unfolding European public space in the specific field of education. I do this through a preliminary investigation into the nature and scope of Europe as an identity category or position as it is built in educational spaces.[13] My substantive examples come from schoolbooks and curricula and public engagements and action around them.[14] Textbooks and curricula reflect the official and codified versions of Europe, but these are increasingly products of the work of an effective network of actors—from teachers, academics and advocacy groups to ministerial and EU officers, and to international organizations of various sorts, UNESCO, Council of Europe and the like. They convene and attend meetings and conferences on teaching Europe, survey and evaluate definitions and histories of Europe, and discuss and develop tools and texts for educating future generations of "Europeans." Through their activities, Europe is revisited, revised, and re-mapped.

I advance my inquiry from an institutionalist perspective. By institutionalist perspective I mean paying attention to the discursive and organizational make-up of a specific policy field.[15] I will focus my discussion on two specific aspects of the Europeanization of identity (or the emergence of the category of European identity): its location and its content. By location I mean the public and social spaces within which Europeanization is "happening." This raises methodological questions for studying Europeanization from an institutionalist perspective: first, the actors and processes on which we focus our analytical gaze, and, second, the level of analysis we choose. By content, on the other hand, I mean the discourses through which claims to identity are advanced, and also the constitution of emerging identities. A discussion on the content of European identity invites us to revisit the two major analytical concerns of the institutionalist theory: first, the issue of convergence and divergence, and secondly, institutional conflict and change.

LOCATION OF IDENTITY: WHERE DOES EUROPEAN IDENTITY HAPPEN?

One of the challenges I see in studying the Europeanization of identity is to locate where it happens. Much of the debate on European integration and identity privileges the legitimate actorhood of nation-states or intergovernmental negotiation and decision-making structures. This stems partly from the disproportionate weight given to economic, political and legal aspects of the European integration process.

However, investigating Europe from the margins, that is from a less formalized and less prioritized policy field such as education, reveals a wider set of actors and processes in action. In the case of education, the rather less structured nature of this EU policy field (unlike the monetary, economic or security issues) provides an opportunity area for various actors to seize initiative outside the strict intergovernmental negotiation structures. Education remains a priority of member-states, until recently touched little by supra-national policy making. Since the Maastricht Treaty, education policy has had its own separate directorate.[16] Also since then, the Union has developed and funded several educational initiatives. Many of these initiatives, however, have been confined to the recognition of diplomas, vocational education, contacts between educational institutions, and exchange and language teaching programs. Curricular development and content are still adamantly guarded by the nation-states, despite successive EU resolutions to insert the "European content/dimension" into school curricula. Many scholars and activists of European integration comment that attempts by the Commission to Europeanize education remain limited and not effective.[17]

Nevertheless, we find enormous activity at the European level, which, when taken in its entirety, contributes to the production of an *affective* Europeanness in the field of education. An extensive set of non-governmental organizations are at work: networks and advocacy groups, teachers' unions and associations, publishers of educational materials, minority organizations—all actively taking part in defining and redefining Europe, and mostly under the auspices of UNESCO, the Council of Europe, and other inter- and transnational bodies. Working in conjunction with these non-governmental organizations is an increasing number of advisory committees comprised of scientific experts and technocrats effecting government policy and decision-making through a diverse set of channels. Their activities extend European networks, both organizationally and symbolically, and facilitate a climate of Europeanness and the promotion of European education and ideals.

Among the most significant activities are the works of international committees and organizations that are engaged in revising history textbooks and remedying conflicting histories. In Europe, international attempts to re-examine and revise textbooks predate the European Union, going back to the interwar period. The national and international committees set up by the League of Nations, in cooperation with teachers' associations in different countries, sought to eliminate prejudices and stereotypes from textbooks. In the 1930s, bilateral consultations were already in place between German and French, and German and Polish historians. With the foundation of UNESCO and the Council of Europe after World War II, however, these efforts gained a more institutional basis. Between 1953 and 1958, the

Council of Europe convened six major international conferences, during which "some 900 of the 2000 history textbooks then in use in 15 Western European countries were examined by representatives of Ministries of Education, academic historians, school inspectors, teacher trainers, textbook authors and teachers."[18] The outcome was the adoption of a set of guidelines for textbook authors and teachers on such issues as the teaching of peace and war in Europe, colonialism, religion, and gender equality.

Since 1990, the inter-European activities on textbook revision have proliferated and rapidly expanded to include the central, eastern and southern Europe, and the Balkans. Several such initiatives can be listed: the Baltic, Caucasian, and Black Sea history textbook projects; the southeast European history teachers' education project, and the projects on "history teaching in the New Europe" and on "learning and teaching about the history of Europe in the 20th century." These projects, along with bi- or multilateral committees on textbooks, aim to harmonize the teaching of historical relations between neighboring countries, normalize contentious histories, and bring about a rapprochement among former enemies.[19]

Working towards the same goal, the European Standing Conference of History Teachers' Association (EUROCLIO) conducts teacher training seminars to develop and disseminate "European historical consciousness." They organize workshops to debate the teaching of conflicting episodes and personalities of European history. In one of their initiatives Spanish, Dutch, Portuguese, Scottish, and English history teachers gathered together in Toledo and discussed the "controversial personality" of Philip II and his times—recasting his legacy as one of advancement in arts and literature, rather than the entrenchment of Catholicism in Europe. These are efforts to rehabilitate "unique national heroes and enemies" and the remaking of a European heritage, not of wars and conflicts, but of a positive collective past.[20]

All these conferencing activities and projects in effect create practitioners of Europe, who share objectives and discourses on European education. Having participated in several such conferences and projects during the last three years as part of my research activity, I was struck by the degree of affinity in the goals stated and agendas pursued by actors coming from different national and institutional contexts. The emphasis was invariably on a Europe constituted by dialogue, conflict resolution, tolerance, human rights, and intercultural understanding. This was a Europe taken for granted: European project's necessity and furtherance were not questioned. One other effective form of activity that is worth mentioning is the establishment of European educational statistics, socially and politically unifying an educational space. These statistics make abstract notions of European space "tangible," natural, and self-evident, by fashioning a common language and instituting formal and standardized ways of understanding and measuring success across the terrain of Europe.[21]

All these exercises, in reassessing histories and creating standardized, across-the-board measurements, are a prelude to coordinated teaching and curriculum development and unified educational targets and results. They are also movements in the way to what Cram aptly calls the banalization of Europe: Europe becoming routine, and part and parcel of everyday life and discourses[22]—in other words, a social fact.[23] This is where Europeanization (the creation of Europe, if you will) happens and where European space is enacted: mainly outside inter-governmental structures and formal EU institutions, and through informal institutional processes. Through these processes Europe is realized and communicated.

It is not sufficient, then, to confine our analysis simply to legal definitions, arrangements and formal governmental structures, and those actors who are strategically placed within or connected to the EU institutions. The challenge for us is to expand our analytical agenda to actors and processes, which are often deemed to be ineffective and, thus, remain invisible in much of our analyses. And we should do this by bringing to the fore the non-state associational and networking practices, and by identifying the institutional resources and opportunities they mobilize, both at national and transnational levels.[24]

A second issue regarding the location of European identity is to do with level of analysis. When it comes to explicating European identity, most studies either search for a political identity of the EU itself in the international arena (vis-à-vis other political entities or nation-states), at times secured in commonplace symbols of statehood and cultural collectivity (flag, anthem, heroes, holidays). Or alternatively, European identity is sought in individual citizens' consciousness and dispositions as subjects (a favorite concern of the *Eurobarometer* surveys). The general hypothesis is that the more institutionally integrated the EU, with its distinctive institutions and sovereign governing principles, the greater the likelihood of a shared identity and culture, discernible at the level of individual citizens and, expectedly, replacing or at least undermining national identities.

Such formulations of identity unnecessarily dichotomize the levels of analysis. National and transnational are taken as autonomous levels, and the question becomes either the dominance of one over the other, or the linear transition from one to the other. There is much confusion around this issue and much time and energy is spent in arguing whether we are approaching a transnational stage or not. This is obviously not a productive debate. We need to re-conceptualize the transnational as integral to the very structuration of the national. In other words, transnational and national should be seen as constitutive and a signifier of each other. They are not separate levels of analysis or separate trajectories. In terms of research strategies, this suggests that we should locate the transnational as it factors in the territorially defined spaces and institutions of identity. This also means paying attention to how local and national are re-articulated within the transnational. I come back to this in the next section.

CONTENT OF IDENTITY:
WHAT DOES EUROPEAN IDENTITY HOLD?

To expand upon what I mean by content, I want to take up two specific examples of the ways that European identity is projected and practiced. First, the definition of European identity in schoolbooks and curricula. Second, the discourses employed in educational claims. As narrated in educational spheres, Europe is a diffuse idea and discourse, with contingent boundaries that do not necessarily overlap with the territorial confines of the European Union. Its identity is a loose collection of civic ideals, such as democracy, progress, equality and human rights. As such, Europe represents the "transnational normativity."[25] Its identity is not an exclusive one. With such a definition, everyone can be European, as long as they adhere to the principles.

Europe as normativity, to use Therborn's seductive terminology, is a different way of conceptualizing identity than we normally assume. Unlike national identity categories, it does not find its legitimacy in the deeply rooted histories or ancient cultures and territories. This Europe is future oriented, not past. No doubt, history textbooks glorify Europe's Roman, Christian, and even Greek origins, as particular European achievements. But these origins are treated less and less in ethnic or religious narratives, and increasingly more in terms of universalistic principles they contain. So what are celebrated are the abstract, universalistic principles, attributed to Europe's past, independent of the fact that the same principles have inspired most of the conflicts in Europe's war-ridden history. In recent schoolbooks, Europe appears as a much more peaceful land than its history empirically dictates. Historically, Europe emerged and was sustained more by conflict and division than by consensus and peace, but now what holds Europe together, in textbooks, is a set of civic ideals and universalistic tenets.

The trouble with such a formulation of identity, however firmly they are claimed, is that these universalistic principles and ideals can no longer be affixed specifically to Europe or the member states. The origins of Europe can be traced back to its discursive and institutional position vis-à-vis others.[26] But now it is no longer easy to assert a European past and define a present significantly different from that of others.[27] At the end of the twentieth century, human rights, democracy, progress and equality are everyone's, every nation's modernity—even when they organize their modernity differently and even when they fail to exercise that modernity. This is what makes it impossible to define a territorially and culturally bounded European identity. But this is also what makes possible *a* European identity; which transcends Europe and is legitimated by claims to universality rather than particularisms. This Europe does not exist against its "others. Only in economic competition, do America and Asia become Europe's others; but they do not necessarily constitute cultural others. Islam does not make the grade either. Europe, in collaboration with non-Europeans, defended and still defends Muslim Kosovo and Bosnia against a non-democratic Yugoslavian state. Also remember the extent of pains taken by European leaders in the aftermath of the attacks on New York to differentiate their "war against terrorism" (an ambiguous other and not a very passionate one at that) from a "war against Islam." Despite attempts to the contrary, Europe fails to create its cultural, and symbolic, other; and rightly and fortunately so.[28]

As such, European identity lacks originality, a condition of nationness[29] and its identity does not appear as a challenge to national identities. Schoolbooks and curricula testify to this.[30] A significant proportion of history teaching in schools is still devoted to national or local history. But the nation and its history taught are less recognizable to the eye than before. The textbooks increasingly situate the nation and identity within a European context, and in the process, the nation is being reinterpreted and recast.

We increasingly observe a *normalization* of national canons. By which I mean a standardization process that removes the mythical, the extraordinary, and the charismatic from its accounts of nationhood. Take the increasing celebration in history textbooks of the Vikings as part of the European heritage. The warrior forefathers have been replaced with spirited long-distance traders. Similarly, ancestral tribes—Germanic and Gallic, Normans, Francs, and Celts—are all increasingly depicted, not in heroic but cultural terms, through such images as quaint village life, hospitality, and artistic achievements.[31] The Crusades are taught not simply as holy wars and conquests but as occasions for cultural exchange and learning, between Europeans and other civilizations. In English textbooks, we read that Christians learned to use forks and table manners from more civilized Arabs during their attempts to capture the "holy land."

The same normalization applies to national heroes. They are often talked about in a matter-of-fact way, removed from mythical glorification. Jeanne d'Arc, Bismarck, and Francis Drake are treated with sentimental detachment, and invoked not as a personification of a glorious French, German, or British moment but as common historical figures from whom to learn, or persons with ordinary human weaknesses and qualifications. In German history textbooks, Bismarck is praised for having accomplished the foundation of the German empire in 1871. The "blacksmith of the German empire" nevertheless appears as a double-edged character. On the one hand, it is acknowledged that Bismarck installed a foresighted social insurance system, and that, as foreign minister, he managed to avert the latent danger of war in Europe. On the other hand, these positive aspects are compensated by his decided, anti-democratic impetus and by the fact that even the social insurance legislation was introduced for instrumental reasons, to diffuse the power of Social Democrats. This negative, authoritarian side of Bismarck's policies rendered "bad consequences" or even "fatal" effects later on, the textbooks explain. The conclusion the students are expected to draw from this narration is that one should not simply admire but critically approach the times and efforts of the historical hero. This surely contrasts the tenor of earlier textbooks, in which the founding of the German empire is characterized as the fulfilment of the national longing of many Germans and Bismarck is presented as the bright and politically artistic hero of his time, without any remark on his militaristic tendencies.[32]

Like the nation, local and regional are also revised and recast within the European. We have examples in textbooks of how regional specificities emerge as possible identity positions within the Europe of regions. In French geography textbooks, for example, we read that European integration has modified the organization of the French space. Within this new space Alsace-Lorraine looses its contested existence in the national imaginary, and emerges as a region in the heart of Europe; rich, dynamic and with encouraging prospects. In one textbook, published in 1994, in a section entitled "Regional Cultural Diversity," it is explained that "although the 19th century historians invented the 'Nation-State' and proclaimed the Republic as "one and not divisible," regional diversity still exists, especially in the cultural field." This section is supplemented by a map showing linguistic diversity in France, the European Charter of regional and minority languages, and a text about regional languages, which states:

> Linguistic differences are arranged in a rich national harmony [...] French regional languages are similar to some European languages and for this reason they constitute a precious bridge towards the languages of neighboring countries, thus enhancing important political and economic links with Germany, Italy, Spain, and the Netherlands.[33]

This emphasis on regional and linguistic diversity is quite remarkable for France where regions are always undermined in favor of the center, as opposed to Germany where regional autonomy is inclined because of the more federalist political structure.

My analysis of schoolbooks also testifies to divergence in identity projections and formulations. While the "idea" of Europe is accepted and incorporated in school curricula and textbooks in expansive ways, its appropriation varies in form. In German history books, Europe (and also local regions) heavily figures in the narration of history and identity, while the nation virtually disappears. The nation is valorized negatively if not disavowed for its inclination to turn into dangerous nationalism. This is even so in books that cater for Bavaria, a state known for its conservative politics. One such book affirms the pride in one's own nation by connecting it to liberal and social advancements of 1848, such as freedom of the press, and wealth and education for all. If separated from liberal movements, as was the case in the second half of the 19th century in Germany, the text claims, pride "turns into national arrogance as well as the despising and devaluation of other peoples." Even the unification of the two Germanies is greeted without much emotional enthusiasm and sentimentality. That the celebrations staged for unification in 1990 were not effusive but rather reserved is considered to be "certainly quite good" by another textbook. The same textbook also puts strong emphasis on post-war efforts for international reconciliation, with the French, the Poles and the Jews. Hence, the nation is counterbalanced by invoking a normative international perspective and by insisting that one should not make it too big an issue.[34]

This detached attitude towards nation in textbooks is certainly to do with Germany's specific historical trajectory. But another important factor is the specific institutional structure of the German education system and textbook production. In Germany, one finds close connection between educational authorities and other interest organizations—teachers' associations and unions, parent's associations, churches and universities. The very corporatist structure of decision-making regarding curricula and textbooks, by involving different groups and interests in the process, manages to leave out conflicting views and creates a more consensual outcome. So the revisionist historical positions that give primacy and legitimacy to the German nation and national identity do not find resonance in educational curriculum or schoolbooks. The result is a prudent representation of the nation and its history.[35]

The French textbooks, on the other hand, are much more forthcoming in presenting the nation. But, in this case, the French nation, which is historically conceptualized as an abstract and universalistic entity, is equalized with Europe. The books depict the nation as the carrier of positive values, interwoven with notions of freedom, citizenship and laicism, all of which are also defined and elaborated as universalistic principles. France is the location of these principles and the national feeling is simply "to love France." With the introduction of the 1985 curricular program, which explicitly incorporates the teaching of Europe, these universalistic principles are projected as elemental properties of Europeanness. In other words, Europe becomes French. Since the French system is much more centralized compared to most European countries, this universalistic standpoint easily penetrates and dominates every aspect of education. Even though textbooks are produced commercially by private publishers, because of the very detailed nature of the centralized curriculum, one does not find much variation across textbooks published by different companies. The universalistic conceptualization of France and Europe is present in every textbook.

So Europe, as narrated in schoolbooks and as conceptualized in educational spheres, hosts multiple geographies, multiple boundaries, and multiple cultural bibliography. Europe affords national and regional identities, belongings but not in an organic interdependent way as Weiler suggests in his multiple *demoi* model; as these multiple parts hang together rather haphazardly, sometimes affirmatively but often refiguring each others' interpretation and meanings. Europe is fuzzy,[36] no longer historically unique and precise to perpetuate a coherent, homogenous collective. Unlike the national identities and histories, as they were codified in the ardent processes of state and nation-building, Europe cannot afford to develop its discriminating particularisms and authentic markers. It derives its legitimacy from universalistic principles and from the future it projects. And that future, or aspiration for that future, is now entangled with others' futures, making European identity broader than Europe itself.[37]

Complimentary to schoolbooks and curricula, a second source I suggest for investigating the content of the European identity are the discourses through which claims to rights are advanced and legitimated in the public sphere. In my research, I found that minority (ethnic, religious, or regional) groups' engagement in claims-making furthers the Europeanness of the public spheres and identities. When, for example, immigrant associations mobilize around educational claims for group-specific provisions and identities, they connect their claims to European discourses and agendas of human rights. In forwarding demands about mother-tongue instruction, Islamic *foulard*, or *halal* food in schools, they appeal to the dominant discourses of equality, rights, and emancipation. In that sense, their claims for difference are affirmed by the universalistic and homogenizing ideologies of human rights, rather than the particularities of religious or ethnic narratives. By so doing, they participate in and contribute to the reification of European (and global) discourses and ideals, as well as common public spaces.[38]

This is all in line with institutionalist arguments about isomorphic tendencies—that is, the diffusion, reproduction and elaboration of the rules and principles of the wider cultural environment at national/local levels. My example again attests to the involvement of an extensive set of actors in this process, even including those marginal ones, like immigrant associations, which are neglected in predominant accounts. However, by pointing to shared discourses and practices of claims-making, we should not assume harmonious, conflict free public spheres or homogeneous (policy) outcomes. This brings me to another analytical concern that occupies the institutionalist research agenda: institutional conflict and change.

As frequently brought out by the critics of the theory, institutionalist approaches are more attentive to stability and persistence in institutions than change and conflict. Conflicts between different institutional spheres and levels, between institutions and their environments, and between the logics of different organizational systems have already been observed as sources of tension and change in institutionalist accounts.[39] Not much attention has been given, however, to the contradictory principles that institutionalize the very idea of Europe itself. Europe, as a rationalized institutional environment, hosts multiple and often contradictory systems of rules. These conflictual principles and the organizational rules associated with them enable different legitimating discourses, authorize different sets of actors and claims, and thus create a basis for both conflict and change.

To exemplify from my research, I find that in European countries there is significant variation in the accommodation of the types of educational claims advanced by immigrant groups. While some claims face organizational resistance, others are more readily accepted and incorporated into formal state structures. The educational authorities in Britain, for example, are more willing to accommodate the claims for Islamic dress codes, or even the teaching of immigrant languages in schools. On the other hand, religiously codified family laws (or polygamy, female circumcision) that create status disparity between genders are not viewed as legitimate demands. Here, what we see is that the principle of gender equality contests the principle of religious equality. These are principles, which are clearly embedded in European and global institutional frameworks. In Europe, the treatment of women is codified in secular laws and institutions, thus the attempts to confine it to the religious, private domain generate conflict.[40]

By drawing upon conflicting institutional principles, societal actors forge new alliances and open up space to insert their demands. In the Netherlands, for example, as an extension of the pillar system, education is organized along denominational lines. This system allows the Muslim minority to build a case to make demands for separate or single-sex schools. In the process, interesting patterns of alliances take shape. Christian church groups, for instance, support the claim of Islamic organizations arguing for the principle of religious freedom. Similarly, in Britain, Christian and Muslim groups allied against the Labour government's decision to abolish Section 28, the legislation that prohibits the "promotion" of homosexuality in classrooms. They also demanded the right to withdraw their children from sex education classes. Thus, apparently contradictory interests become aligned, creating possibilities for the accommodation of new claims that challenge the (rationalized) order of European education.

EUROPE: FRAGMENTARY UNISON?

Admittedly, the analysis I am advancing here derives upon just one specific narration of Europe, as it is exercised in schoolbooks and curricula and in educational spheres. We may be inclined to fault this narration of Europe as limited and contained. But this is *one* important narration. Schoolbooks and curricula are important not as texts themselves but for what broader social and political debates, struggles and orientations they represent. One should also note that Europe is being constructed and defined differently in different organizational fields. These designs and definitions may follow disparate premises and at times may very well be contradictory. Europe as such develops in fragmentary tracts.

This challenges our conventional thinking and expectations of a public space. Our projections of Europe still derive primarily from the nation-state model and experience. We expect the European public space to manifest itself through a common agenda and purpose. We complain that Europe lacks culturally, as it does not have a shared language and identity. This we consider as "the European void."[41]

I provided a different trajectory of Europe in this chapter. My observations from the field of education render a European space, which is a product of repetitive enactments and diffusions, and exhibit convergences and divergences at different levels. It does not depend on collective emotions or pre-disposed identities. It includes multiple spheres and subjects and it is created through the activities of a growing contingent of social and political actors, who engage in the discourse of Europe and deploy strategic action—with or without institutionalized contact with the EU. The actors involved may not speak the same language or may not have the same cultural disposition, but they create a mutually comprehensible meaning and discourse of Europe across borders.

As such, Europe is a space for participation but it does not imply the existence of a European demos or polity in the conventional sense—based on consensus and uniformity. European public space is open to conflicts and creates its own conflicts. Its inception, existence, and its eventual progress, however much it relies on or proceeds from models of rational communicative process[42] does not necessarily bring reason and will together and create agreeable positions. The European public space implicates an evolving but at the same time ever-extended and ever-fuzzier Europe—beyond the territorial limits of nation-states, though not without its conflicts and ruptures.

The identity that arises in this public space evokes abstract, universalistic principles—democracy, progress, human rights, and gender equality—without requiring the condition of a bounded cultural community. This assemblage of principles and their enactment is what affords "the ties that bind" in the European public space. European identity as it happens is not on a due course to replace the nation as the source of collective or individual subjectivity—it reinterprets the nation to cast it simply as another repository of the same ideals and principles for which Europe stands. The nation then is still a source of pride and identification but is no longer unique or commanding, far from its familiar self. The script of Europe is still open to modifications and re-writing, and it may never end with a coherent narrative. The fact that it is contended however points not to its absence or thinness but to its increasingly taken for granted existence as a framework for reflection and experimentation.

NOTES

1. This paper draws upon my ongoing project "Rethinking Nation-state Identities in the New Europe" funded by the "One Europe or Several?" Program of the Economic and Social Research Council, with additional grants from the Fuller Bequest Fund, the University of Essex, Leverhulme Trust and the British Academy.

2. J. H. H. Weiler, *The Constitution of Europe* (Cambridge University Press, 1999).

3. G. Delanty, *Inventing Europe: Idea, Identity, Reality* (New York, St. Martin's Press, 1995); S. Garcia, ed., *European Identity and the Search for Legitimacy* (London, Pinter, 1993); C. Shore, *Building Europe: The Cultural Politics of European Integration* (London, Routledge, 2000); Weiler, Ibid.

4. For a refreshing challenge to the "crisis" thesis, see T. Banchoff and P. S. Mitchell eds. *Legitimacy and the European Union: The Contested Polity* (London, Routledge, 1999).

5. A. D. Smith, *Nations and Nationalism in a Global Era* (Cambridge, Polity Press, 1995).

6. A. D. Smith, "National identity and the idea of European unity," *International Affairs* 68 (1992), pp. 55–76. Smith is sceptical of the prospects of this project given the habitual communities of already existing national cultures and the historical embededness of nation-states.

7. Shore, Ibid.

8. H. Wallace, "Deepening or Widening: Problems of Legitimacy for the EC" in *European Identity and the Search for Legitimacy*, ed. S. Garcia, (London: Pinter, 1993).

9. A. D. Smith, "A Europe of Nations—or the Nation of Europe," *Journal of Peace Research* 30 (1993), pp. 129–135.

10. J. Olsen, "Organising European Institutions of Government" in *Institutional Approaches to the European Union*, ed. S. S. Andersen (ARENA Report, No 3,

2001); F. W. Scharpf, *Governing in Europe: Effective and Democratic?* (Oxford: Oxford University Press, 1999).

11. L. Cederman, "Nationalism and Bounded Integration: What It Would Take to Construct a European Demos?" *EUI Working Papers, RSC No. 2000/34,* (2000). p. 21.

12. C. Calhoun, *Citizenship, Identity, and Social Solidarity,* Paper presented at the ASA meeting (Chicago, 1999).

13. To clarify, I take identity as a discursive and contingent category to be explained, not as self-evidently analytical or sociologically innate in and of itself. Identities are codified and publicly available categories of classification, providing templates for managing and manufacturing the "self." For a most helpful critique of scholarly deployments of identity see, R. Handler, "Is 'Identity' a Useful Cross-Cultural Concept?" in *Commemorations: The Politics of National Identity,* ed. J. R. Gillis (Princeton: Princeton University Press, 1994). See also, M. Kohli, "The Battle-grounds of European Identity." *European Societies* 2 (2000),pp. 113–37.

14. In my current project, I am explicating the redefinitions of Europe, nation, and citizenship in educational spheres in relation to the ongoing consolidation of Europe as a transnational entity. I carry out this inquiry through a cross-sectional and longitudinal analysis of secondary school national curricula and textbooks in history and civics subjects. The data set for the broader project is constructed by sampling the history and civic textbooks and curricula in four European countries (Germany, France, Britain and Turkey) at three time points, 1950s, 1970s, and 1990s, when major educational reforms took place. I also examine public debates and conflicting claims on national curricula and education.

15. G. M. Thomas, J. W. Meyer, F. O. Ramirez, and J. Boli, eds. *Institutional Structure: Constituting State, Society, and Individual* (Newbury Park, CA: Sage, 1987) and W. W. Powell and P. J. DiMaggio, *The New Institutionalism in Organizational Analysis* (Chicago: University of Chicago Press, 1991).

16. Directorate General XXII for Education, Training and Youth.

17. For a comprehensive review of the EU activities in the field of education see, T. Theiler, "The European Union and the 'European Dimension' in Schools: Theory and Evidence." *European Integration* 21 (1999), pp. 307–341. Complementary efforts to ascertain a European identity through cultural policy and marketing are also underway. See, Shore, ibid.

18. M. Stobart, "Fifty Years of European Co-operation on History Textbooks: The Role and Contribution of the Council of Europe," *Internationale Schulbuchforschung* 21 (1999), pp. 147–161.

19. See the websites of the Council of Europe (www.coe.int/T/E/Cultural_Co-operation/education) and the Center for Democracy and Reconciliation in Southeast Europe (www.cdsee.org) for detailed information on these projects.

20. For an extensive account of EUROCLIO's activities and initiatives regarding the teaching of Europe, both in and outside the EU, see J. Van der Leeuw-Roord, ed. *History for Today and Tomorrow. What Does Europe Mean for School History?* (Hamburg: Koerber Stiftung, 2001).

21. Shore, op.cit.

22. L. Cram, "Imagining the Union: The Case of Banal Europeanism?" in *Whose Europe: Interlocking Dimension of European Integration*, ed. H. Wallace (London, Macmillan, 2001a).

23. L. Cram, "Social Movements: the Case of Women's Movements and European Integration," *One Europe or Several? The Dynamics of Change Across Europe (ESRC), Newsletter*, Issue 6, Spring, 2001b. Cram's own research on women's movements and their participation in European networks, EU institutions and programs (in Greece, Ireland, and the UK) reveals how European discourses penetrate domestic political structures, organizational literatures and activities resulting in the "acceptance of the EU as a given rather than as something remarkable."

24. Placing the emphasis on informal processes and outside the inter-governmental structures is not to suggest that Europe as a process privileges actors and their interests indiscriminately and equally. The participation in European public spaces is often fragmented and diffuse, but by its nature of diffusion it may have more penetration. Weiler (1999), ibid, raises concerns for the perils of such a process for democracy, for not being procedural and transparent. One cannot help but agree with his proposals of improving the participation in the European public space. My point here concerns the analytical foundations of making Europe and European public spaces, not its normative inadequacies and improvement.

25. G. Therborn, "European Modernity and European Normativity: The EU in History and in Social Space," in *Institutional Approaches to the European Union. Arena Workshop Proceedings*, ed. S. S. Andersen (ARENA Report, No 3, 2001).

26. G. Delanty, op.cit.; M. Herzfeld, *Anthropology Through the Looking-Glass: Critical Ethnography in the Margins of Europe* (Cambridge: Cambridge University Press, 1987).

27. cf. Kohli, Ibid.

28. Surely there are attempts to symbolically define America as the other in the meaning of culture (e.g., the resistance to McDonalds by promoting local cuisine), in definitions of justice (e.g., the denouncement of death penalty and gun control), in models of social equality (e.g., the role of the state versus market in providing the social equality and standard of living). Among these, one thing that Europe can still claim of its own, despite all its existing variants in the member states, is the welfare state and some understanding of the shared social (Weiler, Ibid.). However, this is increasingly undermined by the hegemonic discourse of liberal market theories, currently favored by most European governments.

29. Weiler (1999), op.cit., p. 340

30. C. Shore (2000) reports that the Commission officials hold the same image of mutually existing multiple identities when it comes to their approach to European identity. See also Haller, 1999 and Pantel, 1999.

31. N. Y. Soysal "Identity and Transnationalization in German School Textbooks," in *Censoring History: Citizenship and Memory in Japan, Germany, and the United States*, eds. L. Hein and M. Selden (Armonk, New York: M.E. Sharpe, 2000).

32. N. Y. Soysal, T. Bertilotti, and S. Mannitz "Projections of Nation-State Identity in French and German History and Civics Textbooks," in *The Nation, Europe, and the World: Textbooks and Curricula in Transition*, eds., H. Schissler Y. N. Soysal, (Oxford: Berghan Books, forthcoming).

33.   Ibid.

34.   op.cit.

35.   Soysal, 2000, Ibid.

36.   "Fuzzy Statehood" is the title of Batt et al.'s research project on European integration in Central and Eastern Europe. See www.bham.ac.uk/crees/statehood.

37.   My examples in this section come from the core countries of Europe. It is true that one finds Europe more in its core than its margins. In the cases of Turkey and Greece, for example, we observe that the content of education still prioritizes the nation and its chronology. However, in their increasing attempts to reevaluate their positions within and vis-à-vis Europe, both countries have engaged in efforts to revise their textbooks and curricula. This involves both amending the adverse and nationalistic tone of textbooks and elaborating their nation's place in Europe. See, V. Antoniou and Y. N. Soysal, "Nation and the Other in Greek and Turkish Textbooks," in *The Nation, Europe, and the World: Textbooks and Curricula in Transition*, eds H. Schissler and Y. N. Soysal, (Oxford: Berghan Books, forthcoming).

38.   N. Y. Soysal, "Citizenship and Claims-making: Organized Islam in European Public Spheres," *Theory and Society* 26, (1997), pp. 509–27.

39.   R. Jepperson, "Institutions, Institutional Effects, and Institutionalism," in *The New Institutionalism in Organizational Analysis*, eds. W. W. Powell, P. J. DiMaggio (Chicago: University of Chicago Press, 1991); R. Friedland and R. R. Alford, "Bringing the Society Back In: Symbols, Practices, and Institutional Contradictions," in *The New Institutionalism in Organizational Analysis*, eds. W. W. Powell, P. J. DiMaggio (Chicago: University of Chicago Press, 1991); Olsen, ibid.

40.   Soysal, Ibid., 1997.

41.   A. de Swaan, "The European Void: The Democratic Deficit as a Cultural Lack," *European Studies Newsletter*, 4 (2002).

42.   J. Habermas, *The Structural Transformation of the Public Sphere* (Cambridge, Mass.: MIT Press, 1989). See also T. Risse, "Let's Talk: Communicative Action in World Politics." *International Organization* 54 (2000), pp. 1–3.

CHAPTER 6

FROM EVASION TO A CRUCIAL TOOL OF MORAL AND POLITICAL EDUCATION

Teaching National Socialism and the Holocaust in Germany

Falk Pingel

INTRODUCTION: THE EXTERNAL STRUCTURE OF THE CLASSROOM—CURRICULA AND TEXTBOOKS

Not everything pupils are supposed to learn at school is learnt and not everything learnt is memorized. Moreover, what pupils know and what influences their way of thinking is not only learnt in school. School learning is simply one of several factors that help form young people's knowledge and consciousness of history. When we start to examine how history curricula and school textbooks deal with the subject of National Socialism and the Holocaust, we are basically dealing with the ideas of educationalist institutions (ministries; textbook authors; teachers) on what pupils *should* learn, i.e. what society would like to have passed on to the following generation. Youngsters are not always prepared to accept older people's ideas,

What Shall We Tell the Children?, pages 131–153
Copyright © 2006 by Information Age Publishing
All rights of reproduction in any form reserved.

they often discover quite different traditions, which is probably one of the reasons why they do not learn what they are expected to learn, but become interested in other things.

To begin with, a few general remarks on the structure of the history curricula and textbooks in the Federal Republic of Germany. The education system is federally organized, there is no central Ministry of Education, syllabuses are issued by the Ministry of Education and Cultural Affairs of the individual federal states. A "Standing Conference of Ministries of Education and Cultural Affairs" ensures comparable requirements regarding the compatibility of the syllabuses and pupil mobility between federal states. The ministries examine whether school textbooks comply with the curricula, teaching regulations and constitutional principles. Approved textbooks are selected as a teaching basis for individual class levels. There are a large number of different history textbook series in the Federal Republic of Germany containing a broad spectrum of didactic approaches, content and focus. It is only possible to offer a condensed overview here, indicating the most important tendencies, without any strong differentiation according to individual textbook series.

The German school system is highly differentiated. Following a four- or six-year elementary education, the school system is divided into three main branches, depending upon the achievement of the pupil: secondary grade schools (lowest academic level), intermediate schools, and grammar schools or gymnasiums (highest academic level). After nine or ten years, mandatory school education is completed. From then approximately 25% continue their education at a grammar school for the higher secondary level (grade 11 to 13 or—in the future—to 12).

Within the last thirty years, the German school system has been drastically reformed in a pluralistic and democratic sense. More and more children are reaching the level required for entry into grammar schools and thus gaining qualifications to enable them to study at university. "Broader education instead of elitism" has been the motto since the 1970s. While during the 1950s and 1960s only about 10% of students attended a grammar school for their lower secondary education, today 30% are reaching this level. In consequence, the more challenging the school education, the more thoroughly students will have learned about the Holocaust.

The Holocaust and National Socialism are not usually dealt with in elementary school, the curricula neither lists it as a compulsory or optional subject in a context where such schools do not differentiate between history, geography, and social studies. These disciplines are covered in regional studies, dealing mostly with the history and geography of the pupils' town or region. During the course of such a unit topics concerning the persecution of the Jews or the Nazi regime may arise and be thematized, for example when concentrating on a specific part of a town where many Jews lived. Some pedagogues and historians are discussing the possibility of teaching about the Holocaust, or at least about the persecution of the Jews, at the elementary school level.[1] The main topic of this chapter is however secondary education, so I will leave this question open.

The topics "National Socialism" and "Holocaust" are a compulsory part of the curriculum for lower secondary schools in all federal states, especially in history classes. All history courses are constructed to allow for a chronological study of history from the earliest times to the present. National Socialism and the Holocaust are automatically incorporated into this process. From the age of approximately 14 to 16 (8th–10th grade) a thorough study of the Nazi era and the Holocaust is undertaken. As a rule, the Holocaust was—and still is—presented alongside other themes like occupation, persecution, and war. It is often studied again in more depth in higher secondary schools, for students aged 16 to 19 (11th–13th grade).

The subjects of history and social studies each receive one or two periods of fifty minutes per week at these schools. In many federal states history is only taught as an autonomous subject at grammar schools, in other schools it is integrated into geography, social studies and environmental studies. As a result, the curriculum of the grammar schools usually contains detailed coverage of the Holocaust as a central event in contemporary German history, while other schools aim at less detail concentrating on those aspects relevant for contemporary times. The syllabuses issued by several federal states deal with the subject of National Socialism in civics lessons as well as in history teaching. In this analysis I will concentrate on lower secondary level teaching, which contains the last years of compulsory schooling, grades 9 and 10.

The history of contemporary history teaching in the Federal Republic of Germany can roughly be divided into four phases:

1. The immediate post-war period (occupation and the foundation of the Federal Republic of Germany), i.e., approximately 1945–1952.
2. The period of stabilization in post-war society—from the beginning of the 1950s to the beginning of the 1960s.
3. The period of change, approximately from the mid-1960s to the end of the 1970s.
4. The period of stabilization in the 1980s.

Today's perspective is still open. A new phase must be developed due to the breakdown of the socialist system and German reunification.[2]

Occupation and the Foundation of the Federal Republic of Germany: 1945–1952

History teaching was a varied and contradictory experience during this period. The Allies set out the history curriculum immediately after taking over political responsibility.[3] However, textbooks were seldom available or were of an experimental nature. The trial of war criminals and the process of de-Nazification provoked public debate, particularly in intellectual circles, on the "historical disaster" that National Socialism represented for German history. The mass crimes were not left out of public debate but the question of cause or guilt was often pushed aside and the idea of a "collective guilt" was generally denied. It is doubtful that this discussion was conducted in schools although it affected young people, in particular, who had been members of National Socialist mass organizations. Syllabuses, which were again regularly issued from about 1947, reflected this debate only in exceptional cases. National Socialism was not always mentioned as a subject area and whenever it was explicitly included, the subject of the war was usually predominant. This was reflected in school textbooks, in some textbooks of the period half the chapters on National Socialism dealt with the war, the subject of mass extermination was barely touched upon.

There were some new approaches towards developing teaching material among which the most successful history textbook of the time, "Wege der Völker," can be counted.[4] This book dealt with National Socialism including mass crimes and the extermination of the Jews and raised the question of the responsibility of bystanders. In contrast to almost all textbooks that were to follow the authors of this series were not afraid to clearly and morally condemn the persecution of the Jews ("the most cruel and humiliating chapter in the history of the Third Reich"). Individual stages of persecution from the Nürnberg laws to the "fundamental destruction of Jewish life" were presented. Nevertheless, the gas chambers were only mentioned in the edition intended for senior classes. Although the book stated that the population in general had not known the true extent of mass extermination, it emphasized the responsibility of large numbers of the population who had supported Hitler until the end.

At the beginning of the 1950s "Wege der Völker" became the most widely used history textbook. This series stood for a new development that could have meant a breakthrough due to the emphasis placed on contemporary history. The last volume, for the middle grades, covered the period from 1849 to the Potsdam Agreement and the beginning of a new "policy of world security." Authoritarianism, democracy and dictatorship were the diverging points of reference in German history. "Wege der Völker" was jointly produced by a trade union-orientated group of teachers from Berlin who drew their inspiration from socialist tendencies. The book reflects new intellectual approaches that were much in evidence in the post-war period. However, following the foundation of the two federal German states these principles began to fade.

A Period of Stabilization: 1950s to Early 1960s

The few new approaches towards the structure of curricula and school textbooks were more or less abandoned at this time. The history textbooks appearing after the mid-1950s regarded the Third Reich as a wrong path taken in German history, denied factors of historical continuity with the German past and supported the widespread opinion that "the people" had been led astray by a small group of individuals bearing sole responsibility: any crimes mentioned were attributed to this group. The extermination of the Jewish population was usually dealt with in a few sentences and there was little consideration of how this genocide could have been possible. The "Fundamental Aspects of History Teaching" agreed on by the Ministers of Education and Cultural Affairs on December 17, 1953, did not give particular mention to the National Socialist system of power and rule, and merely spoke generally of "dictators" and the Second World War.

However, tendencies towards apology began to increase considerably. One publication, *Geschichtliche Unterrichtswerk,* stated that "the annihilation of the millions of Jews in the East" was an act unequalled in the history of mankind, but this is followed by the sentence, "Hitler knew that his officers and the German army could not be expected to perform such destruction of human beings and so he commanded special troops for the purpose."[5] This error of judgement on the part of the authors can only be understood by the fact that they were not only following the opinion held by the general public but the prevailing viewpoint of historical science.[6] They were certainly also aware that "Western" Jews were not spared from extermination. The longest text on the extermination of the Jews in this book is a ten-line extract from Himmler's infamous Posen speech on October 4, 1943. The authors were unwilling to describe mass murder in their own words or in those of the victims.

In the textbooks of this period, the extermination of the Jews was not treated in separate paragraphs but seen as a component of warfare in general. History teachers (mostly men in grammar schools) had usually served as soldiers during the war and very few had really condemned the National Socialist system. Many avoided the subject so as not to come into conflict with the official teaching doctrines whereby they would have had to adopt an attitude of disapprobation and, thus, question their own actions. Nevertheless, teachers did refer to war experiences, which were often the focus of memory for parents. These adults saw themselves as victims of the system, victims of the Allies' bombing attacks, victims of a system that had sent them to war. There was no change of perspective, few asked, "Who were the persecuted?" and there was no mention of resistance to National Socialism. The question of guilt and collaboration could not be asked in this context. Nevertheless there were attempts to come to terms with the past, for instance in the protest activities against rearmament and the "emergency laws," which did not seem compatible with the anti-military, anti-state power lessons derived from history. But the majority of the population wanted to see the consolidation of society and political normality, accepting many unpleasant consequences, such as rearmament, as the price for Western orientation. This required distance from the past and not reflection upon it.

With this approach, it was difficult in textbooks and classrooms to name the perpetrators and victims explicitly since many perpetrators, and for the most part collaborators, were still alive and among us at the time and were represented among schoolteachers and university professors. They were neither willing to speak about their crimes nor about the victims. The inability to commemorate was characteristic of the collective memory of the post-war period.[7] This was precisely the reason why survivors' memories were not recognized at that time. It was not until the 1970s that school textbooks appeared that gave the victims voices and individual faces.

A Period of Change: Mid-1960s to the End of the 1970s

The historical understanding of young people growing up in the Federal Republic of Germany in this period was influenced to a great extent by traditional opinions. Von Friedeburg and Hübner discovered that the prevailing picture of history was characterized by "overemphasizing the role of the individual, personalized collectives, stereotypical ideas of order and anthropomorphic categories of reference." In terms of National Socialism, this meant that Hitler took an overpowering position as the person with sole responsibility for the horrors of National Socialism, often appearing as the only active participant.[8] The higher the level of education, the more pupils knew of the events of National Socialism, but the categories of analysis did not deepen in terms of reflection and precision. At least senior pupils knew about the policy of extermination; exculpation arguments were used in attempts at explanation—the population had not known about the mass crimes, the majority had followed the National Socialists because of their family-orientated labour and social policies. In a survey carried out from 1958 to 1962, Jaide found that pupils were often far more interested in dealing with the subject of National Socialism than their teachers. The majority of young people had a clearly negative opinion of Hitler, in contrast to their teachers in many cases.[9]

Throughout the 1960s history textbooks underwent a change in terms of methods and content, for the first time victims were allowed to speak. The persecution of the Jews was more frequently described in all its stages—from discrimination in society to ghettoization and subsequent extermination. The development of specialized academic research contributed by examining internal resistance to National Socialism and the institutions of persecution. The prime goal of teaching about the Nazi era was to elucidate why the democratic attempt of the Weimar Republic had failed and why a murderous dictatorship, which could only be defeated from the outside, replaced it. Curricula, school textbooks, and lesson plans in the Federal Republic thus often emphasized the road to dictatorship rather than the dictatorship itself. While neither the authors of textbooks nor the politicians denied the murder the Jews, they nevertheless did not find it appropriate to deal with the Holocaust more extensively. It was not regarded as a central event that would have a durable impact on modern civilization. It did not yet shape the German historical consciousness.

A breakthrough in textbook design was achieved by the book *Menschen in Ihrer Zeit* which for the first time presented primary source material for analysis.[10] The authors referred to Auschwitz and gave the number of Jews murdered as "more than 4 million." It is pointed out that "other undesirable" ethnic groups, for example gypsies, also "were systematically wiped out." The process of extermination was described in the book by a former prisoner and not, as usual, by an extract from the diary of camp commander Höß. The text was illustrated with photographs taken from the ramp at Auschwitz. But the question of responsibility for these crimes remained problematic:

> The victims. It was only much later that people realised what the "Third Reich" really meant for Germany (...) Fear, mistrust, and the evil they faced had seduced countless people to stay silent, look the other way or even help. Many others heard practically nothing about the monstrous deeds perpetrated. They supported the government in the firm belief that they were doing right and did not realise until much later how shamelessly they had been abused.[11]

All in all, the books remained weak in what is, admittedly, the most difficult part—attempts at explanation. Often they merely pointed out the irrationality of the process or the pathological attitudes of National Socialist leaders.

The view of history began to change in the late 1960s as a result of the first economic crisis in the Federal Republic of Germany and the students' movement. The generation growing up at this time had not experienced

National Socialism (except maybe as children) and questioned the interpretations prevalent in society. This "break" between the war-generation and the post-war generation was by no means limited to Germany. The representatives of academic youth, in particular, claimed that the restoration of society in West Germany had required the suppression of the past. Political and ideological security had been given priority over painful self-questioning about what interests made "Fascism" possible in Germany. In general it can be said that the higher the level of education the more probable it was that pupils were confronted with, and actively participated in, this discussion.

Historical research was mainly concerned with National Socialist racial ideology as well as the policies of occupation and extermination. An increasing number of contemporary historians, who had studied after the war and adopted modern social-historical methods from France and English-speaking countries, were lecturing at universities. History books and history lessons profited from these factors. Texts now discussed which social groups had helped to maintain National Socialism and what possibilities for resistance there had been. The extermination of the Jews and other groups was described with relentless openness; it had after all been carried out by people who were, or could have been, the parents or grandparents of pupils. This detailed treatment of the subject of persecution, including primary sources was particularly evident in the new, but not very successful, series Zeitaufnahme.[12] In the chapter entitled, "Their life was hell. Cause and extent of the extermination of the Jews," the "scapegoat theory" and the Jewish contribution to German culture are briefly acknowledged before coverage of the stages of persecution from the boycotting of Jewish businesses in 1933, to the gassing during the war was discussed. The subject of "Resistance against deportation in the occupied areas" is also mentioned.

The increased penetration of National Socialism and its detailed treatment in school history books plus a greater degree of public interest eventually caused the Conference of Ministries of Education and Cultural Affairs to stress in a new guideline "Nowadays too, schools must actively work against uncritical acceptance of portrayals that trivialize or even glorify the Third Reich and its representatives, characterized as it was by dictatorship, genocide and inhumanity."[13]

The Period of Stabilization: Securing the Achievements in the 1980s

Many of the controversial issues of the 1970s that were the subject of public debate became an almost natural component of curricula in the

1980s. The Holocaust was now regarded as a topic in its own right. Not only were comprehensive accounts of the persecution found, some authors also described Jewish life in the ghettos, and made pupils aware of the difficult choices or the dilemmas Jewish families were confronted with: to emigrate or to stay and to hope that they could at least survive in Nazi Germany as they had endured so much suffering in previous generations. New questions, however, were raised about the efficacy of teaching such horrible events to 14-year olds. Could children understand the full extent of terror, violence and inhuman behavior that denied all the values that they should learn to follow? Could they deal with the emotional impact of descriptions and pictures displaying the gas chambers and corpses in concentration camps? To provide an adequate account of these aspects it was suggested that it was no longer sufficient to simply describe what had happened. Advocates of change argued that the material must be open to question and to further inquiry. It was not enough to tell the story; that quite different stories existed became apparent not through the writing of new schoolbooks but through a TV series.

The series "Holocaust" gave public discussions on the past a new dimension. The suffering of the persecuted, the willingness of "normal" citizens to "join in" even in the face of the most atrocious crimes, was voiced more clearly than ever before.[14] I personally participated in numerous debates in various educational institutions, where—I believe for the first time in public—a genuine discussion between the generations took place. Nevertheless, such discussions came too late for some, as many of the generation who could speak of their experiences were no longer alive. Perhaps this dialogue only became possible when the generation that should have protested and offered resistance during the era of National Socialism no longer bore responsibility in the Federal Republic of Germany.

But certainly many young history teachers were able to strengthen their commitment in this dialogue with the older generation and went on to teach children how people can be harnessed to systems of enforcement.[15] In contrast to previous stages of development, this new impulse was reflected in a number of pupil activities. One example was a school competition under the patronage of the Federal President where children carried out research on a particular topic. This competition is now held every two years. In 1980–81 and 1982–83 it was devoted to the period of National Socialism, by far the largest number of participants ever took part. Children carried out research on the history of their hometown, their schools or on individuals persecuted under National Socialism. They asked mayors, teachers and relatives such questions as "How much did you know?; what happened to the Jews in our area?; what did you do?" Textbook authors no longer spoke about "extermination" in a general way but mentioned the places where many of the Jews and other persecuted groups were murdered. Auschwitz became the symbol of genocide under the Nazi regime.[16] When the Georg-Eckert-Institut for International Textbook Research presented the German-Israeli textbook recommendations in 1985, which were compiled by Israeli and German historians as well as geographers, one could read about the presentation of the Nazi period in German history textbooks.

The most detailed portrayal in the textbooks is that of the history of the Jews in the modern world. However, the density of information in the survey period is extremely uneven. The ideological defamation and—even more so—the persecution and murder of the Jews under National Socialist rule stand quite unmistakably in the foreground. The fate of Jews during this period is neither hushed up nor trivialized. The intensity of reporting in general has increased considerably in comparison with earlier textbooks. This manifests itself not only in the scope of the portrayal and in a consistently very broad documentation of text and picture sources, but also in the way that—especially in the more recent works—the persecution is no longer dealt with as part of Hitler's biography but is placed more strongly in its social context. The crucial question of responsibility and co-responsibility for the persecution of Jews is posed more sharply than in earlier textbooks, even if it does not always receive a clear enough answer. Some shortcomings concerning the authors' perspective were criticized:

> Persecution is described in most of the books in the sequence of state measures, often, however, using self-styled terminology or the terminology of the National Socialist era, intended to play the matter down. This means words such as "Reichskristallnacht," "destruction," "extermination," "Final Solution."[17]

Even today warnings must be issued with regard to such terminology even though there are now books on the market that have found a new language better suited for pupils' needs. It is also true that today criticism aims at didactics rather than at specialized knowledge.[18] The amount of information on National Socialism now offered in school textbooks is perhaps too much for many pupils. The dry style and highly rational argumentation are factors that prevent pupils from developing a high degree of emotional involvement with the subject. Most textbooks have a separate section containing source material but it is unclear to what extent this material is used during lessons. Trying to "prevent undue pressure," a lesson learned from National Socialist indoctrination, has led authors to present National Socialist history in great detail but in an extremely emotionless manner.[19] This was certainly a method of gaining access to pupils still in conflict with a generation of parents who had lived in the Third Reich, when both sides were full of emotion, feelings of guilt, accusations, justification, and in need of de-emotionalization. Today this situation has completely changed and such an approach does not comply with the educational needs of a generation who are no longer confronted with eyewitness accounts and the personal experience of one's family.

For many teachers it was impossible to teach this subject without emotion. However, they did not want to create the impression that they were politically prejudiced or that they wanted to force their own negative opinion of National Socialism on their pupils. Therefore, they often started their lessons by describing the processes of mass extermination in a realistic manner so that the students had no other choice than to speak out against such inhuman behavior. This approach, however, often prevented controversial discussion and did not allow students to form their own opinions.

BEFORE UNIFICATION: A GLANCE AT THE GERMAN DEMOCRATIC REPUBLIC (GDR)

In the GDR, the theory of anti-fascist resistance that later became part of the state's heritage and political doctrine offered an explanation that concentrated on communists as victims and as active opponents of the Nazi system. It excluded others and was clearly discriminating in this sense, probably with long-term effects we are only now beginning to become aware of.[20] Jews were rarely mentioned in textbooks as victims or as inmates of concentration or death camps until the late 1980s. Generally, one spoke of "prisoners" when referring to Jewish prisoners. Terms like "racism," "anti-Semitism," or "the persecution of the Jews" did appear in the official teaching guidelines and school textbooks. However, during the 1950s and 1960s they were perceived as ideological conditions of capitalism. Excessive crimes against the Jews as something new and previously unheard of remained under-emphasized. The first careful steps towards portraying the Holocaust were taken by textbook authors during the 1970s and 1980s. Dogmatic positions declined and a greater emphasis on social history and everyday lives could be found in textbooks. This development went hand in hand with a modernization of didactical strategies leading to the incorporation of pictures, photographs and short primary sources into textbooks that now offered an impression of the Jews' difficult living conditions in Germany during the 1930s. Anti-Semitism was defined as the driving force of National Socialism.

Commemorating the victims of resistance and persecution had a high standing in the official memory culture of the GDR. This was expressed in numerous marches, talks, conventions, and holidays, and found its way into the classroom in the form of commemoration periods or history projects. Every new generation of students reacted differently to this indoctrination into historical anti-fascism that served to legitimize the politically immobile socialist system. Some students of later generations resisted the exaggerated formalization of commemoration and especially rejected the political messages associated with it. Of course this does not mean that they were not in favor of a political and historical condemnation of fascism. After reunification, it suddenly became possible to openly voice ambivalence to the GDR's proclaimed anti-fascism and to regard National Socialism more as an historical phenomenon. In the most extreme cases, the social pressure on young people brought about by economic and ideological change lead to a growing youth culture that adopted neo-Nazi role models from Western Germany. These young people rejected the strictly prescribed educational indoctrination of the GDR, as well as the "foreign," dominant pluralistic society a united Germany was starting to create.

CURRENT CURRICULAR DEVELOPMENTS

After the breakdown of socialism and the unification of Germany, many federal states began to revise and renew their curricula. The new and revised history courses of several federal states placed more emphasis on dealing with the period after 1945. National Socialism and the Weimar Republic are thus now dealt with in the context of early modern history, beginning with the French Revolution. In the former syllabi, the First World War was seen as the major turning point and the last year of compulsory schooling was devoted to the time period from the First World War to today. Now the end of the Second World War replaces this caesura. However, this shift has not lead to a cut in the time allotted to the teaching of the Holocaust. A less elaborate teaching of medieval and ancient history provided more time to teach contemporary history. The topics of National Socialism and the persecution and murdering of the Jews have become central elements in teaching modern history during the last decade even if this is not explicitly required by the syllabus. Today the Holocaust is regarded as a topic in its own right and it is treated in separate chapters in curricula and textbooks.

During the 1980s and 1990s, a growing pedagogical concern emerged: not why, but how to deal with the topic became the crucial issue. Teachers were asked to make more use of activities outside the classroom setting. Ministries of Education recommend and financially assisted visits to memorials. The educational staff of the memorial sites increased, and enriched teachers' pedagogical efforts by planning seminars and developing educational materials. They developed pedagogical approaches for schoolchildren and offered special tours, task sessions, and seminars, which usually went hand in hand with teachers' efforts so that school classes and visits to memorials could complement one another. This change in interest again reflected an international trend caused by generational change. As the shift in the consciousness of time took place in other modern industrial societies the general didactic requirements of history teaching in Germany and in other Western European countries no longer differs as strongly.[21] In Germany, teachers do not have to follow the syllabus slavishly, they have a certain leeway in preparing their courses. At present, in contrast to previous decades, this often leads to a more extensive coverage of the Nazi era than is prescribed. In addition to textbooks many teachers include didactically valuable teaching methods like excursions, films, and talks with eyewitnesses. In every federal state, teachers find in-service and resource centers offering a wide range of printed material, as well as electronic and other media. The Georg-Eckert-Institute for International Textbook Research in Braunschweig collects all history textbooks and additional material designated for the use in German schools. Its latest catalogue on teaching materials dealing with "The Persecution of Jews in the Third Reich" contains more than a hundred titles published in the 1980s and 1990s. Again in contrast to previous times, today a micro-historical or biographical approach is emphasized. The Nazi regime is not presented as an impenetrable and incomprehensible system of terror for the individual that left absolutely no possibility for decision-making. Certainly it remains important to convey basic facts concerning widespread suppression and genocide, but the possibilities of helping those who were persecuted, and resistance should also be discussed.

CONTEMPORARY HISTORY AND POST-WAR HISTORY?

Little doubt remains that the majority of pupils today have at least a basic knowledge of the Third Reich and are aware of the fact that millions of Jews and other ethnic groups were murdered. It is true, however, that the National Socialist era is becoming increasingly strange and distant to pupils. To many of them it is incomprehensible that a civilized society could be in favor of organized mass murder. These pupils no longer see National Socialism as a part of their own world, as a part of contemporary history. To them this period belongs to a history, like the Kaiserreich or other phases of German development, with which they feel no involvement. They find it difficult to compare the barbarous activities of the National Socialist era with racist behavior today.[22] The living conditions that the youth of today aspire to are mainly connected with the economic rise of Western Germany, if a historical perspective is attributed to such wishes at all. This is the only historical background against which pupils in Western and Eastern Germany want to see the future of a reunited Germany.

Unquestionably new didactic approaches are required to fulfil the needs of pupils today. Arguably approaches adopted in the United States where teaching the Holocaust tries to establish common factors and conditions and seeks to find similar historical events in order to penetrate the distance and feelings of strangeness towards history are appropriate for German students.[23] For German historical science and didactics, the use of comparison as a means of understanding the Holocaust was taboo for a long time. Mass murder was viewed as an occurrence so monstrous and unique that it could not be explained in terms of comparison. This was an adequate approach only as long as we had the feeling that National Socialism belonged to our time and had happened in the German society of our parents or grandparents—but the chain of memory has torn over the generations. The conflict between the National Socialist and post-war generations has itself become history and it is becoming increasingly difficult to make the pupils of today realize that this is not just history but contemporary history, the history of our and their time. Recently mass murder has occurred in other nations such as Cambodia, the former Yugoslavia and other parts of the world. These horrors are also brought to us in immediate proximity and in graphic detail by the media. Surveys show that the majority of young people today are strongly rooted in the present; their political convictions, moral opinions and expectations for the future hardly arise from reflection on the past—only a small minority are consciously involved in the historic experiences of their parents or grandparents.

FROM OLD TO NEO-NAZIS

But is this conclusion not contradicted by the existence of neo-Nazi groups gathering beneath Nazi symbols, proclaiming anti-Semitic slogans and spreading hate of everything "non-German?" It would be too simple to assume they do this through lack of knowledge about the significance of National Socialism. These Neo-Nazis prefer to see it as a sign of the times when Germans were privileged over other members of society who are regarded as "inferior." They would like to re-establish these times as they feel threatened by economic insecurity and competition on the job market that no longer guarantees well-trained youngsters employment. When social benefits are cut, and chances for employment jeopardized, members of neo-Nazi groups attempt to protect themselves in a society in which all people are equal by constitutional law. On the one hand, globalization and the dissolution of ideological blocs have proved traditional social-political patterns outdated and without place in a society which apparently has no borders. On the other hand, German reunification seems to offer a different model—a truly traditional pattern of political identity which has survived changes in the political landscape: namely nationalism.

Thus, young people in particular question the principle of equality in our society by attacking people who still have to find a way of adapting to this national society and whose social position is not yet assured. These young people feel resonance with some parts of our society. Their orientation to Nazi history provides legitimation as well as the ideological framework and organizational structures required for their activities. To them it is not a question of imitating National Socialism or reviving it as a system because that would be contradictory to modern ways of living that are desirable even for neo-Nazis or at least their less organized supporters. Therefore, these groups adopt a selective view of the past; they imitate what seems worth imitating. History lessons alone can do little against this as the neo-Nazis are in favor of exactly the passages from history that should have a deterrent effect and deny all those which appear too monstrous. This means they can combine anti-Semitic activities with statements of their own that no Jews were gassed in Auschwitz. It is not a lack of knowledge of the facts that is the problem but imparting the desired moral message.

Why do young people choose National Socialism for their purposes? It is probably because it is the most recent historic example of nationalistic ideology. On the other hand it is long enough ago not to mobilize the protest of large groups of affected individuals. However, I believe that the neo-Nazis have misjudged this factor. It is evident that among the general population, as well as the political-economic leaders and intellectuals in Germany, that a defensive attitude towards nationalist, racist thinking and activities is so great that the hoped-for social acceptance of xenophobic actions has not taken place. Thus a degree of learning from history has taken place, even though it has not reached society as completely as could be hoped.

It is important to recognize the reasons that today lead a small minority of youths to orientate towards National Socialist ideologies. Dissatisfaction with the present situation is probably a greater reason than identification with the historical model. Contemporary teaching should address the deeply held beliefs of neo-Nazis and right-wing radicalism and should incorporate and not just try to show the catastrophes caused by National Socialism. The extensive research on right-wing radicalism, xenophobia and neo-Nazism currently carried in Germany is included in teaching material for these subjects.[24] In my opinion the greatest chance for intensive teaching on the subject of National Socialism does not lie in trying to convert those already belonging to neo-Nazi groups but in strengthening the defensive attitude of others.

THE CHALLENGE OF "LEARNING" FROM MASS DESTRUCTION IN HISTORY

The evaluation of National Socialism has perhaps become more strongly polarized among pupils than in previous decades. In considering views of National Socialism pupils today associate phrases such as "war and pointless destruction," "murder of Jews and gypsies" far more often than the harmonizing stereotypes of "work for all" or "safety and order" which were still used in the 1950s to explain acceptance of National Socialism.[25] Young people today are far more aware of the terror of this era than its so-called "good sides." Gerd Steffens, a teacher at a German Gymnasium, has the good fortune to teach in a particularly favorable classroom situation but his opinion of his students probably reflects the attitudes of majority of pupils at German Gymnasium schools:

> Moreover, genuine national motives are not so widespread among the pupils. On the whole they are more universalistically than ethnocentrically orientated, more cosmopolitan than national. The Gulf War, for example, affected them more than their own national reunification and questions of ecology, peace and mass poverty in the Third World, i.e. questions regarding humanity, bring more to bear on their view on life than national feelings. Maybe this is why it seems to some of them to be unfair that they have to live with the memories of National Socialism despite having no inner relationship to national claims.[26]

Some perceive National Socialism as an historical burden that they have inherited but are not responsible for and which, particularly abroad, makes communication and the ability to declare themselves to be Germans very difficult. Examples, given by students at an international conference in Lübeck show that this period of history remains tangible even if the chain of generative experience seems to be broken.[27]

Schoolbooks and lessons are by no means the only media, and often not the most important media, that transmit knowledge and emotional access to National Socialism. It is the media that confronts pupils with the subject. The great historical debates on the place of National Socialism in German history and the comparability of the Holocaust with the crimes of Stalinism have given the subject a prominent position in the media, the reporting and presentation of which is also dealt with in schools. Pupils, however, are often only superficially aware of these issues. They feel they are confronted with the subject in nearly all media and that after a certain time they know enough about what happened. At school they show an attitude of rejection when the subject is to be dealt with "yet again."

Nevertheless, it is often reported that students feel insecure, and sometimes even guilty, abroad. This seems odd, as almost no teacher, or parent, or politician would consider making young people of today guilty for the crimes of National Socialism. In turn, many in the public sphere, including many Ministers of Education speak, of the "responsibility" of this generation for the history of their country. The students themselves overwhelmingly confirm that it is necessary to take responsibility for the history of one's nation, but it is probably difficult for students between the ages of 14–16 to distinguish between "guilt" and "responsibility," which seem abstract to them. Those authors adhering to psychoanalytical models of explanation go further postulating that students are shouldering the guilt that the generation of perpetrators refused to accept.[28] In light of the fact that these two generations are far apart this assumption seems highly speculative. Interestingly many members of the post-war generation rejected the notion of having to shoulder the guilt of their parents' generation, and publicly, as well as privately, made the whole of the older generation responsible of having been bystanders. Today's student generation is usually no longer subject to these familial conflicts involving rejection of facts, interrogation, and blame.

Purely factual and informative lessons are not of much help in dealing with transferred or assumed feelings of guilt, which are directed in anger and recriminations against the Nazi generation, but hardly lead to a deeper understanding of how completely normal people could become willing servants of state terrorism. In comparison to the 1970s and 1980s, young people today are more prepared to generally condemn the generation of those who "joined in" National Socialism without any examination of the subject as they have a preconceived notion that this generation is guilty in general. In this respect, the younger generation's view of the Holocaust differs a lot from the beliefs their grandparents held in that they acknowledge wide responsibility for the horror of the Third Reich but reject personal guilt.[29]

APPROPRIATE TEACHING APPROACHES

The vast amount of supplementary teaching material published in recent years is suitable for dealing with National Socialism as it allows a higher degree of identification than school textbooks, which often have to present their material at a relatively general level.[30] Detailed treatment includes, for example, personal research in archives, exhibitions and museums or even interviews. These cannot often be managed in the course of regular lessons so the subject is dealt with in long-term projects or projects involving several school subjects. The concentration camp memorials that have developed their own educational departments over the past few years are growing in importance. These educational centers are run by qualified, knowledgeable personnel, mainly teachers transferred from school service for a limited period, who offer an exchange of information on their work with school classes and have learnt to deal with the particular questions asked by students. In addition, several institutes for further education have specialized on the subject. The best known is the Fritz-Bauer-Institut in Frankfurt that reports continuously on practical teaching experience and theoretical concepts for educational work.

Most teaching approaches still presume that the Holocaust has to be dealt with as part of recent German history. Dealing with this subject needs no justification but certainly requires special didactic considerations with regard to teaching aims and methods. In contrast to many other countries, particularly the United States, no intensive discussion on this has taken place in Germany. When asked about their aims in teaching this subject, teachers often reply that humanistic values should be strengthened in young people and an emphasis placed upon ensuring that there is no repetition of what happened in the past. Although strong agreement with these aims is possible they contain two theoretical dilemmas:

1. If the Holocaust is treated as a unique and hitherto unheard-of occurrence that cannot be compared with other forms of genocide, then it might be argued that there is little point in assuming any danger of repetition. Moreover, when dealing more closely with the subject, the pupils often are too overwhelmed at what happened to be interested in examining potential parallels or extrapolations in the future.

2. By its very nature the Holocaust exposes the radical denial of humanistic values. Fundamentally, it deals with the destruction of human civilization in a highly civilized country. Dealing with the Holocaust therefore does not create trust in human values but shows their fragility.

Memory of the Holocaust as a field within the teaching of history entails more than mere description. This memory should conjure empathy for the victims. Just as important as the cognitive, is the emotional aspect, which is often difficult for German teachers to manage because they are trained to teach rationally and are asked not to show "ideological bias" or to put students under moral pressure. This was one of the main lessons learned from the example of ideological teaching during the Nazi era. I experienced this emphasis on rationality in the course of the German-Israeli teachers' seminars, which the Georg-Eckert-Institute conducted during the 1990s in cooperation with the Israeli teachers' union in order to implement the German-Israeli school textbook recommendations. The German teachers were eager to present the methods and materials they used for the teaching of the Holocaust. The Israeli teachers, on the other hand, could not understand how the German teachers could remain so "objective," since they found it impossible for both teachers and pupils to comprehend the subject matter without emotion. The philosophy behind the teaching of history in Germany implies giving the pupils the chance to express their emotions when they are dealing with primary sources. The teacher's presentation should remain free of judgements that could lead to an emotional response from students. In the last few years, however, a discussion has been taking place as to whether or not it would be wise to promote an affective aspect in the teaching of the Holocaust.[31]

In some federal states, children have to deal with the subject for the first time in the fifth or sixth grade in lessons on "The World and the Environment."[32] Authors of school textbooks for this age group generally avoid direct allusions to the extermination of people. The effects of persecution are dealt with through examples of resistance and the fate of individuals. The higher the age group the greater the lack of specific didactic considerations regarding the introduction of National Socialism. For older students the topic is often dealt with simply because it is in the chronological period in question. The dilemma for teachers is that whereas one approach remains too factual, the other might prevent open discussion and exert too much moral-political pressure on pupils.

THE INNER-GERMAN DIVIDE

The context of lessons on the persecution of the Jews has altered with the changes in German society. More and more frequently teachers at seminars and conferences are reporting that they have to take into consideration the multicultural nature of their classes. Those belonging to other persecuted minorities ask to what extent their fate is dealt with in lessons in Germany. For example, for a Kurd, whose nationality is hardly mentioned in lessons about Turkish or Ottoman history, or for refugees from the wartorn areas of the former Yugoslavia, parallels with the Holocaust are more apparent. As a consequence calls for greater inclusion of comparative aspects of history may have some justification. Since reunification one can hardly speak of generally similar conditions for the teaching of contemporary history. Knowledge of the history of persecution, patterns of judgement and the emotional occupation of the National Socialist past are too different in the east and west to render it wise to presume the same kind of questions and teaching approaches are relevant in both geographic locations.[33] Coming from outside after numerous courses of further education in East and West Germany, Chaim Schatzker issued an early warning against simply transferring West German teaching methods to East Germany. The terminology had different connotations. For example, "anti-Semitism" would mean practically nothing to East German pupils so that a comparison of National Socialist discrimination with anti-Semitic statements or attitudes after 1945 would be meaningless. "Anti-Zionism," on the other hand, would appear to many to be justified today and would be translated as "anti-Israeli" or "anti-imperialist" and would not be associated with an anti-Jewish attitude.

Following reunification, a strong nationalist attitude began to spread among some young people leading them to equate Jews with foreigners in general, and making both these groups subject to prejudice and violence. In many cases, individuals adhering to these attitudes had never consciously been in contact with Jews. They assimilated a xenophobic ideology coming from the radical right in Western Germany that stood in contrast to the sociological situation in Eastern Germany. With few exceptions there was only one group of foreigners, the Vietnamese, who were ever represented in East German society. Xenophobic tendencies were largely geared toward phantoms. These young people nevertheless constructed an ideal picture of a homogenous society without ever having lived in a pluralistic society. The old social order, which had formerly provided them with cultural orientation and social welfare, was diminished with the fall of the socialist system. The only thing that could now take the place of this security was their awareness of being "German," an awareness entailing nationalist or even neo-Nazi attitudes.

The particular starting conditions and the comparatively small amount of knowledge about Jewish-Israeli history in eastern Germany was taken into consideration by the Sächsische Akademie für Lehrerfortbildung when they developed courses in cooperation with the Israeli Embassy on the subject of "Judaism and the State of Israel" or "Anti-Semitism, xenophobia and right-wing extremism." These have been supplemented by extracurricular and outside activities such as school twinning arrangements with Israeli educational institutions and school competitions. However, even with all of these measures it must be noted that pedagogical methods only achieve minimal success in influencing right-wing attitudes among young people. In spite of the fact that civics claims to be able to contribute to the development of democratic behavior and multicultural openness, sociological research has shown that the school has little authority over the students and is largely unable to alter attitudes that have already shaped the individual. In these cases, external political and social measures must be taken within the school setting, in the form of programs such as "awareness groups," where students can learn to control their behavior in and outside of school, and to adapt to generally accepted moral norms and values.[34]

Nevertheless, teaching the Holocaust should not be over-saturated with questions pertaining to problems of our daily societal situation. In a pedagogical sense it could be destructive to instrumentalize the Holocaust in order to encourage currently appropriate forms of behavior, or to expect students to take a stand on current xenophobic attitudes as a direct conclusion of teaching the Holocaust. We do not need the Holocaust to impart in our students the conviction that it is important to combat anti-Semitism or other forms of discrimination. We should teach it because it happened. It had grave consequences for the Jews, the Sinti and Roma, handicapped people, political dissidents, and those of the social underclass. But most of all, it was a threat to our very humanity.

NOTES

1.   Vocational schools that some pupils attend after their compulsory education are not included in this analysis.

2.   P. Pingel (1990) "Geschichte unserer Zeit—Zeit für Geschichte? Geschichtsdidaktik und Geschichtswissenschaft in ihrem Verhältnis zur Zeitgeschichte in den Westzonen und in der Bundesrepublik," in *Tel Aviver Jahrbuch für Geschichte,* Volume XIX, pp. 233–258.

3.   U. Mayer, *Neue Wege im Geschichtsunterricht. Studien zur Entwicklung der Geschichtsdidaktik und des Geschichtsunterrichts in den westlichen Besatzungszonen und in der Bundesrepublik Deutschland 1945–1953,* Köln, 1986.

4.   Arbeitsgemeinschaft Berliner Geschichtslehrer (Ed) *Wege der Völker. Geschichtsbuch für deutsche Schulen,* vol. I-VIII, Berlin 1948–49, Volumes IV and VIII.

5.   R. H. Tenbrock, et al., *Geschichtliches Unterrichtswerk für höhere Lehranstalten,* Mittelstufe, 4 vols., Paderborn, Volume IV, p. 153, 1957.

6.   The "Geschichtliche Unterrichtswerk, Volume 4, p. 96, presented Hitler's anti-Semitism through a wrong perspective, which could easily be slightly directed against foreign countries in the pupils' eyes: "Hitler's National Socialism was aggravated by his having grown up close to the German-Czech border and experiencing all the ethnic problems arising from the bitter, intolerant battle against Czech nationalism."

7.   A. Mitscherlich and M. Mitscherlich, *The inability to mourn: principles of collective behavior,* New York, 1975.

8.   L. von Friedeburg and P. Hübner *Das Geschichtsbild der Jugend,* München (1st ed. 1964); cf. R. Raasch, *Zeitgeschichte und Nationalbewußtsein,* Berlin, 1964.

9.   W. Jaide, *Das Verhältnis der Jugend zur Politik. Empirische Untersuchungen zur politischen Anteilnahme und Meinungsbildung junger Menschen der Geburtsjahrgänge 1940–1946,* Darmstadt, p. 93, 1964.

10.   *Menschen in ihrer Zeit. Geschichtswerk für Realschulen, 6 vols.,* Stuttgart 1965–66, Volume. 6, p. 64.

11.   *Menschen in ihrer Zeit,* p. 64, 1965–1966.

12. C. Schatzker, *Die Juden in den deutschen Geschichtsbüchern*, Bonn 1981; M. Kolinsky and E. Kolinsky "The Treatment of the Holocaust in West German Textbooks," in *Yad Vashem Studies* X, pp. 149–216, 1974.

13. Sekretariat der Ständigen Konferenz der Kultusminister der Länder in der Bundesrepublik Deutschland, 1997.

14. F. Pingel. "Nationalsozialismus im Geschichtsunterricht—Neue Perspektiven seit "Holocaust'?", in *Geschichtsdidaktik* (1979), 4, pp. 306–318, 1979.

15. C. Hopf, et.al, *Wie kamen die Nationalsozialisten an die Macht: eine empirische Analyse von Deutungen im Unterricht*, Frankfurt/M, 1985.

16. J. Lietzke, *Alltag im Nationalsozialismus: die Kriegsjahre in Deutschland. Schülerwettbewerb um den Preis des Bundespräsidenten*, Hamburg, 1985.

17. Deutsch-israelische Schulbuchempfehlungen. "Zur Darstellung der jüdischen Geschichte sowie der Geschichte und Geographie Israels in Schulbüchern der Bundesrepublik Deutschland. Zur Darstellung der deutschen Geschichte und der Geographie der Bundesrepublik Deutschland" in *israelischen Schulbüchern*, Braunschweig 1985, Frankfurt/M. 1992 (2nd. ed.)

18. E. Kolinsky, "Geschichte gegen den Strom. Zur Darstellung des Holocaust in neuen Schulgeschichtsbüchern," in *Internationale Schulbuchforschung* 13, pp. 121–145, 1991; P. Pingel, "Jüdische Geschichte in deutschen Lehrbüchern," in *Geschichte lernen* 6, 1993; W.F. Renn, "The Holocaust in the school textbooks of the Federal Republic of Germany," in *Holocaust Literature*, Westport (CT), pp. 481–520, 1993.

19. B. Mütter, and U. Uffelmann, *Emotionen und historisches Lernen. Forschung—Vermittlung—Rezeption*, Frankfurt/M, 1992; P, Malina, "Auschwitz: Betroffenheit statt Einsicht: Schulbuchtexte als Indikator öffentlichen Geschichtsbewußtseins," in: *Materialien zur Geschichtsdidaktik*, 1995.

20. S. Küchler, S., "DDR-Geschichtsbilder. Zur Interpretation des Nationalsozialismus, der jüdischen Geschichte und des Holocaust im Geschichtsunterricht der DDR," in *Internationale Schulbuchforschung/International Textbook Research*, 22, 31–4, 2000. p. 124; Weißer, A.*Die Darstellung des Dritten Reiches und des Holocaust in Geschichtslehrbüchern und Unterrichtsmaterialien der DDR 1949 bis 1989. Hausarbeit für die Erste Staatsprüfung für das Lehramt*, Universität Münster, 1999)**; B.B.** Weber, *What shall we tell our children?: The presentation of Nazi atrocities in East and West German textbooks*, Vermont, 1995.

21. See Aktion Sühnezeichen Friedensdienste e.V.: *Rencontre Pédagogique Internationale. La mémoire d'Auschwitz dans l'enseignement. Problèmes et perspectives*, Brüssel, 4.- 8.11.1991.; R.L. Braham, *The Treatment of the Holocaust in Textbooks. The Federal Republic of Germany, Israel, The United States of America*, New York, 1987; R.L. Braham, *Anti-Semitism and the Treatment of the Holocaust in Postcommunist Eastern Europe*, New York, 1994; R. Steininger (ed.), *Der Umgang mit dem Holocaust. Europa-USA-Israel*, Wien 1994; M. Heyl, *Erziehung nach Auschwitz. Eine Bestandsaufnahme. Deutschland, Niederlande, Israel, USA*, Hamburg 1997; "Unterricht über den Holocaust/Teaching the Holocaust," *Internationale Schulbuchforschung/International Textbook Research* 22, 1; M. Heyl, *Erziehung nach Auschwitz. Eine Bestandsaufnahme*, Deutschland, Niederlande, Israel, USA, Hamburg, 1997.

22. H. Hötte, "Museumspädagogische Arbeit mit Jugendlichen im Dokumentenhaus KZ Neuengamme," in: *Internationale Schulbuchforschung* 6, 1984,

pp. 173–185; B. Mütter and F. Pingel, *Die Ideologie des Nationalsozialismus. Unterrichtsmodell und Arbeitsbuch für die Sekundarstufe II*, Bochum, 1988.

23. H. Freiling, "Der Holocaust als Thema amerikanischer Schulcurricula," in *Internationale Schulbuchforschung* 11, 1989, pp. 255–282.

24. K. Fritzsche, and M. Hartung, (ed), *Der Umgang mit "Fremden." Eine deutsch-deutsche Schülerbefragung zum Thema Schulbuch und Fremdenfeindlichkeit. Eine kommentierte Auswahlhilfe von Unterrichtsmaterialien*, Hannover, 1997.

25. B. von Borries, "Vorstellungen zum Nationalsozialismus und Einstellungen zum Rechtsextremismus bei ost- und westdeutschen Jugendlichen. Einige empirische Hinweise von 1990, 1991 und 1992," in *Internationale Schulbuchforschung* 15, 1993, pp. 139–166; K. Pohl, *Bildungsreform und Geschichtsbewußtsein*, Pfaffenweiler, 1996.

26. G. Steffens(1991)"Die nationalsozialistischen Verbrechen und der Völkermord. Bemerkungen zur Unterrichtspraxis in der Bundesrepublik," in Aktion Sühnezeichen Friedensdienste e.V.: *Rencontre Pédagogique Internationale. Le mémoire d'Auschwitz dans l'enseignement. Problèmes et perspectives*, Bruxelles, 4–8 novembre.; S. Küchler, S. Ibid, p. 124, 2000.

27. *Time to Remember—Zeit des Erinnerns*, Lübeck, 9–11 November 1999.

28. H. Stierlin, *Der Dialog zwischen den Generationen über die Nachkriegszeit*, Stuttgart, 1982; Müller-Hohagen, J.Verleugnet, *verdrängt, verschwiegen. Die seelischen Auswirkungen der Nachkriegszeit*, München, 1988.

29. T.R. Henschel, *Young German Europeans divided memory in a united Germany*, unpublished presentation at the conference on "European Historical Consciousness: Empirical Evidence and Experience," Essen, 13th–15th January, 2000.

30. Georg-Eckert-Institut für internationale Schulbuchforschung, 1999; E. Fuchs, et al. (ed.) *Holocaust and Nationalsozialismus*, Wien, 2000.

31. B. Mütter and U. Uffelmann, *Emotionen und historisches Lernen. Forschung—Vermittlung—Rezeption*, Frankfurt/M, 1992.

32. This subject deals with geography, history, civics and even biology in an integrated manner.

33. S. Wolf, "Antisemitismus and Schoah als Unterrichtsgegenstand in Ostdeutschland—ein Fragment," in T. Lange (ed.), *Judentum und jüdische Geschichte im Schulunterricht nach 1945*, Wien, pp. 125–139, 1994

34. Fritzsche and Hartung (ed.), 1997.

CHAPTER 7

WHOSE HISTORY?

Portrayal of Immigrant Groups
in U.S. History Textbooks, 1800–Present

Stuart Foster

As a result of a continuous flow of immigrants to the United States during the past three centuries, modern America currently houses the most diverse ethnic, cultural, and linguistic school population on earth. In 50 of the largest 99 school districts embracing such cities as Chicago, Los Angeles, Washington D. C., New York, Seattle, and San Francisco, half or more of public school students are persons of color.[1] Between 2000 and 2020 the percentage of Hispanic school-age children will increase by a staggering 60%, and by 2040 white, non-Hispanic students will represent a minority in U.S. public schools.[2] Recent decades have seen a boom in immigration not witnessed since the end of World War I. In 1993 alone, for example, almost one-third of the increase in U.S. population occurred as a result of the influx of 895,000 immigrants, the largest number in a single year since 1914.[3] Although immigrants arrive from all regions of the world particular concentrations in recent decades have originated from Mexico, the Philip-

What Shall We Tell the Children?, pages 155–178
Copyright © 2006 by Information Age Publishing
All rights of reproduction in any form reserved.

pines, Cuba, El Salvador, China, Korea, and Vietnam. Today, several large school districts wrestle with the fact that over one hundred distinctive languages are spoken by children attending school and approximately ten million children (or almost 1 in 5 of the current school-age population) originate from homes where English is not the first language.[4] Today, as in the past, these striking demographic features have a profound impact on all aspects of American public education.

Although the issue of how best to educate such a heterogeneous school population challenges contemporary teachers, the question has confronted educators for generations. Because school history traditionally has been regarded as the primary place in the curriculum for students to cultivate a sense of national identity and heritage, the issue has proved especially pertinent for history teachers and authors of history textbooks. Important questions have endured: What history gets told? Or, perhaps more importantly, *whose* history gets told? Should the experiences of various ethnic groups be portrayed in such a way as to value the various histories of America's multicultural past? Or, alternatively, should history textbooks principally strive to present a "common" history that places emphasis on a "shared" national identity and an inclusive national history? To understand how textbook writers in different periods of American history have responded to these questions also is to appreciate the dominant values and ideology of the age in which the textbooks were written. Moreover, it reflects the extent to which certain societal forces have validated the historical contributions of identified groups over the claims of others.

The influence of the history textbook in shaping how children come to understand their past and what it means to be "an American" should not be underestimated. Scholars have long noted the central place of the history textbook in classroom instruction. In the eighteenth and nineteenth centuries for example, apart from the Bible, the most widely read texts were schoolbooks written by an assortment of amateurs who, no matter how ill qualified to do so, helped to create and solidify an idealized image of the American type.[5] By the end of the nineteenth century so distinguishing was this heavy reliance on the textbook that Europeans characterized it "the American system."[6] The reasons for this unbridled loyalty to the textbook were simple to understand. At the turn of the twentieth century few teachers were educated beyond the high or grammar school level. Faced with the daunting prospect of teaching classes of up to 60 students in more than ten separate subject areas, teachers understandably took refuge in the security of approved texts.[7] One educational administrator in Kentucky, who decried the "poorly prepared corps of teachers" in state schools, echoed the concerns of others when he reasoned that the only viable solution was to equip teachers with the best possible textbooks. "The poorer the teacher, the better the textbooks need to be."[8]

Despite the prevalence of alternative forms of print media and significant developments in audio-visual communications, evidence suggests that the textbook held a pre-eminent position in American education for much of the twentieth century. For example, a 1935 study of a select group of 104 of the "best teachers" in New York city suburban schools conducted by Professor Thomas Briggs of Teacher's College, Columbia concluded that the vast majority continually engaged in traditional recitation and that 80 percent were "teaching from the textbook."[9] The results of subsequent studies conducted since the 1970s has proved remarkably similar to Briggs' earlier findings. Indeed, a comprehensive National Science Foundation report concluded that not only did the "conventional textbook" continue to dominate classroom instruction but that teachers tended to "rely on" and "believe in" a single textbook as the principal source of knowledge.[10]

To suggest that textbook content neatly equates to what teachers teach, or, more importantly, to what students learn would be unwise.[11] How students and teachers understand, negotiate, and transform their personal understandings of textual material is a complex process and not a simplistic one in which textbook content is simply absorbed and then regurgitated by students. Nevertheless, sufficient evidence exists to suggest that the influence of the textbook is profound.[12] Textbooks not only illustrate the historical content transmitted to the young, but they also offer a window into the dominant values and beliefs of established groups in any given period. Textbooks are socially constructed cultural, political, and economic, artefacts. Their contents are not pre-ordained but are "conceived, designed, and authored by real people with real interests."[13] Essentially, textbooks appear as gatekeepers of ideas, values, and knowledge. For, no matter how superficial history textbooks may appear in their construction, they prove ideologically important because typically they seek to imbue in the young a shared set of values, a national ethos, and an incontrovertible sense of identity.[14]

Throughout much American history the contents of textbooks principally have been determined by a white, male, Protestant, middle or upper class which has often sought to construct an idealized image of American values and American character. Accordingly schoolbooks have championed the capitalist system, endorsed traditional lifestyles, urged unquestioned patriotism, and preached reverence to the "Western tradition." Coursing through American history textbooks is the strain of unceasing progress and of manifest destiny, a respect for individual rights and recognized authority, and a reflexive suspicion of collectivist ideals. For the most part history textbooks never were intended to promote reflective thought, to stimulate critical analysis, or to celebrate cultural diversity. The function of history in American schools essentially has been to instill in the young a sense of unity and patriotism and veneration for the nation's glorious heritage.

TWO CENTURIES OF CHANGE: CONTEXT, CONTENT, AND PRODUCTION

To suggest however that history textbooks have remained totally unchanged for the past two hundred years would be grossly misleading. One of the most obvious changes during the past two hundred years has been the textbooks' intended audience. Undoubtedly this impacted how textbooks were written. For example, in most schools today U.S. history typically is mandated for study by all children at grades five, eight, and eleven. However, this was not always the case. In the eighteenth and early nineteenth centuries students' historical knowledge chiefly was formulated through fleeting appearances of inaccurate and mythical portrayals in the ubiquitous Noah Webster *Spellers* and the McGuffey *Readers*.[15] Although the teaching of United States history appeared in some schools in the 1830s, it was not generally accepted as part of the curriculum until much later in the century.[16] By 1900, a few states such as New York, Massachusetts, and Illinois made U.S. history a required subject. But it was not until immediately before World War I that American history became a widespread feature of public schooling.

Moreover any American history that was taught reached a very a limited audience. This was particularly true at the secondary level where schooling was for the few. For example, whereas in 1940, seven in 10 students aged 14 to 17 were enrolled in high school, in 1900, only one in ten were.[17] Despite this striking statistic compulsory free public education was rapidly changing the character of American society. Massachusetts had adopted the first compulsory attendance law in 1852, and many other states soon followed suit. By 1900, enrolment in high school had doubled from the previous decade and new schools were appearing at the average rate of one per day.[18]

Not without coincidence large publishing houses quickly recognized the attraction of such a rapidly expanding market. At the end of the nineteenth century, five large houses including A. S. Barnes, Appleton and Co, and Harper Bros., combined their textbook offerings to form the American Textbook Company.[19] The consolidated company controlled 80% of the market and determined the content of virtually every subject in the curriculum. Understandably, this dramatic shift in the locus of control led to changes in the nature of textbooks. Books written after 1890 generally were written in terse, declarative sentences, and although the authors clearly held their own viewpoints, in contrast to authors of previous centuries, they were not foisted upon the reader. Rather, their tone was more authoritative and neutral. Less prominent were the idiosyncratic eccentricities and opinions of individual authors prominent in the eighteenth and nineteenth centuries. Furthermore, whereas the nineteenth century texts choked full of lively anecdotes and tales of colorful personalities those of the twentieth century focused on more distant political and economic undertakings.[20]

Much in the same way as the writing style of textbooks has shifted over time so too has the form in which the texts were presented. Modern texts are distinguishable by their alluring visual appeal. Their pages overflow with cartoons, color photographs, works of art, maps, charts, diagrams, and at-a-glance time lines. On every page at least one visual image appears and not infrequently more textual space is devoted to pictorial representations than to the written word. In contrast books produced only a few decades ago offered a format that endured for over two centuries. Prior to the 1960s, books appeared visually dull and drab. Typically print size was small and visual relief rare. *The Growth of the American Republic* written by Henry Steele Commager and Samuel Eliot Morrison exemplified the mundane nature of old style secondary texts.[21] Despite the fact that the 825 page book was one of the most widely adopted textbooks from the 1930s to the 1950s, the tome offered the reader only 19 maps or illustrations, none of which appear in color. No matter how polished the writing or appropriate the narrative, such a text would be unthinkable in the glitzy "pop-culture" market of the twenty-first century.

Differences in the central purpose of history textbooks also have emerged over the ages. For although a perennial aim of American history texts has been to inculcate a sense of civic pride and national consensus, some textbook authors have pursued other, though not incompatible, goals. Most history textbooks produced in the eighteenth and nineteenth century, for example, were far more intent on fostering a middle class Protestant morality than in engaging children in meaningful historical study. Zealous attention to morality and virtue appeared a peculiar hallmark of American education in this period.[22]

The most widely circulated textbooks reflecting these aims were Noah Webster's *Elementary Spelling Book* and William Holmes McGuffey's *Readers*.[23] First appearing in 1783 Webster's *Speller* sold over 20 million copies in 60 years. In 1828 alone, 350,000 editions were purchased and two decades later sales had approached a million copies a year. The McGuffey *Reader* enjoyed similar success selling over 122 million copies in the years following 1836. Dominating American education in the eighteenth and nineteenth centuries these books stressed the Puritanical virtues of honesty, truth, temperance, obedience, industry, and thrift. Their moral catechisms were memorized by young Americans throughout the nation and they set the tone for books in other areas of the curriculum.

Textbook emphasis on Protestant values proved particularly important during a time of rapid Irish immigration in mid-nineteenth century America. Between 1815 and 1845, over a million Irish entered the United States.

Textbook writers appeared eager to thwart the threat of Catholic insurgency.[24] Children were taught to accept that America was developing into a unique and glorious nation not by accident but because God willed it. To sustain this triumphal march, to preserve the republican form of government, and to aid man's frail nature, children were left in little doubt that the Protestant religion, virtue, and morality were essential.[25]

Although textbooks written in the twentieth century commonly adhered to the vision of America as a place of virtue the heavy handed moral tone is less explicit. By contrast, professional historians who, though often naively unsuccessful, took pride in presenting history in more objective terms authored most textbooks written in the decades after World War I. Acutely less prominent in the twentieth century texts is the incessant preaching and the unashamed lack of neutrality so apparent in textbooks of the previous centuries. In particular uncomfortable and explicit anti-Catholic rhetoric is not immediately apparent. However, despite these nuances of change and development, striking and enduring themes have emerged in American history textbook writing. In particular ethnic groups have received remarkably consistent treatment during the period from the early 1800s to the 1960s.

Enduring Themes: Immigrant Groups in U. S. History Textbooks, 1800s–1960s

Significantly most history textbook writers in this extensive period held views predicated upon the underlying assumption that some nationalities, races, and civilizations were innately superior to others. This overtly racist perspective was particularly evident in textbooks written in the nineteenth century. Most textbook writers of the 1800s, for example, propagated the widely accepted scientific theories of race expounded by Joseph Gobineau, Houston Stewart Chamberlain, John Calhoun, and George Fitzhugh.[26] Central to their belief was the notion that nature had conferred certain immutable characteristics on each member of a racial group. According to the theorists the white or Caucasian race was considered the paragon of all races: intellectually, morally, and physically superior to all others. Throughout the nineteenth century, geography and history textbooks pushed these racial theories on the young. Typically, children were required to memorize these "inherent" racial characteristics and rank them in an established hierarchy. In descending order of racial worth the Caucasian always appeared at the top commonly followed by the Mongolian, the Malaysian, the Negro, and the American Indian.[27]

Children also learned to appreciate that nationality, like race, presupposed certain biologically determined qualities. Some nationalities were, therefore, considered inexorably superior and hence more desirable than others. Most favored were those national groups who mirrored the ideals of a staunchly Protestant New England society. As Ruth Elson's richly detailed study of nineteenth century texts illustrated, northern European groups were held in high esteem. Scotland and Switzerland proved pre-eminent in the national pecking order. One text revealed that "like the inhabitants of New England" the Scots and Swiss are "religious, moral, and industrious."[28] Other northern European nations received similar admiration. The Germans, for example, commonly were considered to be "an industrious, honest, and thrifty people." And although some textbooks questioned their unsavory "military character," they alone among the European nations are praised for having the same kind of "mechanical ingenuity that characterizes Americans."[29]

Despite their military rivalries in the eighteenth and nineteenth centuries, the English were similarly held in high esteem in school textbooks. Britain commonly was regarded as the "progenitor of the United States," the mother country, whose national character generally was well respected. Even though textbook authors of the late nineteenth century did not accept all the onerous trappings of their British heritage, the majority took particular pride in stressing the legacy of English culture, language, and law and many considered it a necessary means to differentiate themselves from the newer immigrant classes.

In contrast to the favorable representation of northern Europeans and Protestant nations, Catholic countries and nations from Southern Europe were treated with varying degrees of disdain. For example, one textbook written in 1844, typified representations in other textbooks,

> The Irish in general are quick of apprehension, active, brave, and hospitable; but passionate, ignorant, vain and superstitious.... The Italians are affable and polite; they excel in music, painting and sculpture; but they are effeminate, superstitious, slavish and revengeful.[30]

Nations beyond Europe also fell victim to the jaundiced views of American textbook writers. For example, Latin Americans were regarded as "naturally weak and effeminate," dedicating "the greatest part of their lives to loitering and inactive pleasures."[31] Chinese immigrants who settled on the west coast in the post Civil War period, received particularly vicious treatment. Children learned through texts written in the 1880s that in San Francisco the Chinese live "huddled together in hovels, almost like rats" and that in Chinatown "one may see opium dens, idol temples, theatres, dirt, squalor and wickedness."[32]

The accepted tradition of elevating the status of selected racial groups to the determinant of others continued into the twentieth century. This practice was particularly significant as educators responded to the demands of the period of intensive immigration that occurred in the years from 1890 to 1920. Between 1881 and 1910, for example, more than five million immigrants arrived in the United States; by 1910 the total had climbed precipitously to more than seventeen million. The impact on public education was profound. By 1909, when the U. S. Immigration Commission investigated the ethnic origins of students in thirty-seven of the nation's largest cities, officials discovered more than sixty nationalities and noted that 57.8% were of foreign-born parentage. In New York, for example, where from 1899 to 1914, school enrolment increased by more than sixty percent and some school classrooms choked with up to eighty students of various nationalities, it was a staggering 72%.[33]

In response to this period of intense immigration, American educators principally sought to divest recent arrivals of their native culture and compel them to conform to the "virtues" of Anglo-Saxon traditions. Ellwood P. Cubberly of Stanford University who declared in 1909 that the primary task of educators was "to assimilate and amalgamate these people as part of our American race, and to impart in their children...the Anglo-Saxon conception of righteousness, law and order, and popular government" persuasively encapsulated this position. In keeping with a robust tradition established for more than two centuries typically the schoolroom was not viewed as a place to legitimate diversity or to celebrate multiculturalism. Rather, its primary function was to impose an orthodox set of traditions and values typically prescribed by a white, Protestant, elite in which no place existed for distinctive ethnic groups. President Wilson's address to new citizens underscored this fundamental conviction. "You cannot become thorough Americans if you think of yourselves in groups," he told his audience in Philadelphia in May 1915. "America does not consist of groups. A man who thinks of himself as belonging to a particular national group in America has not yet become an American."[34]

In general, therefore, attitudes toward immigrants reflected widely held beliefs that newcomers were innately inferior; that to progress in America immigrants must completely repudiate their native culture; and that the middle class standards of the WASP[35] establishment were the benchmarks against which they would be judged. As many historians have noted broad acceptance of these established beliefs meant that for thousands of immigrants the American experience would be a painful one.[36]

School history textbooks did nothing to assuage American students of this dominant assimilationist creed. To the contrary, textbook presentation of ethnic groups provided powerful endorsements of the Eurocentric tradition for much of the twentieth century. Indeed, textbooks written in the years surrounding World War I proved strikingly representative of viewpoints consistently held until the 1960s.

In many respects the period from 1910 to 1930 signified the heyday of American textbook writing.[37] Written by professional historians credited with a flair for reaching young audiences several of the textbooks written in this period were used in schools into the 1950s and beyond. Especially popular was *American History,* authored by David Saville Muzzey, professor of history at Columbia University, New York. First published in 1911, the text immediately became a best seller. In subsequent decades Muzzey's books out sold all competitors. It represented the standard historical diet for the majority of American school children from the days of the horse and buggy to those of the jet aircraft.[38] Incredibly, Muzzey's book, which was still available in the 1970s, remained largely unaltered at the time of his death in the 1960s.

Like most other textbook writers of this period, Muzzey was a product of New England patrician society. Born in Massachusetts in 1870, he descended from a line of preachers and teachers who could proudly trace their roots back to the Puritans. In both heritage and outlook Muzzey symbolized the tradition of the WASP intellectual elite. As a representative of most textbook writers of the era, his literary treatment of immigrant groups proved particularly revealing. In general, Muzzey portrayed immigrants not blessed with Anglo-Saxon blood as a "problem" for America. They fell outside the purview of what Muzzey considered to be "we Americans" and were constantly referred to as an unassimilable "they." Accordingly, Muzzey perpetuated the fear that "they" threatened to become "an undigested and indigestible element of our body politic, a constant menace to our free institutions." Read by native born and immigrant alike, Muzzey's textbooks constantly reminded children of the threat that "aliens" represented to American life. Variously, immigrants were chastised for falling "prey to the manipulations of political bosses," presenting "problems for agencies of Americanization," turning cities into "breeding places of crime," and for contributing to huge "city debt."[39]

The following passage from a 1927 edition of Muzzey's *The American Adventure* typified his pessimistic portrayal of immigrant people,

The aliens were coming faster than we could assimilate them. They were bringing from centers of social turmoil and proletarian revolution ideals which were repugnant to an orderly freedom and the voluntary respect for the law....There were Polish, Hungarian, Russian unions in our labor organizations, with their interest and sympathies primarily with the fortunes of the lands from which they had come. There were communists who "took their orders from Moscow" and set the Russian soviet above the American Constitution. Over one thousand newspapers printed in thirty foreign languages were in circulation. Eleven percent of the population over ten years of age could not speak the English language. Great numbers of immigrants showed no desire to acquire American citizenship. The unassimilated and unassimilable elements of our population were growing to alarming proportions.[10]

As this extract graphically illustrated what particularly troubled Muzzey was the way in which Anglo-Saxon traditions were either being ignored or diluted. To preserve the purity of the American race Muzzey clearly believed that some immigrants were more desirable than others. Topping the list were those of northern European Protestant stock. Others were less welcome. To Muzzey, for example, "the Chinese remained Orientals, unassimilable, with furtive traits and incomprehensible habits."[11]

Muzzey's jaundiced opinions were shared by other prominent textbooks authors of the period. At a time when hordes of immigrants poured into the United States, textbook authors keenly celebrated their ancestry. Children learned that the success of America was founded on the desirable qualities of northern European civilization. *History of Our Country*, published in 1923 by the hugely influential American Book Company, for example, devoted an entire section to "our debt to the northern races" and appeared particularly eager to herald America's English ancestry and the "thrifty, hard working, and God fearing" nature of their forefathers.

Authors routinely echoed Muzzey's concern that unabated immigration both threatened tradition and polluted the quality of American stock. One text suggested that just as the United States "excludes foreign horses, cattle, and sheep that are not sound and healthy," so too should immigrants be carefully screened and selected.[12] Others talked of "race suicide" and were critical of the dramatic increase in non-Anglo immigrants. They also lamented the "rapid decrease in the birth-rate of families of the older American stocks (especially of the New England stock)."[13] Even the archetypal progressive historians Charles and Mary Beard did not disguise their concerns regarding the literacy rate of new arrivals who also knew nothing "of American history, traditions, and ideals."[14]

To a limited extent textbooks written in the 1940s and 1950s softened their prejudicial portrayal of immigrants. Short "biographies" appeared in books celebrating the contributions of immigrants such as Andrew Carnegie, Leopold Stokowski, Albert Einstein, and Irving Berlin.[15] In addition, the term "melting pot" was used more extensively in the decades surrounding World War II. These changes were deceptive however. With few exceptions textbook authors continued to judge immigrant groups against the perceived norm of the Eurocentric tradition. Immigrants were only esteemed if they supported the thesis that America was a land of opportunity for those who worked hard, embraced the English language, and accepted the superior traditions of the dominate culture. As such the "melting pot" appeared a bogus term. It presupposed the equality of the many ethnic groups who contributed to the American mix, including those of native colonial stock. In the first fifty years of the twentieth century, however, few textbook writers subscribed to this seemingly radical notion. Indeed, not until the 1960s were many of these deeply held social and racial attitudes seriously challenged.

IMMIGRANT GROUPS IN U.S. HISTORY TEXTBOOKS, 1960s–PRESENT: THE ILLUSION OF CHANGE

By the mid 1960s the social fabric of the United States was under severe strain. Ideological struggles over the cold war, social conflicts over sexual and racial equality, the catastrophic impact of the Vietnam War and cultural fragmentation evidenced by student radicalism and the chasm between emergent and traditional values had dramatic and profound effects on all aspects of American society. Not surprisingly, as a mirror to the temper of the times American history textbooks underwent important changes.

One of the goals of the Civil Rights movement was to attack racial discrimination in educational settings. As a result, intensive and successful Civil Rights campaigns, which originated in Detroit, Michigan and Newark, New Jersey, forced publishers to eliminate from their texts explicit evidence of racial bias. The protest movement spread like wildfire. Soon other minority groups joined the assault on school boards and the textbook industry each claiming that their groups' histories had for too long either been ignored or undervalued.[46]

In response, publishers grew keenly sensitive to issues of inclusion and diversity. Reflecting these changing times a string of studies conducted in the 1970s and 1980s revealed the increasingly positive treatment accorded ethnic minorities in history textbooks. For example, one study reported that "by the 1960s, minorities had moved to the center stage of American history," and further concluded that textbooks authors had "transformed the texts from scarcely mentioning blacks [and other minorities] in the 1940s, to containing a substantial multicultural (and feminist) component in the 1980s."[47]

Many authors of these studies, however, were troubled by the shifting emphases in textbook writing. Of particular concern to them was that textbooks appeared to sacrifice "essential elements of American history" on the altar of multiculturalism and "political correctness." Nathan Glazer and Reed Ueda argued that textbooks had gone too far in their treatment of ethnic groups. "The old myths of racism which were prominent in American texts of the twenties and thirties," the authors complained "are now replaced by new myths proclaiming the superior moral qualities of minorities, and we find a Manichaean inversion in which whites are malevolent and blacks, Indians, Asians, and Hispanics are tragic victims."[48] Other critics voiced similar concerns. Arthur M. Schlesinger in his widely read, *The Disuniting of America*, offered one of the most articulate and incisive critiques of the apparent trend towards what he termed "the cult of ethnicity."

Fundamental to Schlesinger's anxiety was his belief that America was losing its sense of common purpose and shared ideals and changing into "a nation of groups, differentiated in their ancestry, [and] inviolable in their diverse identities."[49] The very idea that school curricula and American history textbooks should encourage this development was particularly abhorrent to Schlesinger and others who shared his beliefs. As Schlesinger reasoned the stakes were high:

> What students learn in schools vitally affects other areas of American life— the way we see and treat other Americans, the way we conceive the purpose of our republic. The debate about the curriculum is a debate about what it means to be an American. What is ultimately at stake is the shape of the American future.[50]

Despite their disapproval of what one critic deemed "ill considered efforts of textual affirmative action,"[51] most conservative commentators acknowledged the need to address the shortcomings of textbooks written before the 1960s. Increased attention to the contributions of Hispanics, Asian Americans, African-Americas, American Indians and other ethnic minorities was, they argued, warranted. Certainly no place existed for the overtly racist narratives so pervasive in textbooks of previous generations. What troubled critics most, however, was the perception that the "main story line of American history" consistently was being submerged in a sea of political correctness. As Gilbert Sewall concluded in his 1987 study, "Textbooks should not act as cheerleaders for minorities and special causes at the expense of the central stories that mark the nation's political and economic development."[52]

The casual observer might sympathize with the views of those conservative critics who argued that textbooks written after the 1970s accorded too much attention to ethnic groups. Closer scrutiny, however, reveals that far from presenting a vision of American society based upon cultural pluralism most textbooks of the modern era continue to celebrate the Western canon and a society founded on Anglo centric traditions and values. In particular, textbooks written in the past four decades continue to perpetuate three enduring and essentially conservative themes.

First and foremost contemporary portrayals of American history remain nationalistic ones. The primary function of modern texts is not to critically examine America's past but to celebrate the achievements of its people. The ideology of unceasing progress and nationalistic pride is enshrined in every textbook written today.[53] One can tell merely by looking at the cover of textbooks that the essential message is to be a triumphant one. Almost every United States history textbook published today is adorned with patriotic symbols: the eagle, the Statue of Liberty, Independence Hall, the Lincoln Memorial. Moreover, as James Loewen remarked, "the titles themselves tell a story: *The Great Republic, The American Way, Land of Promise, Rise of the American Nation.* Such titles differ from the titles of all other textbooks students read in high school or college. Chemistry books for example, are called *Chemistry* or *Principles of Chemistry,* not *Rise of the Molecule.*"[54]

In keeping with this untarnished image of American society, most textbooks agree that America offered a "golden door" through which immigrants passed as they pursued the American dream of material prosperity and personal liberty. Thus, although contemporary textbooks do reference the hardship and discrimination endured by newcomers, the overriding message is that America presented newcomers with a land of hope and opportunity.[55]

The implications for such a selective interpretation of American history are profound. Most importantly the cult of progress serves to preserve the status quo. It solidifies the argument that because society constantly is improving little needs to be done to address social ills. Furthermore, it often places the blame for any lack of success not on the system but on the ethnic minority. As one textbook study noted, history texts are proficient at trumpeting the achievements of society on the one hand and blaming the victims on the other, thus:

> Native Americans were dispossessed of their land "because they did not understand the concept of private land ownership;" Asian workers received low wages because they were willing to "work for very little;" Blacks could not find good urban jobs because they "were unskilled and uneducated;" Chicanos face problems because "they are not fluent in English...[56]

The standard against which all ethnic groups are held is that of the dominant class. Those who do not share in the conception of a society predicated on the ideology of progress are considered obstacles to America's manifest destiny. Accordingly, textbooks justify the removal of the Cherokees because they stood in the way of western advancement.[57] They interpret the story of Texas Independence not to illustrate the aggressive capture of Mexican land but to celebrate the noble and heroic conquest of the West.[58] To find one's place on the pages of American history, therefore, one must both contribute to, and accept the idea of, progress as embodied in the Western tradition.

The absence of conflict and controversy constitutes the second identifiable theme in contemporary textbooks. In this respect textbooks are particularly conservative in their approach to issues of race. For example, rather than portray racial injustice and discrimination as conscious acts perpetrated by white society they appear in textbooks as amorphous "problems" for America. As Frances FitzGerald argued, "No one can be held responsible for problems, since everyone is interested in solving them. In all history, there is no known case of anyone causing a problem for someone else."[59] This a common feature in American history textbooks: if someone does something positive they are named and accorded full credit, if something negative occurs the actions are presented almost anonymously. Thus, slaves endure "harsh conditions," Asian Americans "face prejudice," and Hispanics are "discriminated against." Typically, however, no one is to blame. Seemingly, everyone shares in the quest for a better society. Controversy is avoided and consensus championed.[60]

Contemporary textbooks are also very cautious in their attention to movements of social protest. Most texts prefer Booker T. Washington's "moderation" over W. E. B. DuBois radicalism. Martin Luther King's nonviolent dignity is emphasized over the bitterly confrontational style of Malcolm X. Furthermore, the Martin Luther King who emerges from the pages of textbooks is not the acerbic, anti-poverty, anti-war activist of 1965 to 1968, but the visionary Christian integrationist leader of 1956–1964. Similarly, textbooks continue to perpetuate the belief that America can resolve social and racial injustice through existing institutions. *American History for Today*, for example, informed its young readers:

> Americans throughout our history have believed that all men must obey the law if democracy is to continue. If a law is wrong, the Constitution provides a way of changing the law. No man need break it. No man can put himself above the law.[61]

However, As the Council on Interracial Books for Children remarks, the historical reality was very different:

> The United States itself was born in violent revolution, and throughout our history, people have agitated and struggled against injustice. Abolitionism, women's suffrage, civil rights, union organizing, and anti-war activities are among the struggles which have utilized extra-legal tactics of boycotts, passive resistance, civil disobedience, and breaking of law. Changes in the law to correct injustice have often resulted *because* of extra-legal types of agitation.[62]

Typically textbooks ignore issues and events that continue to divide American society. Overall what stands out in most contemporary textbooks is the bland coverage afforded historical topics. Conflict, controversy, and contention are for the most part avoided. Optimism and consensus abound. Problems remain but they are solvable given the strength of the American nation. Indicative of such sentiment is the conclusion of one textbook, "As the twentieth century approaches its sunset, the people of the United States can still proudly claim in the words of Lincoln, that they and their heritage represent 'the last best hope on earth.'"[63]

The third trend or theme discernible in contemporary textbook writing concerns the issue of "mentioning." Mentioning involves adding content to the text without altering the books organizing framework or central message. Textbooks appear particularly guilty of this trend with regard to their portrayal of immigrant groups in American history. For although, textbooks written today afford much more space to ethnic groups than those written prior to the 1960s, the nature and quality of the representation has changed very little.[64] As Cornbleth and Waugh observed the tactic textbook authors employ results in "simply adding more historically excluded people...[but] minimizing serious examination of racial and ethnic conflict."[65]

Because publishers are obsessed with the compulsion to mention, textbooks of the modern era have become an uninviting and intimidating classroom resource. High school history textbooks typically weigh four to five pounds and contain between 800 and 1,000 pages.[66] Increased coverage of ethnic groups, however, generally has not led to improved treatment. People from minority groups may pop up on the pages of textbooks more frequently but they are commonly portrayed as people with little or no history, no sense of diversity within their respective groups, and with no reflection on their contemporary experiences. Furthermore, as Banks has argued, "the infusion of bits and pieces of ethnic minority groups into the curriculum not only reinforces the idea that [they] are not integral parts of U.S. society, it also results in the trivialization of ethnic cultures."[67]

Textbooks underscore the conviction that the experiences of ethnic groups are only important in so far as they contribute to the larger story of an American history dominated by white society. Numerous studies have revealed, for example, that textbooks rarely show ethnic groups interacting with one another.[68] Instead, minority groups appear only in relationship to white society. Blacks serve as slaves, Indians appear fighting soldiers, Chicanos boycott fruit growers, and Chinese immigrants construct railroads. In reality, however, American history is rich in diversity of experience. As Sleeter and Grant point out: "Black cowboys were in the West with Native Americans; Mexican Americans were in Texas with Native Americans; Chinese Americans, Japanese Americans, and Filipino Americans were all in California...[but] these groups are only shown interacting with whites."[69]

Finally, despite the fact that most modern textbooks do accord more space to minority groups several studies conducted in recent decades suggest that certain ethnic groups continue to be underrepresented. For example, scholars widely acknowledge that Asian Americans, particularly those originating from Japan and China, have received very superficial coverage in textbooks.[70] Furthermore, arguably the most glaring under representation in U.S. history textbooks concerns the treatment of Hispanics. Indeed, several contemporary studies continue to support the conclusion reached by O. L. Davis almost two decades ago that Hispanics "have long been ignored or casually mentioned in conventional U.S. history textbooks."[71]

Overall, therefore, although textbooks written since the 1960s have paid greater attention to ethnic groups in American society, the central story line has changed little for more than two centuries. Contemporary textbooks perpetuate the vision of America as a land of opportunity to be shared by all ethnic groups. Common experience and consensus are championed over racial conflict and controversy. And, above all, students learn that the story of America, despite setbacks and obstacles, remains one of unremitting progress and triumph for its people to enjoy. Reasonably, therefore, one may ask why has American history textbook writing changed so little over time? And, why do history textbooks written today continue to portray the experiences of ethnic groups in ways that have endured for generations? The answers to these questions are undoubtedly multi-faceted and complex. However, a few fundamental explanations are apparent.

WHY SO LITTLE REAL CHANGE?

Part of the answer lies in the peculiar nature of the American textbook industry. For many decades twenty-two states, principally located in America's "sun belt," have adopted school textbooks based upon the judgements of a centralized state agency. In other words, educators in local settings have little or no say in what textbooks are selected for use in their schools. Typically most states appoint expert panels to review submissions from publishers and after a complex process of hearings and analysis a number of texts (often between two and five in each subject area) are placed on an "approved" adoption list from which local school districts can select.[72]

Of significance, because California and Texas, which together represent 20% of the educational market, are textbook adoption states publishers consciously develop texts that will please these two states.[73] Textbooks adopted in Texas, Florida, or California, therefore, largely determine the content of textbooks produced throughout the nation. The stakes are high. School textbooks constitute more than 16% of all printed materials sold in the United States and command sales worth several billion dollars. The textbook market offers publishers a very lucrative market. Part of the attraction also lies in the fact that most textbooks have a print run of several million copies, are adopted for five to seven year cycles, require little marketing once adopted, and are exceedingly simple to distribute.

Recognizing the potential for profit, publishing houses have devoted increasing attention to the school textbook market. Not without coincidence, this trend has occurred at a time when the publishing industry has seen an enormous concentration of power in the hand of a few major houses. At the beginning of the 1990s for example, the "Big Three," Macmillan, Harcourt, Brace and Jovanich, and Simon Schuster, controlled an estimated 45% of the textbook market and the five largest companies (including Scholastic and Houghton Mifflin) cornered 58% of all national sales. Of even greater significance, many of the companies do not stand as isolated economic units but appear part of such huge multinational corporations as IBM, Xerox, RCA, Paramount, and Time-Warner, Inc.[74] Because textbook companies want to appeal to the broadest possible audience in order to maximize profits the implications for history textbooks are particularly profound. Typically modern textbook publishers will go to great lengths to avoid controversy or to exclude material that might offend special interest groups. Indeed, because a major history textbook series may involve initial research and development costs exceeding $500,000, publishers are particularly anxious to avoid areas of contention.

Furthermore, conscious that their primary goal is to have their textbooks "approved" for statewide adoption, publishers are acutely aware of the power of special interest politics in the United States. Without question, adoption committees are influenced by pressure groups that aggressively lobby for their attention. These pressure groups span the ideological spectrum. Christian fundamentalists, civil libertarians, patrioteers, corporations, racial minorities, feminists, and church-state separatists all compete to influence the contents of history textbooks.[75] In recent decades the religious right has proven particularly well organized and influential in exacting control over state adoption policies.

The result of this complex process is that textbook companies aim to appease a galaxy of audiences. Ultimately, as educational analyst Raymond English notes, "Profit is the aim, and profit, when you are serving a quasi-monopoly, is made by satisfying bureaucrats and politicians and by offending as few vocal and organized interest as possible."[76] For this reason school history textbooks aim to avoid passages that raise serious questions regarding racial conflict and social inequity. Their presentation of the history of ethnic minorities and immigrant groups is therefore calm, considered, and non-confrontational. In general minority groups receive attention as they contribute to the development of American civilization. Textbook publishers however appear reluctant to draw too much attention to issues that have divided American society in the past.

A second major reason why the fundamental message of history textbooks has remained remarkably consistent over time relates to the innate conservatism of American society. Many Americans instinctively believe, or

are otherwise persuaded, that the United States represents the most successful nation earth. Few can argue that the twentieth century was in so
many respects the "American century." Today the United States boasts the
strongest economic, military, and cultural force on the planet. Understandably many Americans are proud of their nation's remarkable
achievements and feel warranted in celebrating its success. In these vein
textbook critics Glazer and Ueda keenly point out that, although many
immigrants have received unjust treatment the United States, "another
side to the story" exists,

> That this country has accepted more immigrants, of more varied stocks, than
> any other nation in the world, and continues to do so; that it has been a bea-
> con for immigrants; that the nation presents the world with what is probably
> the most successful example of a complex, modern, multi-ethnic society; and
> that it goes further than any other great nation in creating a partnership of
> varied peoples, all of whom are guaranteed a range of rights and offered full
> participation in the common life of the nation.[77]

Many citizens share these sentiments and further believe that school history should play an important part in championing the success of American society. Of fundamental importance is the deeply held belief that the
story of America is a just and noble one. Thus, the search for common triumphs, common purpose, and a common identity becomes acute. Americans do not want to address the uncomfortable notion that their society
might be fractured and disunited. They do not want their children to read
about oppression or wrong doing but rather to celebrate America's
achievements. Accordingly American history textbooks are deliberately
designed to form part of the glue that helps to bond society together. Textbooks not only respond to the demands of the educational market place
but they also reflect America's visceral need for a common sense of purpose and shared identity. Understandably, therefore, history textbooks
stress unity over fragmentation, nationhood over ethnicity, and common
experience over diversity.

Conscious of the need to attract lucrative educational markets and not
acerbic political criticism, textbooks produced today remain safe, consensual, and non-controversial products. Immigrant groups might receive
greater attention in contemporary textbooks but their stories feature only
in relationship to the enduring Eurocentric themes of American history.

CONCLUSIONS

Without doubt, writing a definitive textbook for U.S. history is fraught with
epistemological, cultural, ideological and historical problems. On the one

hand textbook publishers are pressured to appreciate the cultural pluralism of American society and attend to the distinctive and complex experiences of a galaxy of immigrant and ethnic groups. On the other hand, they
are urged to stress the common ideals, common political institutions, and
common values that unite citizens of the American Republic. Commentators across the political spectrum have offered textbook authors their
response to these enduring dilemmas.

For example, critics from the political left have not only questioned the
orthodoxy of the enduring Eurocentric tradition, they have also proved
scornful of the persistent notion that any single interpretation of American
history exists. Textbooks, they argue, represent a form of social control that
validates the "official knowledge" of the Western canon and renders marginal or invisible the achievements and experiences of ethnic groups.

In direct opposition those from the political right vehemently seek to
protect the cultural traditions of Western civilization. Their influence on
educational policy has manifested itself in the quest for a standardized curriculum, in a renewed emphasis on moral and character education, and
above all, on the celebration of a Western tradition principally crafted by
white European males. Salient among the concerns of "traditionalists" is
the belief that increased attention to diversity in American society would
prove perilous to the future of the republic. Articulating the anxieties of
many others, Schlesinger concluded: "America is an experiment in creating a common identity for people of diverse races, religions, languages,
and cultures. If the republic now turns away from its old goal of one people, what is its future?—disintegration of the national community; apartheid; Balkanization; tribalization?"[78]

Scrutiny of history textbook writing today and in the past suggests that
those who share Schlesinger's anxieties have little to fear. In order to conform to the pressures of a highly competitive market, to stave off damaging
criticism from the influential political right, and to appease those who control the theatre of education, textbook publishers keenly adhere to established practices. Textbooks remain servants of political orthodoxy. They
celebrate national achievements, venerate the Western tradition, and
emphasize a shared American experience. Significantly at the beginning of
the twenty first century when U.S. society appears more pluralistic, more
diverse, and more complex, American history textbooks cling to an idealized image of society based on perceived common traditions established
more than two centuries ago.

NOTES

1. S. Nieto, *Affirming Diversity: The Sociopolitical Context of Multicultural Education* (White Plains, NY, 1996), p. 13.
2. J. Spring, *American Education* (New York, 2002), pp. 130–134.
3. A. J. S. Reed and V. E. Bergemann, *In the Classroom: An Introduction to Education,* (Guilford, CT, 1995), pp. 352–357.
4. Nieto, Ibid., p. 13.
5. R. Elson, *Guardians of Tradition: American Schoolbooks of the Nineteenth Century* (Lincoln, NE, 1964), p. vii.
6. F. Fitzgerald, *America Revised: History Schoolbooks in the Twentieth Century* (New York, 1980), p. 19.
7. L. Cuban, *How Teachers Taught: Constancy and Change in American Classrooms, 1800–1990* (New York, 1993), p. 31.
8. M. W. Apple and L. K. Christian-Smith, "The politics of the textbook" in *The Politics of the Textbook*, eds. M. W. Apple and L. K. Christian-Smith (New York, 1991), p. 9.
9. L. Cuban, *How Teachers Taught* (New York, 1993), p. 71.
10. See, for example, J. P. Shaver, O. L. Davis, Jr., and S. Hepburn, "The status of social studies education: Impressions from three NSF studies," *Social Education* 43 (1979): 150–153; M. T. Downey and L. S. Levstik, "Teaching and learning in history," in *Handbook of Research on Social Studies Teaching and Learning*, ed. J. P. Shaver (New York, 1991), pp. 400–408.
11. M. Apple and L. K. Christian-Smith, "The politics of the textbook," in *The Politics of the Textbook*, eds. M. W. Apple and L. K. Christian-Smith (New York, 1991), p. 9.
12. As Gilbert T. Sewall's 1987 study of American history textbooks neatly concluded, "To many teachers and almost all students, the textbook is taken to be a well of truthful and expert information. It creates a convenient armature on which the unpublished curriculum hangs. The examples, episodes, anecdotes, viewpoints, information, and data that a textbook contains will constitute the essential corpus of American history in the classroom where it is used." G. T. Sewall, *American History Textbooks: An Assessment of Quality* (New York, 1987), pp. 61–62.
13. M. Apple, "Regulating the text: The socio-historical roots of state control," in *Textbooks in American Society: Politics, Policy, and Pedagogy*, eds. P. G. Altbach, G. P. Kelly, H. G. Petrie. L. Weis (New York, 1991), p. 2.
14. See, M. Kammen, *Mystic Chords of Memory: The Transformation of Tradition in American Culture* (New York, 1991), p. 13.
15. See, for example, F. FitzGerald, *America Revised* (New York, 1980), p. 49; S. Rippa, *Education in a Free Society: An American History* (White Plains, NY, 1997), p. 61.
16. R. Elson, *Guardians of Tradition* (Lincoln, NE, 1964), p. 12.
17. D. Tyack and L. Cuban, *Tinkering Towards Utopia: A Century of Public School Reform* (Cambridge, MA, 1995), p. 47.
18. L. Cuban, *How Teachers Taught* (New York, 1993), p. 31.

19. G. T. Sewall and P. Cannon, "New world of textbooks: Industry consolidation and its consequences," in *Textbooks in American Society: Politics, Policy, and Pedagogy*, eds. P. G. Altbach, G. P. Kelly, H. G. Petrie. L. Weis (New York, 1991), p. 67.

20. See, F. FitzGerald, *America Revised* (New York, 1980), p. 51.

21. H. S. Commager and S. E. Morrison *The Growth of the American Republic* (New York, 1951).

22. R. Elson, *Guardians of Tradition* (Lincoln, NE, 1964), p 1.

23. S. Rippa, *Education in a Free Society* (White Plains, NY, 1997), p. 60.

24. Ibid., p. 82.

25. See, M. Kammen, *Mystic Chords of Memory* (New York, 1991), p. 145; M. Bellok, "Schoolbooks, pedagogy books, and the political socialization of young Americans" *Educational Studies* 12 (1981), p. 45.

26. R. Elson, *Guardians of Tradition* (Lincoln, NE, 1964), p. 65.

27. Ibid., pp. 66–8.

28. Ibid., p. 104.

29. Ibid., p. 144.

30. M. L. Fell, *The Foundations of Nazism in American Textbooks, 1783–1860* (Washington DC, 1941), p. 157.

31. J. Garcia, "The changing image of ethnic groups in textbooks," *Phi Delta Kappa* (September 1993), p. 30.

32. R. Elson, *Guardians of Tradition* (Lincoln, NE, 1964), p. 164.

33. See, David Tyack, *The One Best System: A History of American Urban Education* (Cambridge, MA, 1974), pp. 230–231; L. A. Cremin, *The Transformation of the School: Progressivism in American Education*, 1876–1957 (New York, 1964), p. 72.

34. M. R. Olneck, "Americanization and the education of immigrants, 1900–1925: An analysis of symbolic action," *American Journal of Education* 92 (1989), p. 402.

35. White, Anglo-Saxon, Protestant

36. See, for example, L. A. Cremin, *The Transformation of the School* (New York, 1964); D. Tyack, *The One Best System* (Cambridge, MA, 1974); S. Rippa, *Education in a Free Society* (White Plains, NY, 1997); L. Cuban, *How Teachers Taught* (New York, 1993); M. R. Olneck, "Americanization and the education of immigrants, 1900–1925: An analysis of symbolic action," *American Journal of Education* 79 (1989), pp. 398–423.

37. F. FitzGerald, *America Revised* (New York, 1980), p. 52.

38. See, F. FitzGerald, *America Revised* (New York, 1980), pp. 52, 58–60; G. B. Nash, C. Crabtree, and R. E. Dunn, *History on Trial: Culture Wars and the Teaching of the Past* (New York, 1997), pp. 26–27.

39. These examples are taken from D. S. Muzzey, *The American Adventure: A History of the United States* (2 vols., New York, 1927), pp. 47, 802, and 475.

40. D. S. Muzzey, *The American Adventure: A History of the United States* (2 vols., New York, 1927), p. 787.

41. Ibid., p. 154. Muzzey's textbook also informed readers, "*Their quarters in Chinatown were squalid, reeking with opium and vice.*"

42. R. P. Halleck, *History of Our Country* (New York, 1923), p. 528.

43. See, for example, W. M. West, *American History and Government* (Boston 1913), p. 653.

44. C. A. Beard and M. R. Beard, *History of the United States* (New York, 1921), p. 607.

45. See, F. FitzGerald, *America Revised* (New York, 1980), p. 81.

46. *As Frances FitzGerald noted*, "Within a few years, a dozen organizations from B'nai B'rith's Anti-Defamation league to a new Council on Interracial Books, were studying texts for racial, ethnic, and religious bias...What began as a series of discreet protest against individual books became a general proposition: all texts had treated the United States as a wealthy, middle-class society when it was in fact multiracial and multicultural. And this proposition, never so much suggested before 1962, had by the late sixties come to be a truism for the educational establishment." *America Revised* (New York, 1980), p. 39.

47. R. Lerner, A. K. Nagai, and S. Rothman, *Moulding the Good Citizen: The Politics of High School History Texts* (Westport, CT., 1995), p. 84.

48. N. Glazer and R. Ueda, *Ethnic Groups in History Textbooks* (Washington, DC, 1983), p. 60.

49. A. M. Schlesinger, "The Disuniting of America," *American Federation of Teachers* (Winter 1991), p. 22.

50. Ibid., p. 21.

51. G. T. Sewall, *American History Textbooks* (New York, 1987), p. 75.

52. Ibid., p. 75.

53. See, J. W. Loewen, *Lies My Teacher Told Me* (New York, 1995), pp. 249–65.

54. Ibid., p. 3.

55. J. Garcia, "The white ethnic experience in selected secondary U. S. history textbooks," *The Social Studies* (July/August, 1986): 174.

56. Council on Interracial Books for Children, *Guidelines for Selecting Bias-Free Textbooks and Storybooks* (New York, 1980), p. 91.

57. See, C. E. Sleeter and C. A. Grant, "Race, class, gender, and disability in current textbooks" in *The Politics of the Textbook*, eds. M. W. Apple and L. K. Christian-Smith (New York, 1991), p. 86.

58. See, J. Arries, "Decoding the social studies production of Chicano history," *Equity and Excellence in Education* 27 (1994), pp. 39–41.

59. F. FitzGerald, *America Revised* (New York, 1980), p. 158.

60. A number of scholars also have noted how textbooks written during the 1980s and early 1990s closely reflect the conservative political, religious, and cultural values of the Reagan-Bush era. For example, Leah Washburn's compelling study of textbook portrayal of slavery 1900–1992 noted an acute shift in emphasis from the more multicultural texts of the 1960s and 1970s to the conservative ones of the 1980s and 1990s. In particular, Washburn argued that textbooks written in the latter period were keen to emphasize "gradual social and political change," "the religious experiences" of slaves and abolitionists, and the "traditional values and gender roles" of mid-nineteenth century America. Above all, textbooks written in this period sought to de-emphasize conflict and celebrate consensus. See, L. Washburn, "Accounts of slavery: An analysis of United States history textbooks from 1900–1992," *Theory and Research in Social Education* 25 (1997): 478.

61. As cited in, Council on Interracial Books for Children, *Guidelines for Selecting Bias-Free Textbooks and Storybooks* (New York, 1980), p. 92.

62. Ibid., p. 92.

63. As cited in J. W. Loewen, *Lies My Teacher Told Me* (New York, 1995), p. 252.

64. See, for example, C. E. Sleeter and C. A. Grant, "Race, class, gender, and disability in current textbooks," in *The Politics of the Textbook* eds. M. W. Apple and L. K. Christian-Smith, (New York, 1991), pp. 83–86; J. Garcia, "The white ethnic experience in selected secondary U. S. history textbooks," *The Social Studies* (July/August, 1986),p. 173.

65. As cited in L. Washburn, "Accounts of slavery: An analysis of United States history textbooks from 1900–1992," *Theory and Research in Social Education* 25 (1997), p. 483.

66. Not surprisingly historian Robert Nisbet reflected with some exasperation that, "No one will every curl up, cuddle up with one of these behemoths." Cited in, G. T. Sewall, *American History Textbooks* (New York, 1987), p. 64.

67. As cited in C. E. Sleeter and C. A. Grant, "Race, class, gender, and disability in current textbooks," in *The Politics of the Textbook*, eds. M. W. Apple and L. K. Christian-Smith (New York, 1991), p. 99.

68. See, for example, C. E. Sleeter and C. A. Grant, "Race, class, gender, and disability in current textbooks," in *The Politics of the Textbook*, eds. M. W. Apple and L. K. Christian-Smith (New York, 1991), p. 85; J. Arries, "Decoding the social studies production of Chicano history," *Equity and Excellence in Education* 27 (1994); J. Garcia, "The white ethnic experience in selected secondary U. S. history textbooks," *The Social Studies* (July/August, 1986).

69. C. E. Sleeter and C. A. Grant, "Race, class, gender, and disability in current textbooks, in *The Politics of the Textbook*, eds. M. W. Apple and L. K. Christian-Smith (New York, 1991), p. 97.

70. See, for example, C. E. Sleeter and C. A. Grant, "Race, class, gender, and disability in current textbooks," in *The Politics of the Textbook,* eds. M. W. Apple and L. K. Christian-Smith (New York, 1991); N. Glazer and R. Ueda, *Ethnic Groups in History Textbooks* (Washington, DC, 1983); People for the American Way, (ed. O. L. Davis, Jr.), *Looking at History: A Review of Major U. S. History Textbooks* (Washington, DC, 1986).

71. People for the American Way, (ed. O. L. Davis, Jr.), *Looking at History: A Review of Major U. S. History Textbooks* (Washington, DC, 1986), p. 10.

72. See, for example, J. Spring, *American Education* (New York, 1996); G. T. Sewall, *American History Textbooks* (New York, 1987); G. T. Sewall and P. Cannon, "New world of textbooks: Industry consolidation and its consequences," in *Textbooks in American Society: Politics, Policy, and Pedagogy,* eds. P. G. Altbach, G. P. Kelly, H. G. Petrie. L. Weis (New York, 1991), pp. 61–69; S. Keith, "The determinants of textbook control," in *Textbooks in American Society: Politics, Policy, and Pedagogy,* eds. P. G. Altbach, G. P. Kelly, H. G. Petrie. L. Weis (New York, 1991), pp. 43–59.

73. J. Spring, *American Education* (New York, 1996), p. 248. See also K.A. Crawford "The Manufacture of Official Knowledge: the Texas textbook adoption process," in *Internationale Schulbuchforschung,* No, 26, Hanover, Hahnsche Buchhandlung, 2003

74. G. T. Sewall and P. Cannon, "New world of textbooks: Industry consolidation and its consequences," in *Textbooks in American Society: Politics, Policy, and*

Pedagogy, eds. P. G. Altbach, G. P. Kelly, H. G. Petrie. L. Weis (New York, 1991), pp. 61–69

75. Ibid., pp. 15–16.
76. Ibid., p. 13
77. N. Glazer and R. Ueda, *Ethnic Groups in History Textbooks* (Washington, DC, 1983), p. 2.
78. A. M. Schlesinger, "The Disuniting of America," *American Federation of Teachers* (Winter 1991), p. 31.

CHAPTER 8

THE ISLAMIZATION OF PAKISTANI SOCIAL STUDIES TEXTBOOKS[1]

Yvette Claire Rosser

Assuming that history textbooks are narrated with the intent of developing students into patriotic, productive citizens, this paper highlights interpretations of history found in a selection of school textbooks from the Pakistan Studies curriculum. Examples from state sponsored social studies textbooks used in classrooms in Pakistan graphically illustrate the appropriation and application of historiography to create and reinforce a national philosophy or ideology. Textbooks are the result of social and political pushes and pulls, pressures rising from larger issues of state building and identity formation. Within many nations historical interpretations have become codified, predetermined, and concretized.

In this highly charged atmosphere, where history is seen as a powerful tool to mould a nation's youth, interpretations of historical events are isolated and manipulated, heroes and villains exchange places across the borders of neighboring countries,[2] an antinomy of point of view renders interpretation laden facts from the vast legacy of shared historical events

What Shall We Tell the Children?, pages 179–194
Copyright © 2006 by Information Age Publishing
All rights of reproduction in any form reserved.

mutually exclusive. Selective history often distorts and disconnects historical moments from their context and biography often becomes hagiogra-
phy particularly when social science discourse is based on narrow
nationalist interpretations and ethnically or religiously driven political
mandates. Sometimes the influence is overt, as in the discourse of chauvinistic Islamic nationalism that pervades *Pakistani Studies* textbooks, a narrative based on "Islamization,"[3] an indoctrination strategy institutionalized
during the decade of General Zia ul-Haq's military rule.

PAK STUDIES: PROPAGANDA VERSUS HISTORIOGRAPHY

All students in Pakistan are required to take courses called *Pakistan Studies*
and must pass standardized tests. There are numerous textbooks published
under this title for the 9th class to the BA level. In general, the curriculum
is a composite of patriotic discourses, justification of the Two-Nation Theory, hagiographies of Muslim heroes, and, endemic in the discourse,
polemics about the superiority of Islamic principals over Hinduism. The
rubric in these textbooks must be learned by rote in order for students to
pass the examination.

Many students in Pakistan not only dislike this course but openly mock
it. A student at a women's college in Lahore told me that "Pak Studies
classes were usually scheduled at five or six in the afternoon" and "hardly
any students attend," choosing instead to spend their time studying for
"important classes such as Math or Urdu or English." "Besides," the student
continued, "we've covered the Pak Studies material year after year, it's just
the same Lucknow Pact, Two-Nation Theory ... we don't have to study for
the test, the Ideology of Pakistan has been drilled into us."

Textbooks in Pakistan must be approved by the Curriculum Wing of the
Ministry of Education in Islamabad after which they are published by the
provincial textbook boards located at Jamshoro in Sindh, Quetta in
Balouchistan, Lahore in Panjab,[4] and Peshawar in the North West Frontier
Province (NWFP). The social studies curriculum in Pakistan, as both product and propagator of the "Ideology of Pakistan," derives its legitimacy
from a narrow set of directives. The textbooks authored and altered during
the eleven years of General Zia-ul-Haq's military rule between 1977 and
1988, are still in use in most schools—they are decidedly anti-democratic
and inclined to dogmatic tirades and are characterized by internal contradictions.[5]

Since the terrorist attacks on September 11, 2001, the popular media in
the West has begun to pay attention to the vitriolic anti-Western narratives
that are pervasive in textbooks in several Islamic countries, including allies
such as Saudi Arabia. For years, scholars have warned that the textbooks in

Pakistan were fomenting hatred and encouraging fundamentalism. It is well known that for several decades, textbooks in not only Pakistan, but many Islamic nations have promoted a radically restrictive brand of Islamic exclusivism, and exported that perspective to other nations, as in the case of Pakistani born Taliban.

The teleological nature of the civic responsibility to create patriotic citizens finds a malleable tool in the social studies curriculum where myth and fact often merge. The many textbooks published in Pakistan under the title *Pakistan Studies* are particularly prone to the omissions, embellishments, and elisions that often characterize historical narratives designed for secondary level social studies classes. During the time of General Zia-ul Haq, social studies, comprising of history and geography, were replaced by *Pakistan Studies,* which was made a compulsory subject for all students from the ninth grade[6] through the first year of college including engineering and medical schools. Curriculum changes, institutionalized during Zia's Islamization campaign, required that all students also take a series of courses under the title Islamiyat, the study of Islamic tenants and memorization of Quranic verses. Committees formed under Zia's guidance began to systematically edit the textbooks. The University Grants Commission (UGC) issued a directive in 1983 that textbook writers were:

> To demonstrate that the basis of Pakistan is not to be founded in racial, linguistic, or geographical factors, but, rather, in the shared experience of a common religion. To get students to know and appreciate the Ideology of Pakistan, and to popularize it with slogans. To guide students towards the ultimate goal of Pakistan—the creation of a completely Islamized State.[7]

In 1985 when Zia's policies were in full swing in "Rewriting the history of Pakistan," Hoodbhoy and Nayyar commented on what they perceived as the inevitable and eventual blowback from General Zia's efforts to Islamize the educational system, "the full impact of which will probably be felt by the turn of the century, when the present generation of school children attains maturity."

Nayyar and Hoodbhoy explain that the UGC's directives centered on four themes:

1. The "Ideology of Pakistan," both as a historical force which motivated the movement for Pakistan as well as its raison d'être.
2. The depiction of Jinnah as a man of orthodox religious views who sought the creation of a theocratic state.
3. A move to establish the "ulama as genuine heroes of he Pakistan Movement.

4. An emphasis on ritualistic Islam, together with the rejection of interpretations of the religion and generation of communal antagonism.[8]

The broad expanse of South Asian history is a *tabula rasa* upon which
Pakistani historians and policy makers have created the story of a new
nation replete with cultural roots and ancient socio-religious trajectories.
This manufactured view of the past narrates Pakistan's emergence as an
independent country: in just seven short years, under guidance of Mohammed Ali Jinnah, Quaid-e-Azam, the father of the country, Pakistan rose
from the strife and oppression of religious communalism in Hindu dominated India to join the comity of modern nations. Nayyar and Hoodbhoy
explain, "The 'recasting' of Pakistani history [has been] used to 'endow
the nation with a historic destiny.'"[9]

STITCHING CAPS AND STAGING COUPS

During the past three decades, the Pakistani military[10] has helped to
empower a vast cadre of politically motivated, religiously conservative
Mujahideen, evidenced by the accelerating crisis in Kashmir, the war like
situation in Kargil, airplane hijackings, and the Talebanization of
madrassah[11] education. This continuing move towards Islamization is
accentuated against the ominous backdrop of nuclear testing, missile
development, failed diplomacy, and sporadic tit-for-tat acrimonious
exchanges between India and Pakistan. The social studies curriculum in
Pakistan employs a very narrow definition of Islam in the construction of
Pakistani nationalism.

Islamization is a controversial term with a variety of interpretations.
There are subtle distinctions among usages of words such as Islamization,
Islamic nationalism, Islamic Republic, Islamizing, that represent the
manipulation and implementation of religious terminology and symbols as
political tools. Both Maududi of the Jaamat-I-Islami and Ayatollah
Khomeini of Iran saw Islamization as a model for the world-wide community of Islamic Ummah, distinct from Islamic nationalism, which is "essentially a Western, non-Islamic, secular, and territorial concept that
emphasizes patriotism and love of one's nation-state, its sacred territory,
political institutions and symbols."[12]

A more thoroughly Islamized Pakistan, which would finally fulfil the
true Shariat-ruled mandate inherent in the creation of an Islamic Republic
was how General Zia constructed the meaning of his Islamization campaign, which he propagated and popularized as the inevitable evolution of
Pakistani nationalism. Zia institutionalized a kind of paranoia about parad-
ing Islamic symbols, which were seen as essential for the survival of the

nation-state. Unfortunately some of the strategies that Zia and his fundamentalist mullah supporters appropriated and propagated were based on narrow, medieval interpretations of Islam, which resulted in gender-biased attitudes and policies and militarized exhortations to take up arms for the sake of jihad.

The "Ideology of Pakistan" is based on Islamic nationalism. Islamization is what Zia called it, but not coincidentally. He was consciously pushing for stricter adherence to external expressions of religion, placating conservative forces, exerting social control, influencing social norms. Pakistan's ideology of "Islamic nationalism" still has a dynamic and powerful hold over the overwhelming majority of Pakistanis. Professor Mir Zohair Husain wrote in a personal communication:

> Just because Zia used the word "Islamization" time and again, doesn't mean that he was successful in his so-called "Islamization" of Pakistani political and economic institutions. While Pakistan's governing elite may have been relatively liberal, pragmatic and secular, the majority of Pakistanis were always devout Muslims, and Pakistani culture was always "Islamic" [and] thus didn't need any further "Islamizing." If Zia's so-called "Islamization" of Pakistani society had actually occurred, Pakistanis would never have elected two relatively liberal, pragmatic, and secular Muslims to run Pakistan four times in 11 years in free and fair elections based on adult franchise—Benazir Bhutto (1988–1990, 1993–1996) and Nawaz Sharif (1990–1993, 1996–1999). General Pervaiz Musharraf, who usurped power on October 12th, 1999, is also a liberal and pragmatic Muslim, who has said that he admired Mustafa Kemal Ataturk of Turkey [who] is denounced by devout Muslims all over the world for being a secular dictator who tried to Westernize Turkey. Quaid-e-Azam Muhammad Ali Jinnah was not "actually working to establish an Islamic-dominated state." A "Muslim-led government" is by no means the same thing as an "Islamic-dominated state!" Most governments in the Muslim world are led by Muslims, but they are not Islamic regimes based on the Islamic Shariah (like Iran or Afghanistan [under the Taliban])[13]

Husain's observations, contrasting the elites with the more "Islamized common" people highlights the irony of Zia's efforts. Though this impetus to Islamize the outward manifestations of social and political institutions was itself a reflection of a world-wide movement towards religious conservatism and fundamentalism within the Islamic community, the results of twenty years of Zia's Islamization indoctrination program has given rise to more women in burqas, a generation of Pakistani girls prevented by social conventions from riding bicycles, and militant mullahs preaching political jihad from their Friday pulpits. Though certainly, these expressions are part of the international trend among Muslims toward religious conservatism, Zia latched on to that and used it. The Islamization of Pakistan initiated during the eighties brought an end to the liberal secular ambience of the sixties and seventies, inherited from the sophisticated and educated father of the nation, Quaid-e-Azam, when some women still wore saris to weddings and elbow-length sleeves were the norm in a hot climate, and girls still rode bicycles to the market. Middle-aged Pakistani women remember when hijab and traditional headgear was an anomaly.

Men in Pakistan have also adopted more Islamic expressions in their outward attire. Prior to the pressures exerted by Zia to Islamize all facets of society, Pakistani men who sported long beards and short pants could be seen on their way to pray at the Mosque, they were respected as either sincere practitioners or elderly gentlemen who had performed Haj. A friend in Sindh recently told me, "Now, most of the men who dress up as mullahs are quacks and crackpots. Every dacoit, shopkeeper, middle class business-man, and rickshaw wala wants to look like a mullah." He added, "Twenty or thirty years ago Pakistani men were not judged by the length of their pants or their beards."

Once social and political conventions become codified by conservative religious dictates, it is extremely difficult to break or oppose those newly imposed norms that quickly become sacrosanct and in fact, required of "true believers." External expressions of Islamization, such as traditional Muslim fashion—beards and caps for males, burqas, purdah, or at least long-sleeved clothing or females—are also potent symbols of patriotism, proving one's personal commitment to the Ideology of Pakistani.

THE GOAL: COMPLETE ISLAMIZATION

Discourses about Islam and its relationship to the Ideology of Pakistan comprise the majority of *Pakistan Studies* textbooks that delve at length into how Islam can create a fair and just nation. One textbook states, for example, "In the eyes of a Muslim all human beings are equal and there is no distinction based on race or color [...] The rich or poor [are] all equal before law. A virtuous and pious man has precedence over others before Allah."[14] This *Pakistan Studies* textbook also states, "Namaz (Prayer) prevents a Muslim from indulging in immoral and indecent acts." And regarding issues of justice, the 1999 edition of this *Pakistan Studies* textbook, which is in wide usage in Pakistan states:

> On official level (sic) all the officers and officials must perform their duties justly, i.e., they should be honest, impartial and devoted. They should keep in view betterment of common people and should not act in a manner which may infringe the rights of others or may cause inconvenience to others.[15]

Several students in Pakistan have complained that they felt cheated and pessimistic when they read these things. They expressed anger because they could not rectify their cognitive dissonance with what they heard about the corruption of elected officials, wealthy landholders and industrialists buying off cases. With statements from their textbooks such as:

> Every one should be equal before law and the law should be applied without any distinction or discrimination. [...] Islam does not approve that certain individuals may be considered above law.[16]

A textbook published by the Punjab Textbook Board states, "The Holy Prophet (PBUH)[17] says that a nation which deviates from justice *invites its doom and destruction*" (emphasis added).[18] With such a huge disparity between the ideal and the real, there is considerable fatalism apparent among the educated citizens and the school going youths concerning the state of the nation in Pakistan. Further compounding students' distress and distancing them from either their religion and/or their nation-state, are contradictory statements made in this *Pakistan Studies* book that "the enforcement of Islamic principles ... does not approve dictatorship or the rule of man over man." Compared with the reality unfolding a few paragraphs later when the student is told uncritically that,

> General Muhammad Ayub Khan captured power and abrogated the constitution of 1956 [...] dissolved the assemblies and ran the affairs of the country under Martial Law without any constitution.[19]

In Md. Sarwar's *Pakistan Studies* a chapter is dedicated to "Islamization of Pakistan" with subtitles, "Islamization Under Zia," "Hindrances to Islamization," and "Complete Islamization is Our Goal." Other themes and events in the history and culture of Pakistan are judged vis-à-vis their relationship and support of "complete Islamization." Within this rhetoric are found dire warnings that Islam should be applied severely so that it can guard against degenerate Western influences, yet a few pages later the text encourages the students to embrace Western technological innovations in order to modernize the country.

One part of the book complains that Muslims in British India lost out on economic opportunities because conservative religious forces rejected Western education yet a few pages later the authors tell the students to use Islam to fend off the influences of Western education. In doing so, the textbooks eulogize the efforts of conservative clerics who are presented as the last hope of preventing the westernized degeneration of the country through the implementation of the all—encompassing Shari-a Law. This seems to be schizophrenic reasoning, but may reflect the inherent contradiction of British pedagogical constructs underlying and undermining post-colonial Islamized interpretations.

The Sarwar textbook claims that Islam sees no differences and promotes unity among peoples while it also discriminates between Muslims and non-believers. On page 120 the author writes:

> The Islamic state, of course, discriminates between Muslim citizens and religious minorities and preserves their separate entity. Islam does not conceal the realities in the guise of artificialities or hypocrisy. By recognizing their distinct entity, Islamic state affords better protection to its religious minorities. Despite the fact that the role of certain religious minorities, especially the Hindus in East Pakistan, had not been praiseworthy, Pakistan ensured full protection to their rights under the Constitution. Rather the Hindu Community enjoyed privileged position in East Pakistan by virtue of is effective control over the economy and the media. It is to be noted that the Hindu representatives in the 1st Constituent Assembly of Pakistan employed delaying tactics in Constitution-making.

That this claim is exaggerated can be seen in the recent book by McGrath, *The Destruction of Democracy in Pakistan*, in which the author analyses the efforts of constitution making in the first decade after independence before Iskandar Mizra dissolved the National Assembly. In the McGrath book, the productive role D.N. Dutt, a Hindu from East Pakistan, played in constitution making is highlighted. Yet, in *Pakistan Studies* textbooks, anti-Hindu rhetoric and the vilification of the Hindu community of East Pakistan are standard fare.

In this particular, official, version of Pakistani history, General Zia-ul-Haq is portrayed as someone who "...took concrete steps in the direction of Islamization." He is portrayed as pious and perhaps stitching caps alongside Aurangzeb. Though Zulfikar Ali Bhutto is generally criticized in the textbooks, Zia escapes most criticism though he was the most autocratic of the four military rulers who have dominated the political process in Pakistan. Each time that martial law was declared in Pakistan, and the constitution aborted, textbooks describe it as a necessary repercussion responding to the rise of decadent secular values. Dr. Sarwar describes martial law as an inevitable solution stimulated by unIslamic forces:

> During the period under Zia's regime, social life developed a leaning towards simplicity. Due respect and reverence to religious people was accorded. The government patronized the religious institutions and liberally donated funds.[20]

Sarwar's textbook claims that there is a "network of conspiracies and intrigues" which are threatening the "Muslim world in the guise of elimination of militancy and fundamentalism." In this treatment, under the guidance of General Zia, Pakistan takes credit for the fall of the Soviet Union and lays claim to have created a situation in the modern world where Islamic revolutions can flourish and that the vacuum left by the fall of the USSR will "be filled by the world of Islam." The textbook continues, "The Western world has full perception of this phenomena, [which] accounts for the development of reactionary trends in that civilization." Concluding this section under the subheading "Global Changes" the author seems to be preparing for Samuel Huntington's *Clash of Civilizations* when he writes:

> The Muslim world has full capabilities to face the Western challenges provided Muslims are equipped with self-awareness and channelize their collective efforts for the well being of the Muslim Ummah. All evidences substantiate Muslim optimism indicating that the next century will glorify Islamic revolution with Pakistan performing a pivotal role.[21]

Pakistan Studies textbooks are full of inherent contradictions. On one page the text praises the modern banking system and on another page complains that interest, *riba*, is unIslamic. There is also a certain amount of self-loathing written into the *Pakistan Studies* textbooks, the politicians are depicted as inept and corrupt and the industrialists are described as pursuing "personal benefit even at the cost of national interest."

The textbooks portray Pakistan as a victim of Western ideological hegemony, threatened by the perpetual Machiavellian intentions of India's military and espionage machine, together with the internal failure of its politicians to effectively govern the country. This gloomy situation is further exacerbated by textbook reports that the economy is in the hands of a totally corrupt class of elite business interests who have only enriched themselves at the cost of the development of the nation. Ironically, in textbooks intended to create patriotism and pride in the nation, the country is ridiculed and despised. All of these failures of the state and internal and international conspiracies could, according to the rhetoric in the textbooks, be countered by the application of more strictly Islamic practices.

In 1999 and 2000, most of the people I met in Pakistan were alarmed about the "Talibanization of the nation." I was told time and again "the CIA created the Taliban Frankenstein in Pakistan's backyard, then walked away, leaving the monster behind." Some Pakistanis, inspired by the politicized sermons of mullah elites, vociferously call for a "Taliban type system" and are willing to die to Islamize the nation. This may be especially true among the poor, whose only access to education is in a crowded Madrassa where they learn that Sunni Islam is poised to take over the world of kafirs (nonbelievers) and apostates. These economically and emotionally deprived young men have been taught that a Taliban type system could overcome their poverty, their powerlessness and despair. Caught between conspiracies, corruption and the Holy Qu'ran, they see no alternatives. When text-books and clerics cry conspiracy the tendency for Pakistanis to feel betrayed and persecuted is not surprising. During the 1971 war, newspapers in Pakistan told very little about the violent military crackdown in Dhaka nor did they keep the people informed of the deteriorating strategic situation. The role of the Mukti Bahini[22] was practically unknown in the western wing of the country, and when defeat finally came, it was a devastating and unexpected shock that could only be explained by the treachery of Indira Gandhi, who is often quoted as saying, "We have sunk the Two-Nation Theory in the Bay of Bengal." India remains a hyperbolic threat to Pakistan's very existence.

In the thirty years since the "fall of Dhaka" the government controlled curriculum still does not include a historically circumspect version of the causes of the civil war that dismembered the nation. It is no wonder that during and in the aftermath of the Kargil crisis in the summer of 1999, newspapers ran stories referring to the occupation of the heights above Kargil as "revenge for 1971." There is a chronic shortage of objective information available to the majority of Pakistani citizens that can adequately explain the actual events that led to the three wars with India. Kashmir in 1948, the war with India in 1965, and the Bangladesh War of Independence have become national metaphors[23] for betrayal within and a reminder of the constant threat looming from Hindu India. The split-up of the nation and the creation of Bangladesh remains a potent symbol of Pakistan's disempowerment and a constant reminder of what will happen if the Muslim ummah does not remain vigilant.

During the war-like situation in the summer of 1999 at the Line of Control near Kargil, the Pakistani government claimed that the Mujahideen were not physically supported by Pakistan, that the combatants were indigenous Kashmiri freedom fighters. However, the presence of satellite television, the internet, and newspapers that are now more connected to international media sources, offered the possibility of broader exposure than during the two previous wars fought over Kashmir. Perhaps there is at least one positive outcome of the tragic Kargil crisis where hundreds of young men lost their lives; in the aftermath there was an outpouring of newspaper and magazine articles in Pakistan that attempted to analyze the brinkmanship from various angles. Such critical reflexivity is essential in a civil society.

Although some of the essays in Pakistani newspapers prophetically called for the military to take over the government in the wake of Nawaz Sharif's sell out to Clinton, most of the discussions were more circumspect and many authors looked at the Kargil debacle through a lens of history, trying to understand the cause of Pakistan's repeated failures arising from military brinkmanship. Many of the observations made after Kargil, such as the inadequacy of Pakistan's international diplomatic missions, are interestingly, also cited in *Pakistan Studies* textbooks regarding India's perceived manipulation of world opinion during the 1971 war and Pakistan's inability to counter it.

Pakistani textbooks are particularly prone to historical narratives manipulated by omission, according to Avril Powell, professor of history at the University of London, such erasure can have its long-term negative repercussions.[24] Another example of this is the manner in which the Indo-Pak War of 1965 is discussed in Pakistani textbooks. In standard narrations of the 1965 War there is no mention of Operation Gibraltar, even after four decades. In fact, several university level history professors whom I interviewed claimed never to have heard of Operation Gibraltar and the repercussions of that ill-planned military adventurism which resulted in India's attack on Lahore. In Pakistani textbooks the story is told that "the Indian army, unprovoked, inexplicably attacked Lahore" and that "one Pakistani *jawan* (soldier) equals ten Indian soldiers," who, upon seeing the fierce Pakistanis, "drop their *banduks* (rifles) and run away." Many people in Pakistan still think like this, and several mentioned this assumed cowardice of the Indian army in discussions with me while the fighting was raging in Kargil. The nation is elated by the valiant victories on the battlefield, as reported in the newspapers, then shocked and dismayed when their country is humiliated at the negotiating table. Because they were not fully informed about the adventurism of their military leaders, they can only feel betrayed that somehow Pakistani politicians once again "grabbed diplomatic defeat from the jaws of military victory." Operation Gibraltar, the recent debacle in Kargil, and especially the tragic lessons that could have been learned from the Bangladesh War are products of the same myopic processes. The Kargil crisis was a legacy of the lack of information that citizens have had about the real history of their country.

Pakistani textbooks have a particular problem when defining geographical space. The terms South Asia and Subcontinent have partially helped to solve this problem of the geo-historical identity of the area formally known as British India. However, it is quite difficult for Pakistani textbook writers to ignore the land now known as India when they discuss Islamic heroes and Muslim architectural monuments in the Subcontinent. This reticence to recognize anything of importance in India, which is almost always referred to as "Bharat" in both English and Urdu versions of textbooks, creates a difficult dilemma for historians writing about the Moghul Dynasties. It is interesting to note that M.A. Jinnah strongly protested the Congress' appropriation of the appellation "India," but his arguments were dismissed by Mountbattan. Because Pakistani textbook writers are constrained by the imperative to represent all facts and events in the historical record of South Asia so as to prove the inevitability of the Two Nation Theory, there are, by necessity of this agenda, numerous misrepresentations. Geography also falls prey to this ideological orientation, as can be seen in this quote from one of the many textbooks titled, *Pakistani Studies*:

> During the 12th century the shape of Pakistan was more or less the same as it is today ... Under the Khiljis, Pakistan moved further south-ward to include a greater part of Central India and the Deccan. In retrospect it may be said that during the 16th century "Hindustan" disappeared and was completely absorbed in "Pakistan."[25]

Social Studies textbooks in Pakistan have long been victimized by distorted politics. In 1953, prior to Ayub Khan's period, the second half of the seventh grade *Geography and Civics* textbook,[26] published by the West Pakistan Textbook Board, was devoted to a discussion of various political systems, and featured chapters titled "Democracy," "Theocracy," "Military Dictatorship," and "Federalism." In a subsequent edition of this seventh grade *Geography and Civics* textbook[27] published in 1962, four years after Ayub Khan's military government had taken control of the country, the discussions of comparative political systems had been eliminated, and instead, chapters such as "What It Means to Be a Good Pakistani," and "Standing in Queue" are included. Perceived political imperatives shaped by a pervasive distrust of the Pakistani people have motivated previous manipulations of the textbooks.

Another recent example of alterations made in textbooks to conform the narrative to the current political jargon can be seen by comparing two editions of the textbook *Pakistan Studies for Secondary Classes*, published by the Punjab Textbook Board. First, the 1997 edition states on page 206–207:

> India is very advanced in its nuclear energy program and has performed an atomic test in 1974. To divert world attention from its nuclear plans, Bharat launched a propaganda campaign against Pakistan to the effect that Pakistan was manufacturing nuclear weapons. Pakistan categorically contradicted these baseless allegations and proposed that both the countries should adopt such limitations with mutual consent as may be acceptable at international level, putting an end to the possibility of proliferation of nuclear arms in South Asia. *Bharat is not prepared to accept any restriction in this respect and desires that Pakistan should give up its peaceful nuclear energy program. Obviously this is an unrealistic demand.* (emphasis added)

After the nuclear tests in May of 1998, pages 206—207 of this textbook were changed in the 1999 imprint and the substituted comments added in a different font:

> India is very advanced in its nuclear energy program and has performed an atomic test in 1974. To divert world attention from its nuclear plans, Bharat

launched a propaganda campaign against Pakistan to the effect that Pakistan was manufacturing nuclear weapons. Pakistan categorically contradicted these baseless allegations and proposed non-proliferation of nuclear arms in South Asia. *On May 11 and 13, 1998 India detonated five nuclear explosions and threatened the strategic and security balance in the region. Pakistan was compelled to respond in the same language and it conducted its six nuclear explosions on May 28 and 30 of 1998 at Chagi.* (emphasis added)

The day following the nuclear tests, public servants in Pakistan, without their consent, were docked a day's pay to help offset the cost of exploding nuclear devices. Subsequently, Yome Takhbeer Day is celebrated in Pakistan on May 28. The revised curriculum guide suggests that school children draw posters and march in parades to mark the date of Pakistan's ascendancy to nuclear status.

If war begins in people's minds, as the UN Charter suggests, then our minds are prepared for war while we are students. By the time young people become policy makers, the templates of hostility may be deeply embedded in their worldviews. Textbooks can teach students about international cooperation and respect for other cultures, or they can serve as a source of contentiousness—poisoning the diplomatic climate and heightening the chances of war. Notions of militarized nationalism inculcated through the curriculum subvert efforts at international cooperation thereby diminishing the inherent conflict management capacity in South Asia.

CONCLUDING COMMENTS: INVESTIGATING THE POLITICS OF CURRICULUM REFORM

In the countries of the Indian subcontinent, as in most nations, education is viewed as the ultimate social panacea. Claims are ubiquitously made that if properly designed and regulated, education will solve the problems of society and save the nation from an accelerating descent down the road to ruin upon which the citizens, and especially the youth seem to be sliding. Such ideas drive the pervasive machine of educational reform. Education is far more than personal enrichment and skill development; it is the cure-all for a nation's economic and moral woes.

Politicians use education as a rallying cry. Curriculum committees are appointed to transform schools and the contents of textbooks, usually to modernize them and prepare students for the future, and sometimes to return to traditional values, saving the children from "degenerate cultural influences." Education policy may encourage social change or may conversely take the syllabus "back to the basics" to recapture the past glories of bygone eras or guarantee the status quo. These agendas may exist simultaneously, since social paradigms are constantly changing, driven by class conflict and social, religious, and economic cross-purposes. Unfortunately, if educational reform is based on narrow interpretations of religious dogma or the perpetuation of unequal power relations, the society can atrophy. Assuming that education can change a nation's ethos, if curriculum is designed towards basic human values that support individual human rights and international goodwill, it is more likely that future generations will prosper intellectually.

In today's Pakistan, many educators themselves raised on biased, myopic textbooks now see the need to recast the underlying ideologically bound and moribund rhetoric. Hopefully, these forward looking education specialists will be supported in their efforts to develop textbooks which place value on peace and international cooperation, transforming the inherently belligerent orientation of Pakistani social sciences curriculum and contributing to the goal of constructively managing antagonisms in South Asia. A re-evaluation and modification of curriculum policies and educational documents that perpetuate hostile paradigms may help to contribute to the conversation of reconciliation essential for conflict resolution and lasting peace, leading to increased prosperity in South Asia. On the other hand, representatives of the fundamentalist faction, that gained positions of power during Zia's rule when Deeni-Madrassa schools were made equivalent with national universities, still occupy their positions, such as Vice-Chancellors and professors, and are still explicitly involved in shaping the minds of the Pakistani youth through curriculum design and educational policies. Amid allegations of vote rigging, this fundamentalist faction has gained unprecedented political power in the recent elections and continues to hold a dominant position in the socio-political life of Pakistan. This is not a standoff that will be easily resolved.

Investigations into the rhetoric of educational reform can offer constructive insights into curriculum policies though which nations transmit their aspirations for the future. Those seeking peace and justice need relevant information to deal with sources of conflict. Historical perspectives of educational policy can help to shine light on contemporary issues.

Nuclear testing and missile development in the Subcontinent have brought five decades of intermittent animosity and militarization into sharp focus. The expenses and instability associated with hostilities in South Asia have contributed to the economic deprivation of hundreds of millions of citizens. The need for mutual understanding calls for a broader investigation into the sources of antagonism, including the impact of educational policy in the creation of patriotic discourse and political culture.

NOTES

1. This chapter is drawn from a longer study of history textbooks in three nations in the Subcontinent—India, Pakistan, and Bangladesh. That inquiry examined the impact of the politics of pedagogy and of these nations' history books on school children's sense of national identity. See Yvette Clair Rosser, "Curriculum as Destiny: Forging National Identity in India Pakistan, and Bangladesh" (Ph. D. dissertation, The University of Texas at Austin, 2003). Two chapters of that study have been revised slightly and are available in India, published by Rupa: *Islamisation of Pakistani Social Studies Textbooks* (2003) and *Indoctrinating Minds: A Case Study of Bangladesh* (2004). They can also be found at: http://www.observerindia.com/publications/Monograph/monograph.htm

2. The national elections in India, in May 2004, changed the political dispensation, which immediately sought to withdraw the textbooks that were written under the previous government, thus highlighting the political pressures on historiography, also delaying the publication of the volume on Indian historiography. The history wars in India, which are currently in full swing, are indicative of the intellectual forces within a country that seek to control the narrative and base the story of the nation on predetermined politically oriented criteria.

3. "Islamization" is the word that is used in the English editions of *Pakistan* textbooks and in UGC curriculum documents to describe the imperatives of Pakistani Islamic nationalism institutionalized under General Zia ul-Haq. (Abul Ala Mawdudi (Maudidi), founder of the Jamaat-I-Islami, regarded Islamic nationalism as an oxymoronic concept, since, true "Islam" and territorial "Nationalism" are antithetical. Maududi refused to support Jinnah's call for Pakistan because he felt that Islam, an inherently transnational movement, should not be nationalized. Maududi's goal was to Islamize all of India, and therefore saw Pakistan as a territorial limitation. Maududi migrated to Pakistan only after the creation of the nation where he promoted a more exclusively Islamic perspective of Pakistani Islamic nationalism than had been conceived by the founding father, Mohammed Ali Jinnah.)

4. The phonetic spelling of the name of this large linguistic and cultural area that straddles the border between India and Pakistan is "Panjab" meaning "five waters. "The British spelled it as "Punjab" which has been retained in most English language transliterations in Pakistan. Here I have used Panjab, unless "Punjab" appeared in the original.

5. Sustainable Development Policy Institute in Islamabad recently published a study called, "The Subtle Subversion: The State of Curricula and Textbooks in Pakistan" by A.H. Nayyar and Ahmad Salim. This research was strongly criticized by the MMA, the coalition of Islamic political parties.

6. Known as ninth "standard" in Pakistan.

7. University Grants Commission directive, (Islamabad: Mutalliyah-i-Pakistan, Alama Iqbal Open University, 1983), pp. xi.

8. Ibid, p. 165.

9. Ibid, p. 176.

10. This has been accomplished through the ISI (Inter-Services Intelligence), funded largely by the USA.

11.   Religious schools attached to a masjid or mosque.

12.   Thanks to Mir Zohair Husain, Department of Political Science, University of South Alabama, Mobile, for constructive comments regarding Zia's use of the term "Islamization."

13.   Professor Mir Zohair Husain, University of Alabama.

14.   Rabbani, and Sayyid, p. 3.

15.   Ibid.

16.   Ibid, p. 12.

17.   PBUH—Peace Be Upon Him, traditionally added after Muhammad's name.

18.   Rizvi, Hassan Askri, Javed Iqbal, Ghulam Abid Khan. *Pakistan Studies for Secondary Classes,* (Qamer, Lahore: Punjab Textbook Board, 1999), pp. 9–13.

19.   Ibid, p. 65.

20.   Sarwar, p. 136.

21.   Ibid, p. 146.

22.   The Mukti Bahini (Liberation Army) were anti-Pakistani guerrilla soldiers from East Bengal, supported and supplied by India. They spearheaded a nine month civil war which began when Pakistani troops staged a military crack down on March 26, 1971 and massacred thousands of Bengalis/East Pakistanis, including hundreds of students at Dhaka University. On December 16, 1971, Indian troops liberated Dhaka and the independent country of Bangladesh was created.

23.   For example, a headline that ran in the Islamabad edition of the newspaper, *The News,* in June 1999, said, "Nawaz Sharif's Policies are Turning Sindh into Another Bangladesh."

24.   Powell, Avril, "Perceptions of the South Asian Past: Ideology, Nationalism and School History Textbooks," in *The Transmission of Knowledge in South Asia, Essays in Education, Religion, History, and Politics,* ed. Crook, Nigel, (Delhi: Oxford University Press, 1996).

25.   Zafar, M.A. Pakistani Studies for Secondary Education for F.A., etc., (Lahore: 1986), pp. 4–7.

26.   *Geography and Civics, Class VII,* (Lahore: West Pakistan Textbook Board, 1953).

27.   *Geography and Civics, Class VII,* (Lahore: West Pakistan Textbook Board, 1962).

CHAPTER 9

RECONSTRUCTING THE PAST, CONSTRUCTING THE FUTURE IN ISRAELI TEXTBOOKS

Dan Porat

INTRODUCTION [1]

In the short story *The Sermon (Ha-Drasha)*, that captures much of the ambivalence Zionism had towards the Jewish past, Yudka the protagonist argues against the teaching of Jewish history in school:

> It's well known that children everywhere love to read historical fiction. That's where you get action, see, bold deeds, heroes, great fighters, and fearless conquerors. In a word, a world full of heroism. Now, here now, in Palestine, our children love to read, unless they're stupid. I know this for a fact. I've looked into it. Yes, they read, but historical novels about goyim [non-Jews], not about Jews. Why is that so? It's no accident. It's simply because Jewish history is dull, uninteresting. It has no glory or action, no heroes and conquerors, no rulers and masters of their fate, just a collection of wounded, hunted, groaning, and wailing wretches, always begging for mercy. . . . I would simply forbid teaching our children Jewish history. Why the devil teach them about their ancestors' shame? I would say to them: "Boys, from the day we were driven out from our land we've been a people without a history. Class dismissed. Go out and play football.[2]

For Yudka, the teaching of history is aimed at promoting among students national pride, having them feel admiration in their predecessors. Jewish history, however, lacks the elements—courageous actions, admirable heroes, and great victories—that will instill Jewish pride among students. Instead students find in Jewish history suppression, pogroms and poverty. This kind of history discourages students from identifying with their nation. To have a history worth remembering, Yudka continues, a group must gain control over events; that is, one must be physically powerful, guided by nationalism.[3]

Underlying Yudka's concern for the teaching of history is a view that this subject matter is worthy of teaching if, and only if, it promotes students' identification with their nation; history education that deters students' identification with their nation is unworthy of learning. Students read history for national pride, not for national shame. The goal of teaching history as a means for promoting national pride is one possible goal.[4] Those who hold onto this view believe that history education should advance a national collective memory. To achieve this end the historical account is presented as one coherent and progressive story that places the nation at its center. This kind of historical story, writes Seixas, is focused on presenting students with an account that will benefit the nation most, a kind of "best-story" account framed around the nation's history. This kind of "best-story," its advocates claim, has the power to define for students who they are. While these historical accounts have become more inclusive over time, by including, minorities and women, they still retain the "best-story" paradigm.[5]

The term collective memory that underlies this approach is most strongly identified with the views of the early twentieth century sociologist Maurice Halbwachs. Halbwachs explained that the reconstruction of the past "…provides the group with a self-portrait that unfolds through time," a viewpoint that orientates the group towards a common future[6] through education, social interaction, the media, and other forms of communication, the past is reconstructed to form a meaningful past for the citizenry. This historical story helps the group understand its present situation and endure over time as a cohesive and united group.

An approach that Yudka did not suggest is one that views the goal of history teaching as one aimed at advancing critical thinking. This disciplinary approach takes the historian and his professional actions as a model for emulation. Ideally, the students would focus their attention on the analysis of documents, followed by synthesis and culminating with a narrative. The student's narrative would present a multifaceted perspective on history, a view that would highlight the advantages and disadvantages of different interpretations of an event. This view sees the discipline of history primarily as an interpretative method, as a curricular subject that aims to develop the critical thinking skills of students.

Yudka thought it impossible to promote a collective memory approach in the teaching of Jewish history since the nature of Jewish history as a history full of "Oppression, defamation, persecution, martyrdom," did not allow for it. Israel's education system did not, however, adopt the gloomy perspective of Yudka.[7] In Israel, the teaching of history has occupied a central place in the national curriculum over the past fifty years. History education is a key tool in the formation of a national identity for the Jews gathered in Israel after its establishment. This population, especially in the early years of the state, came from the four corners of the world. No language, no culture, no belief system united these Jews. Not much united the one million Jews assembled in Israel, including six hundred thousand who came as new immigrants after the state's establishment in 1948. These Jews spoke more than seventy languages and dialects and came from distinct cultures. Neither did these Jews share one religious orientation. Therefore, history was one potential uniting point and the educational authorities employed it to advance this unity.

In the pages that follow, I focus my attention on the nature of historical reconstruction in Israeli history textbooks since the establishment of the state in 1948. I concentrate upon the way one historical period, the Second Temple era, has been portrayed in textbooks and examine this reconstruction to explore the goal of history teaching as advancing a national collective memory and promoting a critical approach.

In following the altering representation of one historical era in Israeli textbooks from the 1950s to the 1990s, my key concern is to understand the social and political goals that have shaped the nature of this historical depiction. In other words, I examine how the altering social and political circumstances in Israel shaped the history depicted in the textbooks. In my analysis I focus on textbooks that have been most widely circulated in Israel's secular education system.

The Second Temple era is commonly dated between the 538 BCE "Cyrus Declaration" in which the Persian king permitted Jews to return to Zion (*Shivat Zion*) from their Babylonian exile, and 70 CE when Rome destroyed the Second Temple. However, while traditional Judaism marked the end of the Second Temple era with the destruction of the Temple, the Zionist movement shifted the end of this era to the Bar-Kokhba Revolt against the Romans that ended in 135 CE. By shifting the end of the era from a religious disaster to a national revolt, from the destruction of the Second Temple to the Bar Kokhba Revolt, the Zionist movement highlighted its movement away from Jewish history as a religious history to Jewish history as a national history.

Within the Second Temple era, I will focus my attention on three events that have played a key role in the formation of Israel's national collective memory:

1. The Hasmonean Revolt—a second century BCE rebellion against the Greeks. The leader of the rebels, Judah Maccabee, kindled the fire of revolt in 167 BCE, took Jerusalem and purified the Temple in 164 BCE. As a result of the revolt a Jewish autonomy developed in Judea for decades to follow. This event is traditionally celebrated in the holiday of Hanukkah.

2. The Masada episode—an event that took place in 73 CE in which a group of Sicarii, a Second Temple Jewish sect which had its own unique religious philosophy, headed by Eleazar, son of Jair, left besieged Jerusalem, crossed the Judean Desert and occupied the fortress of Masada on the shore of the Dead Sea. After the Romans besieged the fortress the 960 refugees died at their own hands instead of surrendering. With the fall of Masada ended the Jewish Revolt that began in 70 CE.

3. The Bar Kokhba Revolt—in 132 CE the Jews in the Land of Israel revolted against Roman rule. In the first stages of the revolt the Jews were successful; the rebels liberated parts of the country and nominated Simon Bar Kokhba as leader (*nasi*).[8] However, the Roman Empire sent their legions to stop the rebels, and, in 135 CE the Romans reclaimed the land and suppressed Jewish settlement. The Romans killed hundreds of thousands and sold many more into slavery, while those remaining were subjugated by Roman occupation and a series of harsh laws[9]

These three events have served as central events in the public memory of Israeli society and as a result have occupied a significant place in the teaching of Jewish history in Israeli schools.

A UNITING PAST

In a 1961 educational conference, an official in the Ministry of Education, Yochanan Ginat, pointed out that "We dedicate a large portion of our education to teaching the ancient history of our nation and there are reasons for this. Our life in the land connects to the ancient era... [to the] Biblical and Bar Kokhba eras."[10] It was no coincidence that Israeli history education centered upon this historical era. For the gamut of Jews gathered from the four corners of the world the one (and possibly only) uniting point in their history was the history they shared two thousand years ago.

Furthermore, that history was directly associated with the Land of Israel where they planned to establish their new home. Indeed the leaders of the Jewish population in Palestine, later to become the State of Israel, highlighted the link between the ancient past of the Jews in the land and their modern return. Drawing upon this ancient and common past served to establish a common historical frame of reference for the Jews assembled in modern Israel.[11]

The textbooks of the 1950s and 1960s centered on demonstrating the common tradition that united the Jews assembled in Israel. One important means of doing this was the selection of sources cited in textbooks. Authors chose to highlight Jewish sources in their depiction and ignored those which professional historians considered most credible. In the case of the Bar Kokhba Revolt, the account of a Greek historian, Dio Cassius, which "all researchers" described as "the sole consistent survey of the revolt," was largely absent.[12] Instead textbooks cited legends from the Jewish Talmud, a collection of discussions and contemplations on Jewish tradition and law. From a total of fourteen citations that appeared in five textbooks, twelve were from Jewish sources and only one citation was from Dio Cassius.[13]

Alienation from non-Jewish sources also appeared in the historical narrative that guided the textbooks. For example, the introduction to the one hundred years of confrontation between Jews and Greeks during the Hasmonean Revolt one textbook asserts that:

On the seashores of the Mediterranean lived for hundreds of years, two nations very different from one another and very hostile to one another.... And when the Israelite nation, with its high morals and culture, encountered the Greek culture it appeared as a small island in the great sea of Greek culture. Despite that [the Israelite nation] stayed faithful to its tradition and decided to stand up and overcome the great threat facing it. And why could the Israelite nation not adopt the Greek culture as other nations did? Jerusalem and Athens—two worlds distanced from one another!.... in their personal traits and lifestyle the Greeks were foreign to the spirit of Israel. The Greek with their light spirit lived a life of pleasures and indulgences. In contrast, the Jews excelled in simplicity and humbleness, in seriousness and morals, good manners and love of humans ... Not by might and nor by power, but by My spirit– the Israelite nation saw its way in life, and passed it on to its sons. The determined Greek nation, with the military force that conquered the entire ancient world, strived to undermine Judah's weak image, but [Judah remained] strong in spirit and belief.[14]

This text drew a stark contrast between the Jewish nation and the Greek nation. It matched a culturally dominant view in Israeli society in the 1950s in which the few overcome the many, in which the spirit overcomes power, in which the few Jews overcome the many non-Jews. According to this viewpoint the Jewish nation had a unique positioning in the world, one repeated throughout its history until the present. Like the Jews that were outnumbered by the Greeks, so the Jews in Israel outnumbered by the Arab nations would, thanks to their unique spirit, overcome the hostile Arabs. In pointing to the uniqueness of the Jews and to those aspects that distinguished them from any other nation on earth, the authors of these textbooks highlighted the aspects that united Jews into one nation.

While in the case of the Hasmonean Revolt, Jews had been able to sustain their autonomy despite Greek attempts to the contrary, in the case of the Masada and the Bar Kokhba Revolt they were defeated and dispersed. How could such a disastrous history serve as a source of pride for teenagers reading this history almost two thousand years later? How could it advance student identification with the newly formed nation? After all, the warriors on Masada had died, the Bar Kokhba Revolt was suppressed and the Jewish nation defeated.

To resolve this issue, textbook authors attempted to re-focus readers attention in these events from the final defeat to the initial victory. Many books portrayed the Roman conquest as one that almost failed due to the relentless opposition of the Jews. For example, in the case of the Bar Kokhba Revolt the authors portrayed the defeat of the Jews as a prolonged series of events. By placing greater emphasis on the offensive parts of the revolt and downplaying the defensive, by highlighting the initial victory over the final defeat, textbooks presented these periods as great chapters in Jewish history despite their disastrous results.[15]

Authors further downplayed the defeat by linking past and present, by portraying the establishment of the modern Jewish state as a statement of final Jewish victory. The goal was to create a connection between the modern Jewish State and the second century Jewish kingdom. In summarizing the Masada event, the authors of a popular textbook contend that:

> Three years after the destruction of the Temple, Masada also fell, the final fortress of the Zealots, but the memory of the courageous acts of the heroes of Masada is safeguarded in the nation's memory forever, and when we climb the cliffs of that mountain today… our heart will fill with pride to those courageous fighters that have sacrificed as a symbol for generations their life for their own freedom and the nation's freedom.[16]

By leaping some one thousand nine hundred years ahead the authors linked modern day Israelis with their heroic ancestors atop Masada and set the end of the event in the victorious present.

In fact, although the Sicarii group besieged atop Masada was a Jewish sect, the Jews today are associated with a different philosophy, that of Pharisaism. The Pharisaic sect in fact was opposed to the religious viewpoint of the Sicarii and to their religious doctrine. For example, the Sicarii's refused to submit to anyone besides God, a religious perspective that resulted in their suicide atop Masada. The Pharisaic sect, however, opposed this viewpoint. Despite this discontinuity between Sicarii and modern Jews, the author's of textbooks continuously referred to the heroes of Masada as Jews hinting again at a link between the heroes of Masada and modern Israelis.[17]

Textbooks in the Israel of the 1950s and 1960s assisted in the formation of the new Jewish nation. A unified presentation of history to all Israelis, whether newcomers or veterans, was, according to Ben-Zion Dinur, the Minister of Education, vital for the formation of national unity. There would be no compromises. Responding to a demand for a special curriculum for the new immigrants, Dinur stated:

> I revolt against this idea in all my body and soul. Who gave you the permission? In America or in France is there a separate program for immigrants? We bring the new immigrants to Israel and we want their entrance to be complete; an entrance of cultural identification... There will never be different curricula for new immigrants.[18]

Despite the existence of diverse populations, there was only one curriculum that would achieve a united citizenry. The emphasis of history textbooks was on creating a national collective memory, not on developing critical thinking among students.

AN "OBJECTIVE" PAST

In the 1970s new curricular ideas developed among scholars in the United States as well as in the United Kingdom (where it was known as "New History"). American researchers such as Benjamin Bloom, David Krathwohl, and Jerome Bruner, argued that too many educational objectives centered upon simple lower order tasks such as recall.[19] These researchers called for a shift to an approach that included the application of theories and concepts, detailed analysis of material, and the synthesis and evaluation of evidence. The goal was to emulate scientific disciplines, since: "Any subject can be taught in some intellectually honest form to any child at any stage of development."[20]

The Israeli history curriculum published in 1970, pursued students' attainment of academic conceptions as a primary aim. From eight curriculum principles, the majority focused on cognitive goals such as the comprehension of historical concepts and the development of historical thought.[21] Furthermore, students would develop their own assumptions "...to explain historical events;" increase their historical empathy through "entering the web of life embedded in the relics and documents in our hands," as well as seeking "...in a systematic manner, the different causes and results which may serve as possible explanations for historical events."[22] The final goal, however, continued to focus upon forming a national collective memory requiring that history education "...foster [among students] a sense of identification with the nation and the state."[23]

As a result of the new curriculum, historians became an integral part of curricular development teams. This change showed up immediately in the new textbooks and the manner in which authors used traditional Jewish sources differed significantly from their use in earlier books. While early textbooks used legends to illuminate the historical protagonists, the new books focused on informative citations. For example, when these textbooks discussed the history of the rabbis in the aftermath of Second Temple they turned to traditional texts and used them as historical sources, and when it came to the history of military actions the authors avoided traditional texts.[24]

Furthermore, the most detailed and reliable source for this historical period, Josephus Flavius, who had been rejected by Israeli society in the 1950s and 1960s as a traitor since he surrendered to the Romans after his fellow fighters committed suicide, is cited numerous times in new textbooks published in the 1970s. The actions of Josephus when he joined the Roman camp are not held against him anymore, or as the authors of the most commonly used textbook of this period state, "...the central source for knowing the history of event in the Land of Israel [in Second Temple] are Josephus ben-Matatyahu's two books.... Josephus took an active part [in the Great Revolt] as the commander of the Jewish forces in the Galilee. After the destruction of the Second Temple he moved to Rome and there he wrote his two books...."[25] The new textbook made no reference to Josephus's alleged betrayal. In fact, the text hints that he joined the Romans only after the Revolt failed.

The change in the nature of historical sources was clearly expressed in the case of the Bar Kokhba Revolt. While textbooks of the previous generation cited solely Jewish traditional sources, the three new books published during the 1970s and 1980s had a diverse collection of citations: seven from Rabbinic sources, six from Dio Cassius and eight from archaeological findings (especially from scrolls written by Simon Bar Kokhba found in 1960s in archaeological digs).

Not only did the sources alter but also the images of key protagonists lost much of their vitality between the 1950s and 1970s. In the case of the Hasmonean Revolt the leader, Judah Maccabee, no longer played a central role in the depiction of the textbook. His name almost appears tangentially. Instead, the focus of the textbook is centered on the strategic movements of the forces. Judah Maccabee, who appeared in the past as an unearthly figure, is portrayed in the post-1970s textbooks in a very conventional manner. The initial successes of the revolt is attributed not to the revolt's leader, it is accredited to the common troops who emerged every night from the caves and entered villages and cities.[26]

Yet, although they avoided a "glorious" account, the new textbooks failed to achieve the ambitious cognitive goals stated in the 1970 curriculum. Contrary to the goals of the curriculum, the authors did not allow students to participate in the process of reconstructing an historical event, in developing historical hypotheses, or in analyzing sources.[27] In the textbooks, historical material appeared as a fixed and unalterable narrative. The sources validated the authors' "best story" of the past. For example, Elazar Ben-Yair's speech, reported in Josephus Flavius's book, is presented word-by-word without any attempt to have the student analyze it. Rather, the student is presented with the authors' authoritative interpretation, leaving no space for individual analysis and interpretation. The authors frame the historical event from one vantage point, one that, due to its monolithic nature, could help create a shared memory in students' minds.

Furthermore, the authors implicitly continue to attempt to shape students' contemporary identification. Consider, for example, the following excerpt from the textbook account of the Masada event:

[Following the Great Revolt] a few groups of Zealots entrenched themselves in three remaining fortresses and decided to continue the revolt. The most famous of these groups was the one fortified on Masada.... About 1000 people, men, women and children gathered there with a firm decision in their heart: not to surrender to the Romans....But also now [after the Romans broke the fortress's wall] the people of Masada did not surrender.... They gathered and did one of the most horrendous acts that occurred in our nation's history: The men grabbed their swords and in their very own hands killed their children and women. The remaining killed each other and then the last person killed himself. In this way the people of Masada chose to die, instead of becoming slaves. On that day died the people of Masada. But their death continues to live in the nation's consciousness as a symbol of the love of freedom that even death will not deter.[28]

As is clearly noticeable in this text, the authors portray the event of Masada as a model of national admiration. They do not present alternative interpretations and viewpoints on the actions of the Masada people, for example they do not mention the likely possibility that these people killed themselves and their families due not to national dedication but rather due to religious dedication. Also, they do not highlight a viewpoint that sees the acts of the people on Masada as involving the murdering of women and children.[29] Rather, these authors chose to have the event fortify the present day national identification of students.

In sum, the textbooks of the 1970s presented a canonical account of Second Temple, one that, on the one hand, uses valid historical sources, but on the other hand still continues to communicate a "best-story" scenario that enhances student identification with the nation. Consequently, they avoid the central goal of the new history curricula published in the 1970s of promoting critical historical skills. Although they largely avoid the explicit missionary goal of earlier textbooks, these newer textbooks focus on communicating a master narrative for the future Israeli citizenry.

THE POST-NATIONAL PERIOD

The Israel of the 1990s had lost much of the national zeal that had driven it in the first decades of its existence. Yitzhak Rabin, elected in 1992 as Prime Minister, presented a new agenda to Israeli society, one centered not only on achieving peace, but also on transforming Israel's social priorities from a policy focused on the occupied territories to one focused primarily upon internal social issues. In his inauguration speech on July 13, 1992, Rabin stated from the Knesset podium that:

> In the last decade of the twentieth century, the atlases, history and geography books no longer present an up-to-date picture of the world. Walls of enmity have fallen, borders have disappeared....

He then went on to state that,

> It is our duty, to ourselves and to our children, to see the new world as it is now—to discern its dangers, explore its prospects, and do everything possible so that the State of Israel will fit into this world whose face is changing. No longer are we necessarily "A people that dwells alone," and no longer is it true that "the whole world is against us." We must overcome the sense of isolation that has held us in its thrall for almost half a century...[30]

Rabin presented Israel with a new social agenda, one more open to universal trends and morals considerations. He strove to undo many of the ideological tenets underlying Israel's policy over the past decades. This demanded a change in educational values, a change strongly advocated by the different Ministers of Education who served under Rabin and those who served after his assassination in November of 1995.

The political arena was not the only place where the environment in Israel had changed. The late 1980s and early 1990s witnessed the rise of "the new historians," a group of mostly foreign-educated young historians (also commonly known as post-Zionist historians), who called for a more self-critical formulation of Jewish history. This reformulation of history focused upon topics in modern Jewish history—the Israeli-Arab conflict, the treatment of new immigrants—but it also impacted upon earlier historical periods such as the Bible period and Second Temple era.

The changes in the Israeli political, academic and cultural environment shaped similar changes in Israel's education system. The presentation of a new historiography in the academic world and the rise of a demand for a civil society also penetrated the educational realm. A new edition of the national history curricula was published in 1995. This edition signalled a shift away from the national focus of the two previous curricula and highlighted instead social and cultural perspectives. "National history is one component within [history], just as other parts of history make up other components of it: the history of women or the history of sports or modern history. Each one is a frame within the larger frame [of history]," emphasized Moshe Zimmerman, the head of the curriculum committee and professor of German history at the Hebrew University.[31]

In the introduction to the new curriculum the designers reiterated the list of introductory goals that appeared in the 1975 curriculum, including that which required that students acknowledge the uniqueness of the people of Israel among the nations, in their essence and destiny.[32] But contrary to this stated goal the syllabus presented Jewish history as a sub-topic, albeit a recurring one, of a greater global historical framework. For example, Zionism, the ideological foundation of Israel, surfaced only as a sub-topic of nationalism. Similarly, the establishment of the state surfaced only as a sub-topic of the Cold War.[33] Finally, the Holocaust, an event of greatest magnitude for the Jewish people and a central event in Israelis' identity, emerged as a sub-topic of World War II.

In an elementary school textbook on Second Temple history published in light of the new curriculum, the shift away from a national focus was noticeable from the cover's title. The textbook's Hebrew title read *In Greek and Roman Times*. This title made no reference to the Jewish past.[34] In fact the number of chapters dedicated to non-Jewish history exceeded the chapters that discussed Jewish history. Whereas non-Jewish history was discussed in fourteen chapters, Jewish history was the subject of only ten chapters.

In her reconstruction of specific events from within Jewish history, the author, Bruria Ben Baruch, distanced herself from the Jewish-centered national perspective. For example, in the case of the Bar-Kokhba Revolt the author cited only the Greek source of Dio Cassius regarding the revolt.[35] The traditional Jewish sources, which had been the center of the reconstruction of the Bar-Kokhba Revolt in earlier periods, were completely absent. In her account of Bar-Kokhba, Ben Baruch gave a different portrayal of his image from that appeared in earlier textbooks. "The Christians whom he persecuted saw him as a thief and murderer. The sages of Israel, that probably admired his personality, describe him as a strong and heroic figure, a difficult and assertive person...."[36] Bar Kokhba's image comes across in Ben Baruch's account as an ambivalent figure, one who can be seen either as a villain or as a hero.

But this ambivalent figure's actions resulted in disastrous consequences for the Jewish nation. In the introduction to the chapter Ben Baruch points out that "Bar Kokhba and many of his companions were killed in battle. Tens of the thousands were slaughtered, sold to slavery or died in hunger." She then goes on to ask the student, "In light of the revolt's results was it justified? If you would live in the days of Bar Kokhba would you join the revolt or would you oppose it? Why?"[37] While the author does not state it explicitly, it is quite clear from the sequencing of the text and the following question that students are expected to answer these questions in the negative. National values came second to individual ones.

Ben Baruch's account of Masada adopted a critical perspective of the event, anchored in a present day universal perspective. After portraying the people assembled on Masada not as a group of Jews but rather as a group of Sicarii, Ben Baruch goes on to describe their last choice of death not as an act of heroism but rather as a killing of one another "The Zelots of Masada chose to die rather than be taken to captivity. They set the buildings on fire and then each one killed his family members in his very own hands. Ten people drawn by lottery killed the remaining defenders and then committed suicide..."[38] The author gave no reference to the people of Masada as heroes. Rather, she presents the students with an assignment that questions this "heroic" act. This perspective matched growing tendencies in Israeli society of this period to question the validity of sacrificing one's life for the nation. The significance of one's individual life had been raised high above previously shared collective values such as defending one's homeland.

In a similar manner the author put a growing emphasis upon the role that international politics played in the Jewish history of Second Temple. For example, in her discussion of the Hasmonean Revolt the author highlights not only the strategic abilities of Judah Maccabee but also the Hasmoneans' political wisdom in the international arena:

> The Jews that followed Matetyahu and his sons had a very strong religious faith and they believed that God would assist them in overcoming their enemies. But their leaders also knew how to manoeuvre the international situation in their favor. In those days rose a new super-power that got stronger and stronger—Rome.... The Romans offered Judah Maccabee help in his struggle against the Seleucid leader [who was their enemy] and Judah forged an alliance with them. This alliance, with the super power of the period, strengthened the Hasmoneans power significantly.[39]

The Jews' success was not dependent anymore on their actions alone as it was in previous textbooks. Rather the assistance of foreign powers played a significant part in the building up of Jewish power. Jewish independence was not their personal achievement but also part of a global constellation.

Within her narrative, the author of the textbook integrated some critical elements. For example, she constantly uses the words "possibly" or "may have" in her account, as well as acknowledging the lack of historical sources in some cases. Still, she did narrate the past for students and, therefore, did not fulfil her own commitment that students should learn to ask the questions, and develop an independent view and should participate in historical analysis.[10] The author avoided students' analysis of historical sources, or their narration of events. This textbook, as in others before it, communicated the past in a conclusive manner, advancing what its authors believed was the "best-story." It communicated this story with the goal of forming a collective memory for students; however, this time it portrayed events such as Masada and the Bar Kokhba Revolt in disastrous terms as it matched the concurrent political, cultural and academic tendencies better.

DISCUSSION AND CONCLUSION

In the years between the 1950s and the 1990s Israeli history textbooks altered their presentation of Second Temple era significantly. The historical account changed with the changing spirit of times. The Hasmonean Revolt shifted from an event focused on inner-national powers in the 1950s to one focused on international issues in the 1990s. From admirable events in the 1950s the Masada episode and the Bar Kokhba Revolt have become disastrous events in the 1990s. What, therefore, should we make of this change?

To some extent the new textbooks seem to set history straight, or as some educationalists would claim, they incorporate the new findings of historical research into textbooks. But this is a too simplistic, if not misleading, conclusion. Research in the field of history rarely comes to an agreed viewpoint, while history textbooks rarely present a varied account of the past.

A key element in textbook depiction is appeasing contemporary social and political factors. History textbooks communicate a contemporary past, one that matches the prevailing social and political needs. The changes are not dictated by changes in our historical knowledge. Rather, political and cultural issues are the ones that shape the presentation of history in the educational realm. Much of the scholarship included in the new series of Israeli textbooks was known decades ago. The history presented in the textbooks is one that highlights "the true" perspective of the past, a truth that best fits the social and political circumstances of the day. From the array of possible historical accounts the one the authors choose is the one that will appease as many powerful individuals and groups as possible.[11]

What alternative exists to a history dictated by powerful political and ideological pressure groups? Instead of textbooks that present one authoritative account of the past, with a "best-story," we should aspire to have students walk away from the lesson with alternative accounts. By presenting the historical sources and their different readings we will highlight alternative interpretations and even contrasting interpretations of the past. Students exposed to this kind of history education would progress beyond the presentist history that dominates today's textbooks. It would allow them for a more complex way of seeing the past, one that would enhance their critical thinking abilities.

Today history education in Israel appears as a true and unalterable account of the past. By presenting an authoritative past the textbooks convey to students a misleading perception of what the discipline of history is about. Textbooks communicate to students that history as subject matter centered primarily on accumulation of information, not on argumentation. In communicating a fixed and final account, textbooks deprive students of the capacity to know historically. They advance not history education but memory indoctrination.

In contrast to representations of memory, historical accounts never comes to a full stop. It is continuously altered. The past is always dynamic and changing with alternative viewpoints and interpretations. In memory, as in the "best story scenario" history arrives, for some time at least, to final, fixed, unchangeable conclusions, as is the case in Israeli history textbooks.[42] Rather than teach students the national collective memory of an event—an account that they will most likely pick up from the public sphere in which they reside—one should choose to shift back to the teaching of history education in disciplinary terms. This kind of history is the one as it appears in the discipline, as a changing account with continuously differing viewpoints. This kind of history education can educate students to know in a critical sense. It will help advance the ability of students to participate in a democratic society, a society that continuously offers alternative interpretations and viewpoints. By focusing on the disciplinary viewpoint of teaching history, on the analysis of sources as well as on alternative interpretations we will advance instead of memory indoctrination history education, a way of learning that supports society's democratic foundations. That is a journey that the writers of textbooks and the framers of curriculum models in Israel have yet to make.

NOTES

1. This study was possible thanks to the generous support of the Memorial Foundation for Jewish Culture.

2. P. Alter, *Modern Hebrew Literature* (New York: Behrman House, 1975), pp. 273–275.

3. Ibid.

4. P. Seixas, "Schweigen! Die Kinder! Or, Does Postmodern History Have a Place in Schools?" in *Knowing Teaching and Learning History,* eds. P. N. Stearns, P. Seixas and S. Wineburg (New York: New York University Press, 2000), pp. 19–37; A. Segall, "Critical History: Implications for History/ Social Studies Education," *Theory and Research in Social Education, 27* (1999), pp. 358–374.

5. Seixas, Ibid.

6. M. Halbwachs, *The Collective Memory* (1950; reprint, New York: Harper and Row, 1980), p. 86.

7. The Israeli education system is centralized. Since the 1950s the Ministry of Education has published lists of approved textbooks for use in the classroom that have been screened by the Ministry. I base my determination on the basis of data collected by the Ministry in different instances. In 1962 the Ministry of Education conducted a comprehensive survey in 91% of the elementary schools of the textbooks used in the education system (Source: ISA GL 1814 22/14). See also R. Raz, M. Paduah and A. Doron, "Ha-moreh le-historian be-beit ha-sefer ha-mamad u-gishato le-camah me-markevi tochnit ha-limudiem" [The history teacher in the religious school and the attitude to components of the curriculum] *Halacha le-masehe be-tichnon limudiem,* 4, p. 78; J. Wolf, *Mekomah shel ha-haracha be-hachnat tocniot limudiem chadasha be-hisotriah* [The place of assessment in the preparation of a new curriculum in history]. (Jerusalem: The Ministry of Education, 1992).

8. For reasons of diction I translate the word *nasi* as leader and not president.

9. M. Mor, *Mered Bar Kokhba Otsmato ve Hekefo* (The Bar Kokhba Revolt, its Extent and Effect), (Jerusalem: Yad Yitshak ben Tsevi, 1991); M. E. Smallwood, *The Jews Under Roman Rule* (Leiden: E. J. Brill, 1976).

10. Ministry of Education, Israel, *Horat ha-Shoah be-Veit ha-Sefer* (Jerusalem: Proceedings on Teaching the Holocaust in Schools, 1961), p. 75.

11. Y. Zerubavel, *Recovered Roots: Collective Memory and the Making of Israeli National Tradition* (Chicago: University of Chicago Press, 1995); S. Almog, *Zionism and History: The Rise of a New Jewish Consciousness* (New York: St. Martin's Press, 1987).

12. B. Issac and A. Oppenheimer, "The Revolt of Bar Kokhba: Ideology and Modern Scholarship," *Journal of Jewish Studies* 36 (1985),pp. 33–60; See also, M. Stern, *Greek and Latin Authors on Jews and Judaism* (Jerusalem: Israel Academy of Sciences and Humanities, 1980).

13. M. Shmueli, *Korot Amenu* (Jerusalem: Tarbut ve-Chinuch, 1958).

14. B. Avivi and N. Perski, *Toldot Am Yisrael,* Volume 1, (Tel Aviv: Yavneh Publishing House, 1962), pp. 125–126.

15. D. Porat, "A Contemporary Past: History Textbooks as Sites of National Memory," in *International Review of History Education, Volume 3* eds. A. Dickinson, P. Gordon and P. Lee, (London: Woburn Press, 2001), pp. 36–55.

16. B. Ahiyah and M. Harpaz, *Toldot am Yisrael* (Tel Aviv: Srerbek, 1957) p. 192.

17. See B. Ben-Yehuda, *The Masada Myth: Collective Memory and Myth Making in Israel* (Madison, Wis.,: University of Wisconsin Press, 1995); Zerubavel, Ibid.

18. Cited in Z. Zameret, "Ben Zion Dinur Bein Mamlactiyut ve-Tenuatiyut," in *The Challenge of Independence—Ideological and Cultural Aspects of Israel's First Decade*, ed. B. Mordechai (Jerusalem: Yad Ben-Zvi Institute, 1999), p. 50.

19. B. S. Bloom, et. al., *Taxonomy of Educational Objectives* (New York: Longmans, 1956).

20. J. Bruner, *The Process of Education* (Cambridge: Harvard University Press, 1960), p. 33.

21. Ministry of Education, Israel, *Tochnit ha-Limudim be-Historiah le-Kitot Vav-Tet be-Veit ha-Sefer ha-Mamlachti ve-ha-Mamlachti-Dati* (History Curriculum: Grades 6–9 in National and National-Religious Schools, Jerusalem, 1970).

22. Ibid, Objectives 5.32, 5.22, 5.21.

23. Op.cit. Objective 11.

24. S.Shavit, ed., *Shiuriem be-Historia, Kerech 2* (History Lessons, Vol. 2) (Jerusalem: Ministry of Education, 1987).

25. Ibid, p. 55.

26. S. Shavit ed., *Shiuriem be-Historia, Kerech 1* (History Lessons, Vol. 1) (Jerusalem: Ministry of Education, 1974).

27. L. Adar and S. Fox, *Nituch Tochnit Limudiem be-Historyah u-Bitzuah be-Veit ha-Sefer* (An Analysis of the Content and Use of a History Curriculum) (Jerusalem, 1978).

28. Shavit, op.cit. p. 103.

29. Ben-Yehuda, Ibid.

30. *Divrei ha-Knesset*, July 13, 1992, pp. 8–10; See also R. Slater, *Rabin of Israel—A Biography* (London: Robson Books, 1993) p. 417.

31. Zimmerman, interview by author, August 14, 1998.

32. Ministry of Education, Israel, *Tochnit Limudiem—Historiah le-Kitot Vav-Tet ba-Chinuch ha-Mamlachti* (History Curriculum: Grades 6–9 in National Education) (Jerusalem, 1995).

33. Ibid, pp. 25–26.

34. The English title of the book *Greeks, Romans, Jews* includes the word "Jews" while the Hebrew version did not.

35. B. Ben Baruch, *Greeks, Romans, Jews* (Tel Aviv: Tel Aviv Books, 1996).

36. Ibid, p. 161.

37. Op.cit. pp. 158; 163

38. Op.cit. p. 149

39. Op.cit., p. 72

40. Op.cit., p. 6

41. For a discussion of the economic considerations that shape the writing of textbooks in the United States see, F. Fitzgerald, *America Revised: History Schoolbooks in The Twentieth Century* (Boston, MA: Little, Brown, 1979).

42. Samuel S. Wineburg, "On the Reading of Historical Texts: Notes on the Breach Between School and Academy," *American Educational Research Journal* 28 (1991).

CHAPTER 10

CONTROL THROUGH
EDUCATION?

The Politicization of Israeli and Palestinian
School Textbooks

Jonathan Kriener

INTRODUCTION

Since 2002, intense discussions have been held in the European Parliament regarding Palestinian education. Two key issues emerged from these
debates. The first concerned the extent to which the donor states for the
Palestinian National Authorities (PNA) should unconditionally use their
funds to maintain the Palestinian education system. The second revolved
around the issue of whether or not the European community should
attempt to enforce the weeding out of unacceptable content, in particular
anti-Semitic content and those idealizing martyrs' deaths, by threatening to
reduce aid.[1] Although the content of Arabic school books in neighboring
countries far exceeds the Palestinian ones with respect to stereotyping and
anti-Semitism, the debate in Europe (and in the U.S.) has not been nearly
as passionate. But what impact do school textbooks have? Are they the
mouthpiece of elites or do they express the collective sentiment of society?

What Shall We Tell the Children?, pages 211–225
Copyright © 2006 by Information Age Publishing
All rights of reproduction in any form reserved.

If the latter is true, would not an attempt to exert financial pressure on textbook content be in vain? To what extent do their contents correlate with the ruling system and what impact do the vicissitudes of internal and external political processes have on them? In this chapter I examine these issues based upon examples of curricula for human-sciences related subjects in Israel and the PNA. For this purpose analysis will focus upon the findings of the most significant publications available since 2000 when international debates on Palestinian textbooks began.

THE ISRAELI SCHOOL SYSTEM

Under the British mandate the comparatively well organized Zionist-Jewish Yishuv (settling community) established a number of schools in Palestine where Jewish pupils were taught in Hebrew and learnt Jewish national values. At the beginning of the 1950s these were integrated into one system under the control of the Ministry of Education in the new Israeli state. Today the system consists of state-run religious schools (15%); state-run general schools (54%) and private religious schools (11%). Approximately 20% of the school system serves the Arabic sector.[2] For lower secondary education (Years 7–12) the canon of subjects taught stipulates an equal proportion of lessons in the pupils' mother tongue; foreign languages; mathematics; natural and human sciences. A striking feature is the high proportion of Bible lessons and Jewish studies that represents 10% of the curriculum in state-run secular schools. Significantly, state-run religious schools focus upon the Bible and Jewish studies and this makes up almost 25% of lessons taught. The proportion of time devoted to Arabic culture, Islamic or Christian religion in schools in the Arab sector is far lower while a focus is placed upon language training in Arabic, Hebrew and English. Since the foundation of the state of Israel and, in particular, in reaction to the influx of migrants, one of the key aims of the school system has been the integration of groups of immigrants with varying cultures into a Jewish Israeli nation.

STAGES OF DEVELOPMENT IN ISRAELI
CURRICULUM POLICY

Israeli scholars have defined three developmental stages within the Israeli school system.[3] In 1953, an Education Act grouped together the various Jewish school systems established during the British mandate to form the Israeli school system described above. The Ministry of Education followed a curriculum approach where the principal aim of history and social science teaching was to identify young people with the state and to familiarize them with the values prevalent in society. As a consequence little importance was attached to learning about the Arabs and Arab history and culture was given little space within the curriculum. Arabs were presented simplistically as opponents of the Zionist movement. In most cases, Arab motives were neglected and their behavior was explained in terms of "backwardness" and religious fanaticism or their misinterpretation of the Zionist movement.

The Six Day War in 1967 marked the beginning of a second developmental stage for the curriculum. On the one hand the occupation of the West Bank and the Gaza Strip enforced the need for dealing carefully with the inhabitants of occupied territories. Moreover, this occupation led to the Arabs becoming a more visible presence and focus in Israeli public awareness. The pressure to familiarize oneself with the Palestinian cause was also enhanced by the fact that the Palestine Liberation Organization (PLO) was declared the sole representative of the Palestinian people by the Arab League in 1968, having already gained public notoriety through some spectacular guerrilla actions in 1967.

Academics became involved in consultations on the curricula and the debate changed the traditional approach of history lessons that focused on the teaching of collective values to a new approach that heralded historical science and history lessons as constructivist discourses on various aspects and perspectives. School reforms in 1966 saw the introduction of teaching approaches that included the discussion of sources where the emotional world of the learner became an integral part of the curriculum. Unease about the legitimacy of the occupation, and especially about the Yom Kippur War in 1973, as well as fostering a deeper understanding and stronger emotional bond to Zionism also resulted in a reaction to chauvinist attitudes through including an enhanced knowledge of Arab neighbors and opponents.

This was largely due to pressure exerted on the Ministry of Education by parents and teachers alarmed by the lack of teaching about Arabs in school. In 1975 this pressure led to a shift of focus from ancient Jewish history to Zionist and later history of the Diaspora. It also resulted in a concerted focus upon a short period in which The Arab-Israeli conflict (a textbook and teaching unit) became a compulsory part of the history curriculum and an optional topic in civic education (*Ezrahut*) in upper secondary education. According to Mathias the eventual failure of this teaching unit was due to its pedagogical deficiencies, which is why, contrary to the curriculum framework, many teachers continued working with school books written in the 1960s.[4]

The conclusion of a peace treaty with Egypt in 1979, and the Israeli military campaign in Lebanon in 1982, once again unhinged long-standing certainties about the relationship between Israel and its neighbors. As a consequence, a program of Jewish-Arab peace education was developed and introduced in the mid-1980s as a teaching unit in primary education. Arabic became compulsory in the seventh year. Moreover, after survey results among people revealed shocking and inappropriate attitudes towards the democratic system and its values, civic education started to include core teaching units on democratic education. A history book for Year 9, presented the genesis of Israel and the first twenty years of Israeli history using a more varied approach than previously employed with the aim of encouraging pupils to critically discuss material.

However, two other books were far more popular, recommended by the Ministry of Education until the late 1990s for teaching in Year 8, they presented an uncritical view of Zionism and explained Arab resistance against the Zionist project in terms of a militant tendency and also focused upon relationships between Arab political leaders and the Nazis. The Arab-Israeli conflict was tacitly removed from the curriculum. Instead an optional teaching unit "The Arabs—Citizens of Israel" was included for Years 10 to 12 in civic education; this included issues that focused upon the conflict of loyalty between Israeli and Arab identity and discrimination in Israel.[5]

Two changes marked the beginning of a further phase in Israeli curriculum policy. Firstly from 1987, the Intifada made Israeli and international public opinion more aware than ever of the occupation and its implications. Secondly, at the end of the 1980s a number of Israeli historians began to contest some Israeli founding myths, and, in particular, denied the thesis that the active expulsion of Arabs by Jewish combat units had not crucially contributed to the Palestinian refugee problem.[6] These findings have become an integral part of a number of history school books for upper secondary education, some of which empathize with this claim[7] some of which distance themselves from it[8] while others still fail to deal with the issue.[9] Indeed some authors continue to use the terminology that was in common before the 1990s. For example, they do not use the label "Palestinian" and present a discourse with a distinct focus on an Israeli/Zionist point of view.

Moreover, Jewish history has been treated as an element of world history since the mid-1990s, and textbooks were written accordingly. In comparison to former history books, these books shine a more critical light on the history of the conflict before 1948, the Lebanon campaign and the Intifada. They were much discussed and sometimes fiercely attacked but, according to Ministry of Education statistics, are still among the most frequently used books. In the mid-1990s, an optional civic education unit "The Arabs—Citizens of Israel" for higher classes was abolished in favor of the teaching of democracy. Initially, the basis of Israeli democracy was dealt with in privately published school books.[10] In higher classes this issue has, since 2001, been taught consistently with a book published by the Ministry of Education for all schools, whether religious, secular, Arab or Jewish, and attaches great importance to Israel as the Jewish state, as well as to democracy and the idea of the national state.[11] The Ministry requests an equal weighting between these two constituents of the Jewish state and also demands addressing the tension between them and the particularities of minority life in the state.[12] Due to the vagueness of treaty agreements, Israel's borders are subject to various interpretations by different authors. Although commonly referred to by the Israeli public, the notion of "occupied territories" (Shetahim Kevushim) does not appear in school books when referring to the West Bank and the Gaza Strip.

Detailed political maps do, in most cases, contain the green demarcation line. The West Bank is occasionally called by its biblical names, Judea and Samaria, or is referred to as the West Bank. The textbook for civic education in Years 10–12 marks various zones of the Palestinian Authority, briefly stating the differences and providing the most precise presentation of the status quo. A later, privately published, book on geography merely mentions "Zone A" and either disregards the green line or refers to the remaining Zones B and C, the majority of the occupied territories that still remain under Israeli security administration, as "territory on which no data is available." In contrast the Israeli state territory is depicted with data on the various maps in the book. Strangely enough this book devotes a paragraph to even the smallest Israeli minorities, such as Bedouins, Cherkesses, Druses and Christians, while Muslim Arabs are only mentioned in the context of being Sunnites.[13]

Through its curricula and school textbooks Israel presents itself as a society where turning points and geo-political developments have had a major effect on Israeli self-image and the perception of others. The centralization of the civic education curriculum for higher classes and the plans to standardize history lessons must be considered as a reaction to the various schisms which are perceived to be increasing and becoming more intense in Israeli society and an increasing threat in recent years. We can only hope that this development does not have a pronounced detrimental effect on history lessons with respect to the latest achievements in dealing with blame and the failures of Israel and the Zionist movement and that it does not damage the genuine and extremely lively culture of debate in Israel.

CONTINUITY AND DISCONTINUITY
IN THE PALESTINIAN CURRICULUM

The school system in the Gaza Strip and the West Bank, East-Jerusalem included, has always been centrally controlled. Hence, the curriculum issued by the Palestinian Ministry of Education is also binding on private schools, which include six to seven per cent of pupils, and for the schools of the UNWRA (United Nations Works and Relief Agency, established in 1949 for the needs of the Palestinian refugees), which represent some 20% of the school system. Schools in the occupied territories have always suffered from a lack of classrooms and teaching aids, the situation being aggravated by the occupation. Teachers are notoriously underpaid and frequently have second jobs.[14] Until 1967 the education system was run by the administrative states of Jordan and Egypt, the curricula of which were maintained under Israeli occupation, but which were censored by the Israeli civil administration.

This had been perceived as problematic among Palestinians living in the occupied territories. In 1986, staff of Lutheran schools in the West Bank developed for the first time a Palestinian curriculum for social sciences which was in unofficial use in some schools during the Intifada.[15] After the civil administration of the occupied territories was taken over by the PNA, they prioritized the creation of a curriculum customized to the needs of Palestinians. In 1990, a workshop organized in Paris by the PLO, with the support of UNESCO, initiated the development of a curriculum that took into account the three bases of Palestinian identity: the Arab-Islamic heritage; Palestinian culture and an international dimension.[16] For this purpose, in 1994, immediately after the appointment of the PNA, the Palestinian Curriculum Development Center (PCDC) was founded as a department of the Ministry of Education.

Chaired by Director Ibrahim Abu Lughod, a political scientist who completed his doctorate at Princeton and who returned from exile in 1992 to teach at Bir Zeit University, a team of academics published a report on the curriculum in Palestinian schools (PCDC, 1997).[17] In this general and specific stocktaking of the educational situation in the occupied territories the authors stressed the need to adapt the curriculum to the needs of the Palestinians and to modernize it. They condemned the extensive use of Koran quotations; the over-selection of pre-modern texts as sources for lessons in Arabic, History and Social Sciences and the accompanying neglect of other religions and cultures, as well as the uncritical orientation towards authoritarian values of tradition and inherited rule in the Jordanian and Egyptian curricula.

They also claimed that the new curriculum should support a transformation process from a traditionally patriarchal society to a modern society based on scientific standards and should foster in learners a critical attitude towards the society in which they live. Advocates also argued that the curriculum should have a greater interdisciplinary context, define a high level of general education both for academic and vocational studies and also offer more flexible options for pupils. Due to differences in opinion between authors, contradictions such as the relationship between religion and other subjects remained unresolved. Moreover, no concrete proposals were made in order to classify Israel or the Arab-Israeli conflict. In fact, the first official curriculum plan set out by the PCDC (1998) did not consider the major claims of Abu Lughod's team. Instead the plan focused upon anchoring the Palestinians in Arab-Islamic identity and in the belief in God the Almighty. The education of the individual was aimed at the fulfilment of their duties within society whilst consistently depicting an uncritical view of traditions and family.

Palestinian schoolbooks reveal a fervent patriotism. The Palestinian flag appears on innumerable images in both Arab books for teaching in Year 1. The children are requested to name the flag's colors, to paint it, and, judging by the pictures in the book, the flag is hoisted in all Palestinian schools. Already, at this young stage of education, the books deal continuously with the Palestinian experience of being a refugee, of being arrested and of making sacrifices to prevent oneself from having to sell an inherited plot of land. Textbooks for National Education (*At-Tarbiya al-Wataniyya*) and Civic Education (*At-Tarbiya al-Madaniyya*) are similar. The curriculum for history lessons in higher classes envisages the creation of a bond (*Intima'*) between pupils and Palestine and "...the willingness to sacrifice oneself for Palestine" as teaching objectives.[18] The proportion of religious education in the curriculum is relatively high, accounting for ten per cent in primary education and over eight per cent in the higher stages of education. The volume of Islamic content is significant as it is strongly represented in the curricula for Arabic and the Human Sciences. The Koran is frequently quoted in Arabic, History and Geography books, as well as books on Islamic religion where it represents by far the most important source.

The Palestinians are rooted in ancient Arab-Canaanite and even more in Islamic history. The Islamic eras of Palestinian history make up a correspondingly high proportion of the history curriculum. Other periods, such as the immigration of the Hebrews from Egypt and the destruction of their mini-state (*Duwayla*) by the Assyrians and Chaldeans, are dealt with in the history curriculum for Years 11 and 12. The modern Palestinian people are depicted as a collective, who, with the support of the British mandate, fought unwaveringly against Zionist colonial endeavors (*al-Atma' al-Istitaniyya*). The struggle against the Israeli occupation has been as long-standing as the fight against the colonial exploits of a foreign power.

THE EMERGENCE OF TODAY'S "STATE"[19]

Today's Palestinian polity was created by the "Peace initiative," which was adopted by the Palestinian National Council (PNC) "...based on resolution

181 and known as the partition resolution. It was passed on November 29, 1947, by the UN General Assembly...."[20] The initiative was triggered by the Intifada and resulted in the Palestinian Declaration of Independence. As Resolution 181 is seen by Palestinians as unjust the Palestine Authority makes it implicitly clear that they accepted an unfair decision from the UN for the sake of peace following forty years of conflict. November 15 1988, the day when this decision was made by the PNC, is the Palestinian national holiday and pupils are requested to discuss the various contents of the Declaration of Independence.

SELF-IMAGE

Textbook descriptions of Palestinian society are extremely positive. Society is portrayed as a democratic, parliamentarian political system that is economically organized within an active civil society. The family and common values, especially love for one's country, tolerance, non-violence, Jihad and martyrdom, are the cornerstones of this society. Inner-societal problems, such as child labour, early marriage, behavior that is perceived as antisocial, crime and violence also are addressed. Pluralism, the right to found political parties, freedom of expression and their embodiment in history and in conventions such as the Charter of Human Rights, the Palestinian Declaration of Independence or the Convention on the Rights of Children are comprehensively discussed in the book for civic education for Year 8.

A paragraph "questions for discussion" (*Qadaya li-'n-Naqqash*) within each chapter of this book is designed to provide room for debating concepts and principles on the basis of observation and individual experience. The "psychological fundamentals" (*Asas Nafsiyya*) of the history curriculum in higher years, such as "developing an analytical and critical way of thinking ... respecting others' views, self-criticism...." follow the same objective. However, achieving the teaching targets is not realistic if based upon the given material, which does not usually offer controversial theses for discussion and already anticipates the opinion-forming process by stating, "The clinging of the PLO to the armed struggle led to its recognition on an Arabic and an international level" or "The Palestine-Lebanese ... co-operation contributed to the strengthening of the Lebanese stamina (*Sumud*) as well as to the foundation of Lebanon." Facts are illustrated in a positivist way and it becomes clear, partly via literal restrictions, what the pupil "...is to believe (*an Yu'min*)..." This is the context in which peace and tolerance, martyrdom and Jihad and some quite unambiguous allusions to the antiSemitic stereotype are continuously judged as positive. Significantly, Israel is either presented as a merciless occupying power or is neglected. The apparent inadequacies of Palestinian textbooks have received widespread critical attention and typically have been condemned as political agitation, partly attributed to ignorance.[21]

ON A DIASPORA CURRICULUM

The Palestinian Studies Foundation (*Mu'assasat ad-Dirasat al-Filastiniyya*) that is closely connected to the PLO created a standard book on Palestinian history in the 1970s comprising four volumes for history lessons from primary to higher secondary education. They recount Palestine's history from ancient times until the present in three steps each of which is adapted in terms of complexity and comprehensiveness, according to the appropriate age range.[22] The book is detailed and illustrative although descriptive. The framework of historic events and facts is largely identical to standard works on Palestinian history. The clear secular orientation of the book enables the Kings David and Salomon to be described as they were in the Bible, as Kings of an empire that had been founded by the settlement of a tribal alliance after numerous struggles. The Jews were definitely expelled from Palestine by the Romans. Jerusalem is regarded as a holy city by the three monotheistic religions. In modern history, Jews were persecuted in Eastern Europe for three reasons. First, their religious fanaticism prevented them from integrating within the societies in which they lived. Second, they were competitors in European business, and third, due to an "inherited religious aversion [from the Europeans] to them as they were thought to be responsible for the crucifixion of Jesus-Christ."[23]

On the other hand the Islamic conquest is described as a peaceful process and the Palestinian cause is not questioned, neither are the methods used by Arab and Palestinian leaders. However, empty platitudes ("Israel is an imperialist-colonialist entity,… a racist state,… an expansionist aggressive state")[24] and the distortion of facts when blaming their own religious fanaticism for the isolation of Jews, are rather an exception. Furthermore, the authors do substantiate their interpretation of history very precisely with demographic data and detailed maps featuring some of the country's genuinely Jewish cities, such as Tel Aviv and Netania, and by meticulously labelling the Jewish settlements in the occupied territories.

They provide an in-depth report on the Palestinians' situation in Israel, which is not mentioned at all in the current curriculum and prove their profound knowledge of the opponent's narrative when referring to Hebrew and Israeli terms (*Hovevei Zion, Keren Kayemet, Plan Dalet, Alon-Plan*). The killing of numerous Jews in the course of the 1929 riots of Hebron and Safed is stated without any justification. The book also fails to acknowledge the fact that these Jews had nothing to do with Zionism and had been living in the area for generations. In this context reference is made neither to the role of the Palestinian leadership nor to the role of the Jerusalem Mufti, a core leader of the Palestinian national movement in the 1920s and early 1930s and a propaganda source for the Nazis in 1940s Berlin. Both the various approaches towards a solution proposed by Great Britain and the UNO, as well as the positions and motives of Jews and Arabs are regularly described. The Dalet Plan and the general behavior of the Zionists in the 1948 war are portrayed as the Zionists' objective to reverse the demographic population balance in Palestine.

The treatment of Palestinians in the occupied territories of 1948 and 1967, and the massacre of Kafr Qassem, are dealt with from the same viewpoint. The latter is mentioned with regard to the suing of those responsible who received minor sentences from Israeli courts, some of which were remitted. The UN special envoy, Gunnar Jaring's endeavors at the beginning of the 1970s to implement Resolution 242 failed due to Israel's unwillingness to withdraw to the borders defined in 1949, and to integrate the Palestinians into the process as a people with their own rights. The Jordanian proposal to create a federation with the West Bank and the Gaza Strip is rejected as it involves the threat of annexing Jordan, which would put an end to an autonomous representation of Palestinian interests. The disapproval of Israeli attempts to hold regional elections in the occupied territories is explained as warding off a permanent Israeli regime over a Palestinian people without real political rights. If this gives the impression of a certain unwillingness to accept a partial solution or a compromise that sufficiently takes into account the political rights of the Palestinians and their national identity, the question remains why is this unwillingness denied by textbook statements such as, "...the idea of the Palestinian Revolution ... is based on the unfeasibility of achieving a settlement of the Arab-Israeli conflict, with the exception of Arab capitulation to a regional balance of power, which is coined by a strong lead of the imperialist-Israeli axis."

Whilst Israel's actions are mainly connected with the apportioning of blame, the question that is not asked is why it has not been left up to the Palestinian refugees as to the extent to which they wished to maintain their Palestinian identity. Although this history book imposes judgements, it could, by some, be viewed as being educational as it makes some attempt to show the positions of both sides. It bears comparison with the Israeli books from the same period. Instead of repeatedly stressing Palestine's Islamic character, this book states its own point of view: the migrations and conquests, of which those by the Jews of the Ancient World were one of many, continued after their expulsion." Accordingly the textbook states, "until the Arab-Islamic conquest finally created Palestine and made it an Arab country in terms of language, history, culture and fate (*Ja'alaha Baladan Sarih al-'Uruba*) ... The linkage of the modern Jews to Palestine, many of them originating from people who converted to the Jewish religion outside

Palestine in later eras, is a purely religious-spiritual relation, equal to the one connecting other Christians and Muslims with (Palestine)."[25]

Why is the current curriculum constructed in this way considering that the team of authors led by Abu Lughod, and even the exiled Palestinian leadership, chose a modern approach for lessons in History and Social Studies? Although this issue is not as publicly discussed in Palestinian society as it is in Israel, it is obvious that the current curriculum has directly or indirectly been influenced by conservative and extremist religious influences that the Abu Lughod group had failed to overcome. The final result represents a clear attempt to meet the expectations of Islamically oriented Palestinian society, on the one hand, and, at least from a Palestinian viewpoint, the requirements of the Israeli-Palestinian Interim Agreement of September 1995 (Oslo II) on the other.[26] In an attempt to find a compromise between these incompatible goals the publishers of new Palestinian textbooks fail to address some vital questions concerning Palestine today and in the past—such as, where is Israel situated." What kind of peace are we striving for and with whom?

FUTURE OUTLOOK

As evidenced through their recognition of Israel, they are at least prepared to take the first step towards peace. In contrast, a leaf through neighboring countries' school textbooks makes it clear that Jordan and Egypt[27] (despite making peace with Israel), do not share this position. In Jordan and Egypt, as in Syria[28] narratives openly propagate blatant anti-Semitism. The narrative of the Lebanese curriculum for state-run schools seems to be rational and liberal in comparison. Its description of the Arab-Israeli conflict is very similar to that reported by exiled Palestinians in the 1980s.[29] The Palestinians, who have discussed the decentralization of the school system[30] as well as Israel and Lebanon, represent examples of liberalization endeavors being reversed as a reaction to pressure from internal and external conflicts in states that control curriculum content in an attempt to prevent societal disintegration.

Seen from this perspective it is very hard to reach agreement on a desired curriculum as the simple desire for peace as a major condition for learning tolerance, respect and peaceful conflict-solving does not exist. Although in their history lessons pupils in the Middle East, like everywhere in the world, should be exposed to a wide range of perspectives, the attempt to keep extremism away by controlling the teaching content appears desirable. After all, European educationalists are not expected to seriously consider the extreme positions of neo-fascists or extremist religious fundamentalists with their pupils. In the Middle East, the opponent's point of view does, however, play a similar role. One example is the criticism of a history book written by the Israeli author Aharon Megged[31] who asks whether the next step would be to ask pupils to identify with an anti-Semite following the book's request to identify with a Palestinian refugee and with an Egyptian prisoner of war.

Among the Arab public, it is not unusual to equate Zionism with fascism. Advocates of peace education should nevertheless remember that if children are expected to show tolerance and understanding, when they actually feel the opposite, there is a risk of them being brought up to be dishonest. In fact, the history of the Arab-Israeli conflict does not yet supply any proof that non-violence is a winning strategy. Instead reference should perhaps be made to other parts of the world such as South Africa, Greece and Turkey or South Korea and Japan. In the years after the Oslo Treaty, when peace between Israelis and Palestinians seemed only a matter of time, committed Israeli and Palestinian scholars and educationalists started to create educational material that emphasized common points and facilitated mutual respect and the acceptance of differences. This project was supported by the respective Israeli and Palestinian Ministries. Contrary to all expectations, such a group published the results of their work in 2003.[32] but they are, at most, tolerated by the Ministries. As a pioneering project it will probably have an impact on official teaching content as soon as a new thaw replaces the current icy Arab-Israeli relations. In the meantime its influence will be limited to a small target group.

It is to be hoped that a liberal culture of debate might develop in the Arab states and that the PNA, as part of a reform process, would support textbooks that focus upon the inner-societal relationship between the Muslim majority and the Christian minority, relationships with Europe and other topics. At some time in the future such an approach might be applied to the Arab-Israeli conflict. In his article on history lessons in Palestinian schools, the Palestinian educational scientist, Salem Aweiss, calls for a controversial, dialectic treatment of historical texts, which stresses their interpretative character.[33] However, these kinds of history lessons require teacher commitment. To achieve this goal there must not only be appropriate teaching materials, but teachers must also receive sufficient pay and schools must work on a continuous basis that is often impossible due to curfews and the cordoning off in the occupied territories. It is interesting that the Palestinian curriculum despite being centrally controlled neither takes notice of historical developments like Israel's recognition by the PLO leadership or the Egyptian-Israeli peace, nor major geo-political changes, such as the founding of Israel. Instead it seems to be subject to ideological discourse. In contrast, the Israeli textbooks appear to relate sensitively to historical changes but seem to be rather unimpressed by day-to-day party quarrels. On the basis of these observations, the influence of donor states on Palestinian educational policy, whether positive or negative, can hardly be underestimated.

NOTES

1. *Westdeutsche Allgemeine Zeitung*, March 5, 2003; European Parliament, May 5, 2004.

2. The figures represent an approximate number, referring partly to pupils who had started school in 1999/2000 but also to teachers employed at that time, www.education.gov.il/moe/english/facts.htm.

3. Y. Mathias "The Thorny Way to Recognition: Palestinians and Arabs in the Israeli Curriculum," in *Contested Past, Disputed Present. Curricula and Teaching in Israeli and Palestinian Schools*, ed. F. Pingel, (Hannover: Hahn, 2003); E. Podeh, *The Arab-Israeli Conflict in Israeli History Textbooks, 1948–2000*, (Westport/Connecticut: Bergin and Garvey Anders, 2002); in contrast to R. Firer and S. Adwan *The Israeli-Palestinian Conflict in History and Civics Textbooks of Both Nations* (Hannover: Hahn, 2004) who define five stages.

4. Mathias, 2003, Ibid.

5. A. Ramberg *Ha-Aravim Ezrahei Israel (The Arabs—Citizens of Israel)*, (Jerusalem: Ministry of Education and Van Leer Institute, 1988).

6. B. Morris, *The Birth of the Palestinian Refugee Problem 1947–1949*, (Cambridge: Cambridge University Press, 1988); B, Morris, *1948 and after*, (Oxford: Clarendon, 1990).

7. E. Barnavi, *Ha-Meah ha-'Esrim. Toldot 'Am Israel ba-Dorot ha-Aharonim (The Twentieth Century. The Israeli People's History of the Last Generations)*, (Tel Aviv: Tel Aviv Books, 1998); E, Naveh, *Zmanim Modernim (Modern Times) Part 2, 1920–2000*, (Tel Aviv: Tel Aviv Books, 1999); K. Tabibyan, *Ha-Meah ha-'Esrim—bi-Zkhut ha-Herut (The Twentieth Century—Under the Sign of Freedom)*, (Tel Aviv: Matah, 1999).

8. D. Shahar, Me-Galut le-Komemiyut. Toldot "Am Israel ba-Dorot ha-Aharonim" (From Diaspora to Sovereignty, History of the last generations of the Israeli people), part 2, (Grammar School: Rehovot, 1989); D. Shahar, 'Am ve-'Olam. Prakim be-Toldot Israel ve-ha-'Amim (People and the World. Chapter in the History of Israel and the Peoples) 1870–1970, Part 3: 1945–1970, (High Classes: Rehovot, 1998).

9. S. Anbar, *Tequma u-Mdina bi-Israel u-va-'Amim ba-Zman he-Hadash (Renaissance und Staat bei Israel und bei den Völkern) 1945–1970*, (Petah Tikva: Lilakh, 2000).

10. H. Wahrmann, "The Subtle Silencing of Conflicts in Civics Textbooks," *International Textbook Research* 26 (2003).

11. State of Israel Ministry of Education *Lihiyot Ezrahim bi-Israel—Medina Yehudit ve-Demokratit (Being a Citizen in Israel—a Jewish and Democratic State)*, (High Classes, Jerusalem: Ministry of Education, 2001).

12. State of Israel Ministry of Education, *Tokhnit Limudim: Ezrahut la-Hativa ha-Eliyona le-Vatei Sefer Yehudiyim, (Klaliyim ve-Datiyim), Araviyim ve-Druziyim* [Curriculum: Civic Education for High School Level for Jewish (General and

Religious), Arab and Druze Schools], (Jerusalem: Ministry of Education), 2002, p. 7.

13. N. Nahum-Levi, *Israel, ha-Adam ve-ha-Merhav. Nos'im Nivharim be-Geografiya (Israel, Mankind and Space. Selected Geographical Issues)*, all schools, Middle and High Classes, (Jerusalem: Matah, 2002).

14. PCDC (Palestinian Curriculum Development Center/Ministry of Education *First Palestinian Curriculum Plan*, (Ramallah: PCDC, 1998).

15. M. Khouri, (2003) "On the Road to Self-Determination: the Development of the First Palestinian School Curriculum," in *Contested Past, Disputed Present. Curricula and Teaching in Israeli and Palestinian Schools*, ed. F, Pingel, (Hannover: Hahn); S, Ramsden and C, Senker (eds.) *Learning the Hard Way*, (London: World University Service, 1993).

16. Khouri, Ibid.

17. I should like to thank Götz Nordbruch for the summary of this comprehensive report.

18. Palestinian National Authority Ministry of Education, General Administration of Curricula *Al-Khutut al-'Arida li-Minhaj at-Ta'rikh li-'s-Sufuf 11–12 (Guidelines for the History Curriculum for years 11–12)*, (Ramallah : Ministry of Education, 1999), p. 6.

19. The "Palestinian State" (*Dawlat Filastin*), which actually does not exist is frequently mentioned. The heraldic eagle imprinted on the first pages of each school book, for example, is subtitled with this name.

20. PCDC (Palestinian Curriculum Development Center/Ministry of Education *Al-Mutala'a wa "n-Nusus (Lecture and Texts)*, Year 8, Volume I, (Ramallah, PCDC, 2003), p. 74.

21. Center for Monitoring the Impact of Peace (CMIP "Jews, Israel and Peace in the Palestinian Authority School Textbooks," www.edume.org/reports/report1.htm; G. Nordbruch, *Narrating Palestinian Nationalism. A study of the new Palestinian Textbooks*, (Washington, DC, MEMRI: Israeli-Palestinian Center for Research and Information, 2001); J. Kriener, "Palestinian School Textbooks: between international polemics and national apologia," *International Textbook Research* 25 (2003), p. 399–406.

22. Palestinian Studies Foundation, 1980; 1983.

23. Palestinian Studies Foundation (1980a, 1983a; 1980b, 1983b) *Filastin. Ta'rikhuha wa-Qadiyyatuha (Palestine, its History and its Question)*, Lower and Middle Classes (Volume 1, Volume 2), Secondary Education, Beirut/Nikosia, Palestinian Studies Foundation 1980a: 12; 1983a, p. 14; 1983b, p. 20.

24. Ibid., 1980b, pp. 5, 7, 9.

25. Op.cit. 1980b, p. 19.

26. According to the Oslo Accord, both parties agreed that "… their educational systems shall serve the fostering of peace between Israel and the Palestinians."

27. E. Podeh, "Recognition without Legitimisation. Israel and the Arab-Israeli Conflict in Egyptian History Textbooks," *International Textbook Research* 25 (2003): 371–398; W. Rees, "The Jews in Islamic Religious Education. A Comparison of Egyptian, Jordanian and Palestinian School books," (*KNA-ÖKI*, Volumes 49, 50, 51 and 52, 2003).

28. J.Landis, "Islamic Education in Syria," http://faculty-staff.ou.edu/L/Joshua .M.Landis1/Islamic_Education_in_Syria.htm; M, Wurmser, *The Schools of Ba'athism. A Study of Syrian Textbooks*, (Washington: MEMRI, 2000).

29. J. Hayek, *At-Ta'rikh al-'Ilmi (Scientific history)*, year 9, (Beirut: Habib, 1996)

30. R. Rihan, The Palestinian Educational Development Plan: Promise for the Future, *Palestine-Israel Journal of Politics, Economics and Culture*, 8 (2001): 19–33.

31. *Haaretz Daily* September 13, 1999.

32. Peace Research Institute in the Middle East (PRIME) (2003) *Learning Each Other's Historical Narrative*, Beit Jala, PRIME.

33. S. Aweiss, History Teaching in the Palestinian Context: Confronting the Interpretive Paradox!, *International Textbook Research*, 25 (2003), pp. 319–341.

CHAPTER 11

THE DYNAMICS OF HISTORY TEXTBOOK PRODUCTION DURING SOUTH AFRICA'S EDUCATIONAL TRANSFORMATION

Rob Siebörger

In 1993, I participated in two colloquia on "school history textbooks for a democratic South Africa." For me they were events that have come to symbolize the transition from the old to the new South Africa and represent an appropriate marker upon which to reflect on what has been left behind, and what has, and hasn't, come to be in textbook writing and publication since that time.[1] Events in South Africa at that time were dominated by "the talks," which laid the political and constitutional basis for the hand over of power to a democratically elected government. While these high level talks were taking place, they were mirrored by a myriad of smaller meetings and conferences, bringing together people from all groups to talk to each other for the first time and to plan ahead for the inevitable change of government and the establishment of a new post-Apartheid civil society.

What Shall We Tell the Children?, pages 227–243
Copyright © 2006 by Information Age Publishing

One of the questions that was frequently asked of educationists by curious journalists and the public was, "What is going to happen to school history?" The question was always followed by a more specific one, namely, how would the new history textbooks be written? It was a question that, as far as I know, no-one in the higher echelons was immediately concerned to answer, but there were many academics, writers and educational publishers[2] who were very interested in this burning issue. Amongst them were groups who had been ideologically excluded in the past, or had been in exile, those who had been on the margins and had been producing materials that were not published in the mainstream, and those who saw their previous hegemonic positions threatened.

Falk Pingel and Jörn Rüsen of the Georg Eckert Institute for International Textbook Research were interested outsiders at this point and were very keen to assist the process of change that was unfolding. They offered to find funding for a colloquium (which in the event became two) and to help to facilitate it by bringing a number of German participants, who would occupy a neutral position amongst the parties. A committee of academics from around the country was formed, under the auspices of the Project for Alternative Education in South Africa, located at the University of Cape Town. The colloquia, and a follow-up workshop held in 1995, were attended by a range of present and prospective textbook writers and academics. They brought together people who had never been in the same place before, across race, political and language boundaries, all conscious of the significance of the historical moment, none of whom, however, were key political figures. Significantly, no government officials were invited.[3] An aim was to keep the colloquia small enough for participants to sit in a room around a single square of tables, so that there could be free and frank discussion.[4]

Much of the discussion focussed on finding a consensus with which to enter the future, though the past also weighed very heavily. Arguably, the majority of the time was taken up in discussing issues that had been around for many years—some wanting to bury them and begin afresh, others trying to hold on to what they considered non-negotiable. In the second of the colloquia agreement was reached on a statement on new history textbooks for South African schools.[5] The text of the statement is given in full below, both for its historical value and as a device to enable reflection on what history textbook production was like in the "old" South Africa, and what has happened during the first decade of the "new" South Africa. It contains three sections.

TEXTBOOKS AND THE HISTORY CURRICULUM

Attempting to set out the scope and purpose of the history curriculum was particularly contentious. This is because while the majority of participants were eager to comment on the shape of a future history curriculum a significant minority felt this was premature, was a political action and took the discussion out of the realm of textbook production. The debates underlined that in a country where there had always been nationally constructed curricula (and where no-one expected this to change), textbook production would always be closely related to curriculum development.[6] The first section read:

1.1   The curriculum should reflect advances in the discipline of history and in history education, locally and internationally, and should be sensitive to recent and current debates within specific areas of research.

1.2   The approach to the past should be inclusive and democratic: it should explore the experiences of ordinary men and women as well as leaders and heroes, and should deal with the political, social, economic, cultural and environmental dimensions of human experience. The manner in which history is taught should promote democratic values, and democracy should be introduced through the mode of classroom discourse and the experiences of students in the classroom.

1.3   The approach to historical knowledge should be analytical and explanatory, dealing with change, continuity and conflict, and complex historical processes and concepts should be dealt with at levels appropriate to the learning abilities of students.

1.4   Skills and content should be seen as inseparable. The history curriculum should be based on an awareness of how knowledge is produced. History is not a set of given facts. The process of history production should be made clear to students.

1.5   The topics of the curriculum should be selected in such a way that the amount of historical information which the student has to acquire does not hinder the development of historical skills.

1.6   The curriculum should transmit the excitement and fascination of history as an encounter with the past. Historical education should develop empathetic understanding, emotional and moral commitment with the past, and an awareness of the constant interrelationship of the past and the present, and its future perspective.

1.7   With regard to South African history, approaches to the past that exclude, diminish or distort the history of particular groups, classes or communities should be rejected and curriculum revision should strive for an approach that:

    1.7.1 reflects the diversity of our population, while also accounting for the processes (such as conquest, imperial incorporation, the uneven development of a capitalist economy, and industrialization) that have created a single society;

    1.7.2 seeks to reconcile national unity and cultural diversity by making it clear that nationalism, ethnicity, culture and identity have been constructed over time;

    1.7.3 locates South African history within the broader history of the region of southern Africa and of the African continent as a whole;

    1.7.4 illuminates the relationship between South African history and events in world history which have shaped local experiences (such as the rise of capitalism as a global system, the international trade in slaves and other commodities, the transforming impact of imperialism and industrialization, the spread of Christianity and Islam, parliamentary democracy and socialism, etc.).

1.8 South African history syllabuses should contain a common core of content and skills while allowing for regional, local or school-based flexibility of choice, always providing that local or regional history is not constructed on exclusivist communitarian, sectarian or ethnic lines. Core history could, for example, deal with broad issues and events, with regional history providing the specific detail.

1.9 History syllabus documents should, in addition to the content and skills to be learned, specify clearly the forms of assessment envisaged and the appropriate criteria for textbooks which are to be based upon the syllabuses.

1.10 The teaching of history in primary and junior secondary schools is particularly important. Special attention should be paid to how to approach history in a more integrated (rather than subject-specific) way, to thematic methods and assessment by group and project-study methods.

The right to construct national "core" syllabuses in South African school subjects had been vested in the four "white" provincial education departments since the 1960s. The content of these syllabuses, which were constructed by majority Afrikaner committees, was allowed to be supplemented by the other (racially determined) education departments when they drew up their own versions. Usually, however, very few changes were made[7] and, despite the "separate" character of apartheid, all schools used these white syllabuses. While they were regarded as prescriptive the syllabuses were never specified in detail, only topic headings were supplied. This meant that textbooks became crucial instruments in the transmission of the history taught in classrooms, as it was the textbooks that decided the version of history that was taught. In very many schools textbooks (often constituting only one title) were the sole resources available to teach and learn history.

The first paragraph of the statement (1.1) was deliberately positioned as it was held by many participants that a fundamental problem with many of the existing textbooks was that they did not reflect current historical knowledge and research, and were decades out of date in key areas of South African historiography. This was particularly the case with books that had been reissued with small changes since the 1950s and 60s, and it was these books that dominated the market in terms of sales. Examples of content excluded in these textbooks were provided in 1.7 and sub-paragraphs 1.7.1 and 1.7.4, which drew attention to the dominance of interpretations that placed Europeans at the center of historical explanation. Other conspicuous instances were the failure of these textbooks to mention any archaeological research that had shown that the ancestors of the agriculturalist African peoples of South Africa had arrived a thousand years earlier than the first European contact with the country (in contrast to the claim in many textbooks that their arrival had been contemporaneous), and that the interior of South Africa had been well populated at the time of Afrikaner expansion and colonization (in contrast to the claim that the "Great Trek" had been to an empty land).

Paragraph 1.2 reflected the influence of people's history that had grown as a tool of struggle in the 1980s.[8] It was concerned not only to identify the unrecognized prominent people left out of the white narratives but also to develop the capacity for students and communities to research their own histories.[9] Very few textbooks had devoted any attention to ordinary people. People's history was often referred to as "alternative" history, and much of the material produced for schools under its banner was unpublished or not published by mainstream textbook publishers, most of whom were too closely identified with the apartheid system to be interested.

For roughly a decade prior to the colloquia there had been a small number of textbooks and other school history books published that used a source- and skills-based approach.[10] While the books never sold in large numbers, they exerted a considerable influence particularly in schools that were attempting to be more progressive. Often these methods were combined with the introduction of new content from the research of university history and archaeology departments that was possible because they kept to the topics of the syllabuses but approached them differently. These were among the books presented at the colloquia for discussion as possible exemplars of future practice. The weight of this influence is expressed in paragraph 1.4, and below in 2.5.3.

The 1995 workshop took place in an atmosphere of impatient optimism for textbook writers and publishers. Some had already begun to "jump the gun" and produce books prior to changes in the syllabus, reasoning that they could confidently guess future trends in curricula and textbooks (and the colloquia had, in retrospect, played a part in this). This was a commercially risky path to embark upon, as the major impetus for textbooks sales had in the past always been the launch of a new syllabus. Some publishers were prepared to take the chance because they wanted to re-position themselves and to be seen to be contributing to the government's agenda of educational transformation. For others it wasn't much of a risk at all as they continued to sell annual "top-ups"[11] of their best-selling older books—a practice which severely inhibited the penetration of new books into schools. An interim core syllabus had been produced by a history sub-committee of the National Education and Training Forum, under instruction from the Minister of Education to consolidate and evaluate the existing syllabuses of the large number of previous departments of education (now formed into nine provincial departments). The committee had attempted to remove the "inherently biased and ideologically distorted"[12] aspects of the syllabuses and had tried to make history more skills, rather than content, based. Books produced around, and immediately after this time, frequently reflected the trends of this section of the statement, although it was noticeable that people's history was no longer present as a factor, and that identity emerged as much stronger issue than it had been two years earlier.

There was a brief flowering of history textbook publication in 1996 as Gauteng province[13] decided to replace all the old history and geography textbooks in its schools in Grades 4 to 9. It was the only province to do so. For publishers it represented a rare opportunity in an otherwise stagnant market as the interim syllabuses had been drawn up on the assumption that they would not necessitate new textbooks. Many of the authors of these books had been involved or been in contact with those who attended the colloquia or workshops.

1996 also marked the beginning of a change that would drastically alter the fortunes of history in schools. The long-awaited complete revision of the school curriculum began in that year. "Curriculum 2005"[14] was the product of a very hasty and poorly prepared process. It provided a curriculum framework for the compulsory schooling years, Grades R(eception)—9, divided into eight "learning areas." In an attempt to be rid of as much of the past baggage as possible, "subjects" were not permitted to be mentioned at all; what had been history was reduced to "time" within the Human and Social Sciences learning area. It warranted a single content outcome among the nine outcomes of the learning area: "Demonstrate a critical understanding of how South African society has changed and developed." What was more serious was the failure to specify in any measurable way how much history should be taught, or what topics should be covered in a year, leaving it entirely to the planning of schools and classroom teachers.[15]

In an education system that had only ever had experience of centralized curriculum planning and where the majority of teachers had received very inadequate preparation for teaching, this approach was to prove hopelessly optimistic. From the perspective of textbook production it was the antithesis of what the 1993 statement envisaged. With only one or two outstanding exceptions, the textbooks written for this curriculum did no service to history. Any sense of narrative and explanation was lost as historical knowledge was accommodated to fit randomly chosen themes, an ironic development, given that paragraph 1.10 of the statement had foreseen that the school curriculum would develop in this direction—but not go to these lengths. Whereas there had previously been separate history and geography textbooks supplied for each grade, now there was only one, of the same length. In many cases there was simply too little space to present history meaningfully, this served to nullify the effect of the introduction of aspects such as archaeological knowledge into the books.

Fortunately, Curriculum 2005 never reached maturity, though the name was continued as a face-saving measure by the government. A new Minister of Education, alarmed by reports that the new curriculum had led directly to reduced levels of literacy and numeracy, initiated a review of it in 2000. The review committee recommend that the vertical (subject-oriented) elements be strengthened relative to the horizontal (integrative), and proposed that history and geography be re-introduced. It also proposed that content knowledge be specified per grade and that intended achievement in each grade be described in assessment standards.[16] Their recommendations were taken up and a comprehensive overhaul of the curriculum resulted. The *Revised National Curriculum Statements for Grades R–9*[17] was the product. It was followed a year later, in 2003, by the *National Curriculum Statements for Grades 10–12*, which built on its foundation.[18] The notion of progression and the statements of outcomes written in terms of concepts and skills are very similar to those of history in the English National Curriculum (and analogous curriculum documents in other countries). In content specification, they are very close to the descriptions contained in the statement, the suggested History content for Grades 10–12 National Curriculum Statement exemplifying exactly what paragraph 1.7.4 had intended.

The only textbooks that have so far been published for the new curriculum statements are for grades 4, 5 and 6. Publishers have responded conservatively and have not reinstated separate history and geography books, realizing that provincial budgets are not likely to support two books when one might suffice. As a consequence, these books, written for a curriculum that is specified much more clearly than any in the past and that is much more elaborate in what it expects of teachers and pupils, are approximately half the length of those of the apartheid era.

WHAT HISTORY TEXTBOOKS SHOULD BE LIKE

The second section of the statement represented an opportunity for everyone present at the colloquia to be heard and to have a hand in ensuring that it contained their pet likes and dislikes. It was less contested than either of the other sections and some of its provisions may be considered obvious. In keeping with the spirit of the time, however, participants were reluctant to agree to a text that left anything unsaid—and the future events concerning Curriculum 2005 were to emphasize how wise this approach proved to be. The statement follows:

2.1 Historical consciousness is more than a stock of knowledge. Fascination, empathy, and moral commitment are important aspects of the learning of history. History textbooks should stimulate and inspire students, should acknowledge their imaginative capacity and should attempt to connect with their awareness of the presence of history in their everyday lives.

2.2 The language of textbooks should be sensitive to the use and abuse of labels. Textbook writers should not perpetuate discrimination and prejudice on the basis of gender race or class and so help to release women and men, girls and boys from damaging stereotypes. They should create a sense of belonging and enable students to construct the multiple identities which they have of themselves and which others have of them.

2.3 Practical criteria:

2.3.1 The format and layout of textbooks should be appropriate to the needs and the developmental and reading levels of the target group. Writers should be creative in exploring different modes of presentation and books should be produced to the highest possible standards, within the financial constraints which might prevail.

2.3.2 Textbooks should be clearly structured and illustrated in a way which is easily accessible to learners by, for example, an overview or summary at the beginning or end of each section, guiding questions and tasks, and hints for the students how to work with the given materials, etc.

2.3.3 Textbooks should be appropriate to the students' capacities, learning abilities, and language competence of those who use them. They should meet the students' and teachers' needs and problems, and challenge and extend their intellectual abilities.

2.3.4 Textbooks should be structured as interactive learning materials for the training of students' historical consciousness. They should stimulate independent inquiry and study and be sensitive to the nature of historical sources. To assist this process, textbooks should include reading lists, museum or site information, observation exercises, and community-awareness projects.

2.4 Criteria which stimulate perception and experience in textbooks:

2.4.1 They should engage the emotional and visual perception of students as well as their cognitive/intellectual faculties.

2.4.2 They should present the past in a multidimensional way, i.e. economics, society, politics, culture, the environment and their interrelationship should be explored. At the same time, they should make visible chronological change along lines of development.

2.4.3 They should present the past in a multiperspectival way, i.e. from the different points of view and experiences of the people of the past. In presenting critical changes and conflicts, for example, all the main parties concerned should be given a voice. This approach, besides affording learners the chance to exercise their freedom of choice, also lays bare the nature of the historian's craft and the inescapable necessity of constantly rewriting history in the light of current understandings of human events.

2.5 Criteria which stimulate understanding and interpretation:

2.5.1 Accepted standards of historical discourse and writing should not be neglected.

2.5.2 Textbooks should develop an appreciation of the value of narrative and the use of narratives in history. (There can never be only one narrative.)

2.5.3 Textbooks should offer the opportunity of learning the elementary skills of historical thinking such as: questioning, analyzing sources, interpretation and reflecting on the limits of historical understanding. Source materials in books can be used simply to illustrate a narrative or they can be used to enable the construction of a narrative(s) by students.

2.5.4 History should be presented as a dynamic process in a multiperspectivity way. In this instance, multiperspectivity is related to the different ways in which people of today look at the past and the ways in which historians construct their theories (for example, the different interpretations of the Mfecane). Multi-perspectivity does not, however, imply relativity, as not all perspectives are of equal weight and value.

2.6 Criteria reflecting the role of history in present-day life: The past should be presented in a comprehensive perspective so as to avoid ethnicity, racism, sexism, nationalism and other exclusive attitudes. History should reflect the universalisation of values, which enable men and women to respect each other's historical identity, bearing in mind that an era cannot be judged outside its own historical context.

The contribution of Jörn Rüsen, then of the University of Bielefeld, to the colloquia is particularly apparent in the references to "historical consciousness" and "multiperspectivity." These were not terms that would have been used before then by most of the South African participants, and both became important aspects of the negotiated agreement represented in the statement. Though participants were unfamiliar with the term historical consciousness (and the theory of historical didactics of which it formed a part), they readily embraced its characteristics. Empathy and imagination were seen as very important in enabling a better understanding of the history of those who had for so long been denied a history, despite all the difficulties they presented for assessment. Being able to appreciate what it must have been like in the past was seen as a vital contribution that history textbooks could make.

Paragraphs 2.1, 2.1.1, 2.2 and 2.6 prefigure the Bill of Rights of the South African constitution (1996) and the subsequent work of the Human Rights Commission. In both the original Curriculum 2005 and its revision, the commission played a role in the drafting process, monitoring the wording of the documents and seeking to insert as many aspects of human rights as possible into the curricula.[19] The result of this otherwise commendable emphasis has been entirely contrary to what Rüsen would have desired, in that some history textbooks have, arguably, become human rights checklists, and that "rights consciousness" has been greater than historical consciousness.

"Multiperspectivity" (paragraphs 2.4.3 and 2.5.4) in the statement had two meanings. At the level of people in the past, it referred to the variety of their individual standpoints and perceptions, while at the level of historical interpretation it meant that more than one possible interpretation of the past always existed. Colloquium members found little difficulty accepting these views, though they were very wary of the term, as it smacked of multiculturalism, for which most had a healthy disregard, associating it with the efforts of apartheid apologists to emphasize cultural difference. South African history and its historiography are ripe with opportunities to develop multiperspectival insights, yet when the booklet illustrating the statement[20] was complied, it was difficult to find examples in textbooks where these approaches were well developed. Contemporary textbooks have, thus far, showed no improvement. New textbooks will have to respond to the crucial demand to develop multiperspectivity more substantially if they are to do justice to the assessment standards of the National Curriculum Statements. The test will be to see whether this is done consistently or merely to satisfy the requirement that it be taught.

Hidden in the wording of paragraph 2.3.3 is the reality that roughly 90% of South African children will study history in their second or third languages, an issue also specifically referred to in 3.7 below. In the late 1980s and early 1990s there had been a number of concerted attempts to give special consideration to creating history textbooks at appropriate reading levels without losing the conceptual emphasis. These efforts had rested on the goodwill of the publishers alone. In a harsher commercial climate such attempts appear to have ceased and what has replaced them has been a considerable diminution of written text in favor of illustrations in all lower grades. This tendency was promoted by the first Curriculum 2005, but remains widely prevalent in recently published textbooks.

THE MAKING OF TEXTBOOKS

The final section of the statement reflects a desire to correct past wrongs and inadequacies in the production of history textbooks and a fervent hope that things will improve in the future. It states:

3.1 It is essential that the process of publishing, recommending and selecting history textbooks be transparent, open and fair.

3.2 Students, teachers and parents should be consulted, and if possible be involved, in the production of all textbooks used in the classrooms of a democratic South Africa.

3.3 History textbooks have suffered in the past from having to be written and produced under unrealistic time constraints due to bureaucratic procedures. Sufficient time should be allowed for research, consultation and the trialing of materials, before they are due to be implemented.

3.4 All official curriculum information must be public information, made available to all simultaneously.

3.5 There should be no conflict of interest between textbook writing and employment by an education authority, and no member of any committee should be able to gain materially as a result of the decisions of the committee in respect of the history curriculum or history textbooks and learning materials. Syllabus committee members who are not education authority officials should, however, not be barred from textbook writing, provided that membership of a syllabus committee does not place them at an undue advantage over other writers.

3.6 History textbooks cannot stand on their own. Innovations should be accompanied by appropriate pre-service and in-service training and retraining of teachers.

3.7 The question of multilingual textbooks in history requires special attention. The basic principle should be that students learn history in their home language (or the language of their parent's choice), provided that the necessary human and material resources are available. Textbooks should also present basic terms and concepts in different languages, where appropriate, so that it is apparent that historical thinking is closely related to language.

The initial paragraph was the most important. The political economy of textbook publishing pre-1994 reflected all the characteristics of an enterprise closely tied to the apartheid state apparatus. It was in the hands of privately owned companies that depended on orders from state education departments for the overwhelming majority of their profits. The largest of these companies were Afrikaans owned and did their business exclusively with education departments serving black schools (the largest market sector by far). They were frequently subsidiaries of the companies that served the white education departments, indirectly subsidizing this market. The smallest of the companies were those that concentrated on the white education departments. English owned companies tended to have a smaller market share than the Afrikaans owned companies,[21] something that was attributed to political influence or patronage. This operated at two levels: in the selection of textbooks for the "approved lists" maintained by each education department, and in the placing of orders for books, which was intended to be done at school level but often occurred at departmental level. It is easy to understand how difficult it was for new publishers to enter a market controlled by what came close to being cartels and how difficult it was to sell any history textbooks that were alternatives to the mainstream in significant numbers. This was particularly so when ideological selection criteria were applied, as was the case in all but a couple of departments. Thus, textbooks of quality, which met the criteria of sections 1 and 2 of the statement, were published but were seldom purchased in any numbers.

Paragraphs 3.3 and 3.4 refer to a practice of changing syllabuses simultaneously for all subjects and expecting publishers to provide new textbooks at extremely short notice. The penalty for missing selection review deadlines for the approved lists was that a publisher would miss the opportunity of bulk sales, and would, in effect, not make any money on such books. A few progressive publishers had engaged in special projects to trial new history textbooks in schools in the period prior to 1993 (and between it and the 1995 workshop). This was not common practice and in these instances history was treated as a special case because of public interest in how new history textbooks would be written. The favorable experiences of developing books under such desirable conditions reported at the colloquia were the background to the second half of paragraph 3.3.

The system had always worked to the advantage of those who sat on curriculum committees (paragraph 3.5) and either wrote textbooks themselves or passed advance information to publishing associates. There were anecdotal stories of curriculum committee members who had written their books before the committees had completed their work. Material gain was a real prospect for textbook writers whose books were purchased in bulk orders, as the author royalties were high (10—15%) and it was uncommon for authors to bear any of the costs of production against royalties.

What was missing from the statement, apart from an oblique reference in paragraph 3.2, was mention of the fact that prior to 1993 it was rare to find a textbook that was not written by an entirely white author team.[22] One of the objectives of the colloquia and workshops was to involve black writers and prospective writers, although the numbers were small, they remain very under represented in recently published textbooks.

What has changed since then? The most important change has been in the publishing market that has shrunk significantly. What for a long time had been a relatively easy environment in which to make profits, from 1995 became a difficult market in which to survive. It was evident that the new government was not able to prioritize textbook provision amongst the many competing demands for funding. This remained the case despite the introduction of Curriculum 2005, which many would have considered an obvious time to replace all the old school textbooks, and there remain many apartheid era history textbooks in use in schools written for syllabuses that last changed in 1983. There have been many mergers of publishing companies and most companies now have some degree of black ownership, in part a consequence of the government's policies of black economic empowerment.

The market changes (together with prevailing international trends in publishing) have resulted in a far more ruthless and, dare it be said, careless approach to publishing, which has favored the rapid production of books without the substance, care in language, source material (because of the costs of pictures and research) and production features, that were evident in the best of the books of the 1993–1995 era. The Department of Education has made some attempt to put a workable textbook provision process in place, but has met with limited success in trying to control procurement costs and ensuring satisfactory distribution.[23] Curriculum committee members are no longer at any advantage to anyone else and curriculum processes have been essentially open, participatory and transparent. In other respects there has been little perceptible change from the pre-1993 circumstances.

CONCLUSIONS

Textbooks, I believe, will remain the principal means to influence both the content of the history presented and the ways in which it is taught in the majority of South African classrooms for the foreseeable future. This was acknowledged in the report of a Ministerial Panel on History and Archaeology in 2000, which considered that the, "textbook remains at the center of the history learning encounter,"[24] and by the South African History Project, established on the recommendation of the panel, which surveyed the available quality and use of history textbooks in 2003, finding that "there are good, new history textbooks available in the country."[25] It is undoubtedly true that there are some books that fit this description and one can find evidence that some of the lessons of the colloquia have been learned by writers and publishers (though, arguably, and somewhat ironically, it may be argued that the present curricula show more obvious benefit than do the textbooks).

But in many respects the history textbook report card is disappointing one, and a great deal remains to be done. In terms of provision, urgent intervention, along the lines of that taken by the Gauteng Education Department in 1996, is needed to purge schools of the remaining apartheid era textbooks. The government has yet to commit itself to a replacement policy that would enable all schools to replace all of their books.

The government also has been particularly inactive in the very area in which the colloquia sought action, namely, in establishing credible criteria for the provision of textbooks. In circumstances where financial resources are so limited, it is crucial to ensure that state money is well spent. The high stakes environment in which publishers and authors currently operate can be made much more rational by the adoption of simple ground rules, such as whether there should be single books for history and geography or not, and what the dimensions and price ranges of such books ought to be. Additionally, national selection criteria for history textbooks based on the National Curriculum Statements ought to be developed,[26] and, I would argue that the 1993 statement still represents an excellent starting point for this process. The selection of books by schools, likewise, remains far from satisfactory, with too few decisions being made on educational grounds alone. There is still a real possibility that less than good textbooks will find their way into classrooms. This is likely to continue until there is an independent national review panel to evaluate against criteria yet to be agreed.

The colloquia set forth a vision of history textbooks that were orientated towards the discipline of history and understanding its nature. They foresaw books both with significantly improved content and a much greater awareness of the historical process. This vision was completely distorted by the integrated approach of the original Curriculum 2005, which kept a sense of past time, but did away with history. The National Curriculum Statements have made it possible for this vision to be restored. It would be tragic, indeed, if the majority of the present writers and publishers, whose books have yet to appear, were not to endeavor to do realize this vision.

NOTES

1. This chapter is an insider's reflection, rather than an account of research. The author has been variously involved in history textbook production as a writer and editor, the convenor of the colloquia, presenter of materials development courses, critic and research supervisor.

2. 44 Educational publishers were (and are) privately owned companies. Because of the small demand for locally published books in the overall book market, they depend, almost universally, on their sales of school books for their profits.

3. 32 attended the first colloquium, with larger numbers at the second and 63 at the workshop, when publishers sent representatives for the first time.

4. It is difficult assert with any certainty what it was expected that the colloquia would achieve. It is probably true to say that there was no common expectation, other than to be able to talk and, hopefully, to influence the direction of a new generation of textbook writers. The stated objective was, "to produce a document containing policy guidelines for future history textbooks in South Africa."

5. Published in Rob Siebörger, "Reconceptualising South African School History Textbooks," *South African Historical Journal* 30 (May 1994),pp. 98–108, and Rob Siebörger *New History Textbooks for South Africa* (Johannesburg: Macmillan, 1994).

6. It was unsurprising that this should have been so given that it was the first time that many of the participants had been able to discuss the history curriculum in a formal setting. This was also a dominant theme of the1995 workshop at a time when the first post-democracy curriculum change was being negotiated, the so-called interim syllabus. See Janet Reid and Rob Siebörger, *Proceedings of the Workshop on School History Textbook Writing: From principles... to practice* (Cape Town: Faculty of Education University of Cape Town, 1995).

7. The conspicuous exception was the Standard 10 (year 12) syllabus for black schools, which excluded the period 1948–1970 in the South African history section.

8. See, for example, Melanie Walker, "History and History Teaching in Apartheid South Africa," and David Anthony "South African People's History," in *South African History: Alternative Visions and Practices*, eds. Joshua Brown, Patrick Manning, Karen Shapiro, Jon Wiener, Belinda Bozzoli and Peter Delius (Philadelphia: Temple University Press, 1991).

9. For example, Leslie Witz, *Write your own history* (Johannesburg: SACHED/Raven, 1988).

10. They were strongly influenced by the Schools Council History Project in England.

11. Textbooks were (generally) supplied free to schools by the education departments and were intended to last at least five years. Schools were allowed to order limited numbers of new books each year to replace worn or lost books, as long as they were of the same titles. These orders were referred to as top-ups. This practice has been maintained.

12. Stephen Lowry, "A review of the History Curriculum Process," in Janet Reid and Rob Siebörger *Proceedings of the Workshop on School History Textbook Writing: From principles… to practice* (Cape Town: Faculty of Education University of Cape Town, 1995), p. 21.

13. With Johannesburg at its center, it is the smallest province geographically, almost entirely urban, and much more prosperous than any other province. The Gauteng Education Department is known for being innovative and better able to provide for its schools than others.

14. Named for the year in which it was expected to have been fully introduced and ready for its first revision.

15. For a fuller account, see Rob Siebörger, "History and the emerging nation: The South African experience," *International Journal of Historical Learning, Teaching and Research* 1, Number 1 (2000), pp. 39–48.

16. Ministry of Education, *A South African Curriculum for the Twenty First Century. Report of the Review Committee on Curriculum 2005* (Pretoria: Department of Education, 2000).

17. Department of Education, *Revised National Curriculum Statement Grades R–9 (Schools) Social Sciences* (Pretoria: Department of Education, 2002). For an overview, see Linda Chisholm, "The history curriculum in the (revised) national curriculum statement: an introduction," in *Toward New Histories for South Africa. On the Place of the Past in our Present*, ed. Shamil Jeppe (Cape Town: Juta Gariep, 2004).

18. Department of Education, *National Curriculum Statement Grades 10–12 (Schools) History* (Pretoria: Department of Education, 2003).

19. Also the subject of focus of a Ministerial working group into values, education and democracy in 2000. See Wilmot James ed., *Manifesto on Values, Education and Democracy* (Pretoria: Department of Education, 2001), pp. 40–42.

20. Rob Siebörger, *New History Textbooks for South Africa* (Johannesburg: Macmillan, 1994).

21. There were no textbook publishers of commercial significance that were not white owned.

22. The omission was not deliberate. No proposal to specify it was discussed.

23. Duncan Hindle, "Textbooks in the classroom: Challenges and possibilities," in *Toward New Histories for South Africa. On the Place of the Past in our Present,* ed. Shamil Jeppe (Cape Town: Juta Gariep, 2004), pp. 194–5.

24. Department of Education, *The South African History Project. Progress Report 2001–2003, incorporating the Report of the History and Archaeology Panel to the Minister of Education* (Pretoria: Department of Education, 2003), p. 49.

25. Ibid. p. 9, and Duncan Hindle "Textbooks in the classroom: Challenges and possibilities," in *Toward New Histories for South Africa. On the Place of the Past in our Present,* ed. Shamil Jeppe (Cape Town: Juta Gariep, 2004), p. 190.

26. See an initial step towards this in the recently provided Department of Education, *National Curriculum Statement for Grades 10–12 (Schools) Guidelines for Learning Programs History* (Pretoria: Department of Education, 2004), pp. 71–84.

ABOUT THE CONTRIBUTORS

Dr. Keith Crawford is Reader in Education at Edge Hill College of Higher Education, UK where he co-ordinates courses in textbook analysis, educational politics and policy-making and supervises doctoral students. His research interests focus upon international school textbook analysis, particularly history and citizenship textbooks. Dr. Crawford is Director of *"TEXT," the Center for Applied Research in Textbook Analysis* based at Edge Hill College. He is currently working on the politics and ideology of memory through cross-cultural comparisons of Chinese and Japanese history textbooks.

Sir John Daniel, joined the Commonwealth of Learning on June 1, 2004, as President and Chief Executive Officer moving from UNESCO (the United Nations Educational, Scientific and Cultural Organization) where he was Assistant Director-General for Education and headed the global *Education for All* program. He spent four years helping to establish Québec's Télé-université, moved west to Alberta as Vice-President of Athabasca University and then returned to Montreal as Vice-Rector of Concordia University. He then moved to the UK as Vice-Chancellor of the Open University in 1990, and added the duties of President of the United States Open University in 1998. Sir John was Knighted for services to higher education in 1994, the honor recognized the leading role that he has played internationally, over three decades, in the development of distance learning in universities. In 2002, he was named an *Honorary Fellow of the Commonwealth of Learning*, for his contribution to the development of open and distance education world-wide. Sir John has been awarded 20 honorary degrees from universities in 12 countries.

Dr. Stuart Foster was formerly tenured Associate Professor in the Department of Social Science Education at the University of Georgia, U.S. and is now Senior Lecturer in History in Education at the Institute of Education,

What Shall We Tell the Children?, pages 245–248
Copyright © 2006 by Information Age Publishing

University of London where he is Course Leader for the MA in Education (Citizenship, History and RE) and a supervisor of doctoral students. His research interests include the teaching, learning and assessment of history and social studies, the history of education, international education, curriculum studies, and school history textbooks. Recent publications include: *Red Alert!: Educators Confront the Red Scare in American Public Schools, 1947–1954* and *Historical Empathy and Perspective Taking in the Social Studies* (with O. L. Davis, Jr. and Elizabeth Yeager).

Dr. Misook Kim is an associate research fellow in the Research Division of the School of Education at the Korean Educational Development Institute, Seoul, South Korea. Dr. Kim received her doctorate from the University of Wisconsin-Madison, U.S. Her research interests include class and gender relations in education and young North Korean defectors. Her recent publications include *Bodily Regulation and Vocational Schooling, The State and The Politics of Knowledge* (with Michael Apple), *Struggles over Difference* (with Yoshiko Nozaki and Allan Luke). She is currently working on education welfare policies in urban areas.

Jonathan Kriener received his Masters Degree in oriental philology, Islamic and political sciences from Bochum University. From 1987 until 1989 he worked for *Aktion Sühnezeichen/Friedensdienste* in Israel. He was a lecturer in Modern Hebrew at the Federal Office of Languages (*Bundessprachenamt*), Siegen University and at the *Auslandsgesellschaft NRW/Dortmund*. He has been a research fellow at the Georg Eckert Institut fur Internationale Schulbuchforschung, Braunschweig, Germany, since June 2002. His main fields of research are the Arab-Israeli conflict and education in Middle Eastern countries.

Jason Nicholls is a doctoral research student at the University of Oxford's Department of Educational Studies. His current research, funded by the ESRC, involves the comparative analysis of representations of World War Two in the school history textbooks of formerly belligerent and non-belligerent states. In particular, he is interested in the epistemological and methodological dimensions that underpin comparative research. Before commencing his doctorate he taught at schools, colleges and universities in the UK, Japan, China, Argentina and the U.S. He is currently involved in teaching comparative and international education at the University of Oxford.

Dr. Falk Pingel is acting director of the Georg Eckert Institut fur Internationale Schulbuchforschung, Braunschweig, Germany. His particular field of research is modern German and European history, particularly the Nazi era. He received his doctorate from the University of Bielefeld where he taught as an assistant professor from 1976 to 1983, and again from 1997 to

2000. In 1999 he held a guest professorship at the Shanghai International Studies University. He is a member of the Education Committee to the German Commission for UNESCO. He chairs the Goethe Institute's web-based Committee on Holocaust Education and represents the Eckert Institute in the Council of Europe's project *Learning and teaching about the history of Europe in the 20th Century in secondary schools*. He works with a number of European partners, among them the *Fondazione Giovanni Agnelli* in Torino (Italy). Dr. Pingel is also involved in the *International Task Force on Holocaust Education, Remembrance and Research*.

Dr. Dan Porat is Lecturer in Education at the Hebrew University, Jerusalem. Dr. Porat received his doctorate from Stanford University where he was the Wexner Fellow between 1994 and 1998. Dr. Porat also received the Memorial Foundation for Jewish Culture in 1998, and in 2003–2004, he held a fellowship from The International Institute for Holocaust Research at Yad Vashem. Dr. Porat's research interests include collective memory, history education and history learning; he has also published in a number of journals, including the *Journal of Contemporary History* and the *American Educational Research Journal*.

Dr. Yvette Claire Rosser teaches and researches in the Center for Asian Studies at the University of Texas in Austin. After graduating from The University of Texas at Austin with a B.A. in Asian Studies she taught in high school for several years before returning to graduate study to complete her Master's Thesis on an analysis of the treatment of India in the American secondary social studies curriculum. Her Ph.D. dissertation "Curricula as Destiny: Forging National Identities in India, Pakistan, and Bangladesh" was a study of the politics of history in South Asia and social studies textbooks in India, Pakistan, and Bangladesh, with a particular focus on the rewriting of history in India. Yvette has designed and led several workshops for high school teachers to help them better understand and teach about India. She is the co-creator and sponsor of the *International Day without Violence*, held annually designed to promote peace, non-violence, and conflict resolution, by encouraging autonomous events in communities and schools around the world.

Rob Siebörger is an Associate Professor in the School of Education at the University of Cape Town, South Africa where he is the program leader for the PGCE (Secondary) course. His research interests include history education; curriculum materials development and assessment. He has written history textbooks at all school levels and has been closely involved in the development of new history curricula at national and provincial levels in South Africa since 1994.

Professor Yasemin Soysal teaches sociology in University of Essex. She has written extensively on the nation-state, citizenship, education, human rights and international migrations in such journals as the *American Socio-logical Review, Theory and Society, Sociology of Education, Ethnic and Racial Stud-ies,* and *European Societies.* Soysal's books include *Limits of Citizenship: Migrants and Postnational Membership in Europe* (University of Chicago Press, 1994) and *The Nation, Europe and the World: Textbooks and Curricula in Transi-tion* (edited with Hanna Schissler, Berghahn, 2004). Her current research project (funded by the Economic and Social Research Council, with addi-tional funds from the Leverhulme Trust and the British Academy) is on the post-war reconfigurations of nation-state identities as projected in second-ary school history and civics textbooks. She is past president of the Euro-pean Sociological Association (2001–2003).

Dr. Edward Vickers teaches in the school of Lifelong Learning and Inter-national Development at the Institute of Education, the University of Lon-don where he lectures in comparative education and teaches on the MA and doctoral program. His main areas of research are: the comparative study of education as a vehicle for political socialization; curriculum history and history education, identity and cultural politics in East Asia. Dr. Vickers has worked as a writer of English language textbooks for secondary schools in Hong Kong and China, and has also been commissioned by the Educa-tion Department of the Hong Kong Government to write history teaching materials for schools. Recent publications include *History Education and National Identity in East Asia* (editor), New York, Routledge, 2005, and *In Search of An Identity: The Politics of History as a School Subject in Hong Kong,* New York, Routledge, 2003.

Breinigsville, PA USA
10 March 2010
233894BV00004B/52/A